Distribution
Channels

Distribution
Channels

Understanding and Managing
Channels to Market

JULIAN DENT

KoganPage

LONDON PHILADELPHIA NEW DELHI

First published in Great Britain and the United States in 2008 by Kogan Page Limited
Reprinted 2009, 2010 (twice)

120 Pentonville Road	525 South 4th Street, #241	4737/23 Ansari Road
London N1 9JN	Philadelphia PA 19147	Daryaganj
United Kingdom	USA	New Delhi 110002
www.koganpage.com		India

© Julian Dent, 2008

ISBN 978 0 7494 5256 8

British Library Cataloguing-in-Publication Data

A CIP record for this book is available from the British Library.

Library of Congress Cataloging-in-Publication Data

Dent, Julian, 1957–
   Distribution channels : understanding and managing channels to market / Julian Dent.
      p. cm.
   Includes index.
   ISBN 978-0-7494-5256-8
   1. Marketing channels. 2. Business planning. I. Title.
   HF5415.129.D46 2008
   658.7'88--dc22

                               2008011173

Typeset by Saxon Graphics Ltd, Derby
Printed and bound in Great Britain by MPG Books Ltd, Bodmin, Cornwall

With love to my wife, Jan, and to our children, Laura and Ian

Contents

Preface

This book represents the best part of 30 years' personal and shared experience working with distribution businesses of all types in a variety or roles, starting initially as an accountant with Arthur Andersen, through to the last 18 years as management consultant with VIA International, a firm that specializes in routes to market strategy and implementation. In that time I have had the opportunity to work with some of the world's leading practitioners in the field of distribution channels – and some pretty terrible ones too. In many ways, it was from the clients and situations where things were going wrong that the sharpest lessons could be drawn.

At VIA, we are lucky enough to spend most of our time consulting for some of the world's most successful brands and companies (yes, they still ask for help), which means we have seen an enormous amount of best practice. Often though, these companies are challenged by sheer scale, complexity and channel overlap or conflict which prevents them from seeing the business issues quite as clearly as they might. They are usually relieved to find that we can bring some clarity and objectivity to the situation and can recommend strategies that are rooted in commercial logic to deliver the outcomes they need. Many of these situations have found their way into this book, albeit usually with a cloak of anonymity. You will find many real companies and situations named and described in the book too, but these insights are based on facts already in the public domain or well known among the trade.

Even more usefully, much of our work requires us to go inside the distribution models of our clients' routes to market and investigate the actual measures and business model dynamics operating in the distributors and final-tier trade channel players. This provides the basis for much of the insight into each type of channel business model laid out in the different sections of the book.

Finally, we have had the opportunity to work with many smaller companies and businesses, typically following the introduction of an injection of venture finance, which means that all concerned are expecting a sharp uptick in sales. This growth often has to come from a combination of new customer segments, new markets or new products, which usually means new channels too. There have been some hard lessons learnt along the way about establishing a value proposition that will attract the players in the channels needed to deliver the required growth, and these are laid out for you here too.

All of the content in this book has at some time or other been taught to people in real channel roles or distribution businesses, looking for insights, concepts, frameworks, heuristics and practical lessons that they can take away and apply. For many of the people attending these workshops, English has been their second or even third language, so the experience has been a good test of how to communicate business and financial concepts in terms that make sense to people who work in sales and marketing (and sometimes, vice versa too).

For more information on VIA please visit www.viaint.com.

Acknowledgements

The fact that this book was written at all is down to a German channel manager who asked me at the end of a workshop for a list of books on the subject of channel business models. I found I could not think of any. He planted the seed, which took several more years to germinate.

I am indebted to my professional colleagues and partners at VIA, especially Rosemary Wyatt, Michael White and Guy Swarbrick together with Sharon Davis for their support in allowing me time out to write the book. I have borrowed freely from their expertise as well as from the experiences shared with many current and former colleagues. Their review and feedback has added much to the finished result, as has that of Rob Abshire of Publicis who has shared many of our retail experiences over the past 12 years. In the academic world, the late Professor Erin Andersen at INSEAD was a wonderful source of encouragement, as has been Professor Anne T Coughlan at Kellogg. Of course, none of this would have been possible without the continuing patronage of our clients, who continue to share with us some of their more demanding challenges and issues. We can never say enough how much we appreciate their trust and candour. I would especially like to recognize Phil Darnell of Hewlett-Packard whose vision has inspired some of the more exciting projects we have been privileged to work on.

In the production of this book, I have had the most wonderful support from Sean Daly, who has helped with the layout and formatting of every page and redrawn just about every picture and table too. Any mistakes that remain are down to me.

Finally, I'd like to acknowledge the support of my family, who have left me in peace for long periods interrupted only by teas and coffees, with just the occasional enquiry as to whether it was the butler or the gamekeeper who would be revealed as the villain in the final chapter. Well, now they will have to believe me that it just isn't that sort of book!

Part 1

Introduction and why business models matter

Introduction

Who this book is for

This book is for anyone whose role touches the marketing, sales, distribution and service channels of their industry. It is for anyone whose responsibilities include generating demand and fulfilling customer needs through the provision of products and services. If any of the following terminology forms part of your job description, this book is for you:

- routes to market;
- go-to-market;
- distribution channels;
- channels to market;
- sales channels;
- account, relationship or partnership management;
- business to business;
- business to consumer

This book is for the managers of the businesses that market, distribute, sell and service the products and services of *other* suppliers and it is for anyone who is involved in the frontline of these relationships.

If your role has any commercial element, then this book has you in mind. It is written for people who don't consider themselves to be financial experts but recognize that they need to be masters of the economics of their business and the businesses with which they work. It aims to provide pragmatic insight into the challenges faced by each of the parties involved in the marketing and distribution of products and services (the 'players') and the opportunities that this insight unlocks.

Equally, if you are financially literate but are relatively new to the special dynamics of distribution, then this book should give you a fast track through many years of experience to the unique issues, measures, relationships and success factors that apply, whether you are working for a player in the midst of the value chain, a supplier at one end or a customer at the other.

It is for anyone who manages the relationship between two or more players in the distribution system, be they partner account managers, partner business managers, channel managers, sales managers, buyers, programme managers, etc. And of course it is for the managers and ultimate directors of these critical roles. Everyone involved in these roles needs to know how to demonstrate the commercial impact of their relationship with another player to win and retain business. They also need to understand the way their own business works to build relationships that work for both parties, be they the 'buyer' or 'seller' in the relationship.

For any product to reach its targeted customers and to grow its share of that market, the supplier needs to design and manage a distribution model that works as a business model for all of these intermediaries as well as for the supplier itself. This book is for anyone who is trying to improve the performance of their own business or is charged with influencing the behaviour and activities of the other players with whom they engage to mutual advantage.

There are many books and courses about finance. Some are for financial people; many are for the 'non-financial' manager. Most of these books talk about product companies; some even include a chapter or two about service companies. There are also books about distribution channels and systems, often from a sales or marketing perspective, dealing for example with how to minimize channel conflict or increase your power in the relationship with the channel. However, we have yet to find a book that deals with the business models of companies whose role is primarily to distribute products and services, written for people whose job specification does not require a qualification in accountancy... so here it is!

This book does not aim to teach you how to read balance sheets and profit and loss accounts or how to explain depreciation... though we expect you will probably be able to do these things by the time you have finished it. It will help you to understand:

■ why working capital management is critical to distributors;
■ how to address the demands for more margin from your retailers or distributors if you are a market share leader;

- how to secure the resources you really need from a supplier to achieve your growth targets;
- how to increase your share of your partners' business even if they claim that you are not as profitable to them as your competitors;
- how to punch above your weight in the distribution system if you have a tiny market share;
- how to ensure you are allocating scarce resources to the channels that will generate the highest returns;
- how to increase your leverage over partners who may not even sell or distribute your products, but whose recommendation is critical to customer preference.

What do we mean by business model?

As this book claims to be all about business models, we had better explain what we mean by the term 'business model'. A business model is how a business makes money from its activities. It is the financial expression of the role, positioning, strategy and execution of a business plan of a specific player in a specific industry. It is the logical financial result of the economics of the structure of the industry and its distribution infrastructure. It is both static – in the form of certain cost structures, margins, capital turns and the like, and dynamic – in the way that costs behave, key ratios change with growth or margins behave under increased competition. So the business model of, say, a distributor of plumbing supplies will have some predictable similarities and some predictable differences with that of a computer products distributor, and further predictable similarities and differences with a sheet music or a cream cake distributor. The same can be said of different players in the same channel eco-system, with their role, balance of power and strategy determining where and how they will make profits, where they have to deploy capital and the scale of both these factors relative to the size of business being done.

In this book we will show you the connection between these forces and the impact they have on the structure of the business model. We will help you to understand the inherent constraints and continual trade-offs with which the managers of each business model are wrestling. We will take you into the ways to improve the business performance of each type of player, whether you are managing it or negotiating with it. These constraints are also opportunities. For example, many retailers cannot hold much inventory on their premises owing to size or cost constraints (attractive retail locations attract a fearsome rent). An enterprising supplier with an efficient distribution logistics capability can offer to supply just in time or manage the inventory on behalf of the retailer, gaining share of category over other suppliers without this capability. The retailer knows it can't afford to be out of stock, so will give up some of its demands for a better margin in return for assurance of full and replenished shelves. Being able to put these two aspects into proportion – or quantifying them – might not seem like selling or marketing, but it will have a much longer-lasting impact on doing business together than offering a short-term product promotion to gain share.

In this book we aim to teach you to fish, so to speak, rather than catching fish for you. We will point out the major breeds of fish, ie the dominant business models and their inherent characteristics, but more as a way to making you the complete angler. This way you should be able to assess the situation of any business model in any distribution system in any market from any perspective (managing the player or buying from or selling to it), work out the issues and opportunities available and identify the strategy that will best help you achieve your particular objectives.

How this book is set out

This book sets out the business models of all the major types of intermediary in a distribution system, in the following structure:

■ *The role of the player* – although there are some special cases and exceptions, in most industries the roles of the key players are very consistent. However, the labels that are applied in each industry can vary confusingly and in some cases are used interchangeably and in others can carry quite specific meanings. To make sure the labels applied in your industry do not mislead you, we define the key roles, so you can recognize which players you are dealing with.
■ *How their business model works* – the principal characteristics of each player's role in the distribution system determine the fundamental shape of their business model. They will be subject to some well-understood economic dynamics and each will have one or more 'big issues' that define their management's priorities. We orientate you to the key features of the business model and show how these are driven by each player's role and the structure of the industry or distribution system. We explain the business model in plain English and provide a consistent framework for mapping the key numbers. We provide numerous examples of each type of business model so that you can see how the

forces in its market have shaped its business profile and affected its business performance.

■ *The measures that matter and how to manage the business using them* – we define and explain all the key measures and how and why they are used. We provide some basic benchmarks to give you a sense of the norms for each measure and help you understand what can be done to improve each measure. We show you how the measures interact so that you understand the pressures that managers of each player are under and the trade-offs they are constantly juggling. We provide some case studies and examples of how failing businesses have been turned around and how successful players have executed their strategies in detail.

■ *How to sell to that player* – once you understand the key objectives of the managers you are dealing with, you can ensure that you position your own company's value proposition in terms that will mean something. You can show how your proposals will impact their business model to the good. You can demonstrate that allocating more resource to your products and services is good for both of you, and that attacking the segments in which you want to grow is going to deliver a higher return on investment for them. Equally you can defend your corner, when asked to concede margin or increase market development funding, by pointing out how little this will benefit their overall performance. We aim to increase your confidence to go high in your account relationships by understanding the overall business model and taking the conversation up to the strategic level.

At the end of this book, we have provided all the useful quick reference material you might need and a glossary of technical terms.

Although we encourage you to read the entire book to learn what a powerful resource it can be for you with its hundreds of examples and insights, we also encourage you to dip into the book when confronted with specific challenges or new situations. Some of the more technical elements of the business models will not make compelling reading until you are dealing with a real issue and then you will welcome the detail of the explanations and the depth of the examples.

Although we aim to educate you through this book in the general and specific aspects of business models, with lots of practical, real examples, every so often we will express a point of view. It seems that there are still some lessons that have yet to be learnt and entrenched behaviours that defy commercial logic: market share leaders employing the tactics of the new entrant, distributors and resellers discounting products that are in short supply, capital wasted without any understanding of its true cost. We aim to give you, the reader, the benefit of years of hands-on management and consulting insight to help you avoid these pitfalls. Take heed, or you could find your competitor is the first to break the mould and win the business from under your nose!

Why business models matter

Distribution matters

Typically around half the price paid for a product by a customer is absorbed by the activities involved in getting that product to the customer (and the customer to the product). And this is a proportion that has increased significantly over the past 15 years as production costs have fallen while markets have segmented and media and distribution channels have multiplied. Typically, this is the proportion of costs which is least well controlled and least well understood.

Markets are fragmenting as trends in consumer and business demographics create additional and more distinct customer segments. To make matters worse, product and service innovations are multiplying the options available. Even simple, commodity-type products may now be distributed to multiple customer segments through multiple routes that differ by country or region. Many of these routes to market involve one or more types of intermediary, such as wholesalers, distributors, dealers, brokers, aggregators and retailers, or rely upon influencers who shape customer preference or act as specifiers or their behalf, such as architects or designers. Very few companies can tell you what it costs to sell through a particular route to market whether that be direct, one-tier (eg supplier to dealer to customer) or two-tier (eg supplier to distributor to retailer to customer) distribution. Fewer still can inform you of the profitability of specific intermediaries. We have found wide variation in the costs and profitability of channels and specific intermediaries in every industry and distribution system we have investigated. Companies that have invested in analysing and understanding the business models of their distribution system have been able to take significant cost out of their own business, increasing profits or reducing prices to gain an edge over the competition.

Routes to market control access. Without the right routes to market, you simply won't reach your target market. Coca-Cola's burning desire throughout the 1990s was to make it easier and easier to buy a Coca-Cola. Just look at the result – there is virtually nowhere in the world where you are more than a few minutes from being able to buy a Coke at any time of the day or night. Many industrial companies are still struggling with access, unable to find the channels that will (note 'will', not can) take their products to market. Building access can be expensive, requiring extensive internal systems and infrastructure to be able to sense market demand, gather and evaluate sales forecasts, deploy marketing programmes and promotions, plan and execute complex logistics. It is a tough balancing act to increase access to the market while ensuring your network is profitable and capable of handling the growth you want. You may look to your distribution channels to generate demand for your products and services as well as fulfil it. Classically the local agent appointed in foreign markets is charged with exactly this responsibility, with compensation closely tied to the achievement of sales targets with only back office support from the supplier. Alternatively, you may want the channel to fulfil demand you have generated or even generate demand for you to fulfil. Your market access depends on understanding the role you want your channels to play and the cost and investment that are commensurate with the return generated.

Routes to market control brand. How can you deliver and fulfil your brand promise, unless you manage your routes to market properly and control your distribution? If your brand is built on quality attributes, you need your channels of distribution to execute on those attributes. Not only just at the point of purchase, but also if the product goes wrong or when the customer needs ongoing service and support. How well you incentivize and reward your channels will have a big impact on the ultimate customer experience and your brand. And if your brand is built on low price, you need your channels to be aligned in eliminating every unnecessary activity that incurs cost.

Often, routes to market control product differentiation. You want your product or offering to be different from your competitors'. Routes to market play a vital role in enabling this. Often, the channel you use is the sole way of demonstrating that your product is different from your competitors'. Dell in the computer industry is a good example of this, selling a product that is over 95 per cent the same as all its competitors (with the chips and operating software coming from standard suppliers Intel and Microsoft). Its channel – online direct – is its primary differentiator, offering price and flexibility advantages over its competition which, until recently, has gone to market through retail and dealer channels.

And all the time, your chief finance officer wants more for less. Never before have the costs and benefits of marketing and distribution come under such close scrutiny. With a combination of significant costs, complexity, dependencies on external partners and variety by market, it is now critical to understand and manage your distribution business model.

Challenging business dynamics

Distribution businesses are inherently difficult businesses to get right. To see why, we first need to set out the typical types of distribution players and define their role in a distribution system.

In Figure 2.1, you will see that there are three basic structures for a distribution system:

■ **Direct** – in this structure, the supplier owns and manages all the resources in the value chain through to the customer (or a particular set of customers). Companies employing this model have multiplied since the internet enabled online direct distribution. Examples include Dell in the computer business, easyJet in the low-cost airline business, Charles Schwab in securities and Lands End in clothing. Each of these companies has made a virtue out of increasing customer convenience or reducing cost, or both, by employing the direct model. In addition they gain valuable customer insight through the direct interaction and can adjust prices and promotional offers instantly to respond to demand and supply issues. It is a model that also includes the direct sales force typically seen calling on the very large corporate accounts in most business-to-business sectors.

■ **One-tier distribution** – this structure is defined by employing one set of intermediaries between the company and its customers to increase reach (such as overseas agents), provide special services to complete the customer offer (such as conservatory installers) or position the product within established channels for the customer (such as retailers), where

Distribution structures

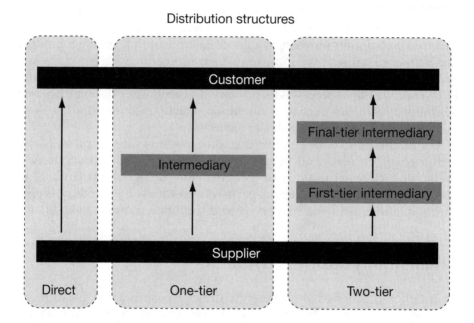

Figure 2.1 Typical distribution structures

it would make no sense for the supplier to try to persuade customers to change their shopping and buying habits. The benefits include easy and often immediate access to well-defined segments of customers or the leveraging of investments made by the intermediaries, such as overseas agents, warehouses and established sales forces. The disadvantages include the need to grant an acceptable trading margin to the intermediary and a degree of dilution of focus because the intermediary sells many brands, including potentially direct competitors (think how many varieties of soft drink or cereal are on offer in the average grocery store). In addition, the distancing of the customer by interjecting a layer of intermediaries can be a major disadvantage, depending on what information the intermediary is willing, or contracted, to share with the supplier.

■ **Two-tier distribution** – in many markets there are potentially thousands of intermediaries who service the customer segments a supplier is seeking to reach. Each of these may handle only a few sales a month and the cost of finding them and managing a commercial relationship with them cannot be recovered from the margin on such a low volume of sales. Imagine yourself to be manufacturer of a particularly tasty chewy toffee. You need to reach the thousands of small boys and girls (and the odd parent and grandparent) across the country who would expect to find your toffees in their local newsagent, kiosk, station, airport, garage forecourt and sweet shop as well as the sweet aisle in the big grocery store. It would be prohibitively expensive in terms of sales people and infrastructure to sell to each one of the thousands of such stores across the country. Fortunately someone has already done this for you, in the form of a relatively small number of cash and carry warehouses, where these stores go once or twice a week to replenish their inventory. To reach them, all you need is to get your product into these cash and carry's (a challenge we address in Chapter 10), and you now operate a two-tier distribution system, from you to the cash and carry to the newsagent to the customer. You will find similar models in the computer and telecoms industries where there are many thousands of local dealers serving small and medium-sized businesses. The advantages are leverage and cost effectiveness, enabling the supplier to reach a wide, mass but low-volume market, at the cost of further distance from the customer and market.

■ **Multiple-tiered distribution** (not shown in Figure 2.1) – This is the same as the two-tier model but with additional tiers required to reach the end-customer. In some challenging markets, perhaps caused by complex geography or economic conditions, there will be a number of players involved, such as for example the cigarette vendor in Zimbabwe who will sell a single cigarette at a time, having bought a packet from the local shop. In many emerging markets, Unilever sells soap in sachets containing enough for a single wash and these are bought and resold by several layers of dealers. In China, it is not uncommon to find five- or six-tier distribution channels moving products into the central areas, away from the burgeoning commercial centres ranged along the east coast.

■ **Original equipment manufacturer channel** (not shown in Figure 2.1) – the concept termed original equipment manufacturer (OEM) describes the situation when one supplier (the OEM) makes a product that is embedded inside another. An example would be the electric motor inside a stairlift, or the silicon chip inside a computer. On their own the electric motor and silicon chip do not comprise complete products, so the route to market is first into the OEM channel (stairlift or computer manufacturers) and then as a part of a completed product into the one- or two-tier channels described above. Although this channel is primarily a direct connection between the OEM and its customers, Intel's well-known 'Intel inside' marketing campaign demonstrates that there is still an end-user marketing dimension even in the OEM route to market.

One-tier and first-tier intermediary businesses such as distributors or wholesalers are offering the supplier efficiency and cost effectiveness through leveraging their assets and infrastructure. This exposes them to the risky combination of long-term fixed costs and short-term visibility of revenues. To compound this they are often critically dependent upon a few major relationships, which can be changed with relatively little notice. They are usually fast-moving businesses which consume significant amounts of capital or people or both and in many industries have typically not delivered high returns. Shown in Figure 2.2 is a set of performance measures for a sample of distributors, which shows that very few make a return on capital above 20 per cent, the sort of rate you'd expect to compensate for the inherently risky nature of the business.

Final-tier intermediary businesses come in many forms. In the business-to-business sector they typically wrap services around the product, using special skill sets that need to be recruited, developed and retained. This means that these businesses can have relatively high fixed costs with lumpy, project-based revenues that can give rise to volatile profitability and awkward cash flow. To survive they need to be well focused on their offer to one or more defined customer segments, and to grow they have to invest in additional resources ahead of the sales curve. In the consumer sector they need to juggle stock levels against fluctuating (sometimes seasonal) demand to minimize over-stocking while avoiding empty shelves and missed sales. Allocating scarce retail space between distinct categories, competing brands and individual product lines has now become a science. The new IT systems introduced by leading UK grocers Sainsbury in the mid-2000s were initially flawed, causing stock-outs of basic items, and highlighted just how difficult it can be to get it right and how costly errors can be, with major market share losses, share price falls and the departure of the CEO and several senior members of the management team.

We go into these dynamics and how to manage the different business models in considerable detail in later chapters, but this introduction should be enough to convince you that these business models are challenging, whether you are managing them directly or need to partner with them as a supplier or customer. And you should view this complexity as an opportunity, because it will give the advantage to the players who invest in mastering their business models and punish those who attempt to muddle through.

Sector and distributor	Gross margin	Operating margin	Net margin (Pre-tax)	Inventory turn	Return on capital employed	Historic PE Ratio (Nov 2007)
Building supplies						
Travis Perkins	35%	10.2%	8.1%	6.3	12.3%	8.6
Wolseley	28%	5.9%	5.4%	5.2	15.1%	9.0
Chemicals						
Ashland	17%	2.4%	2.9%	11.3	4.7%	12.9
AM Castle & Co	18%	7.1%	7.1%	6.0	11.4%	9.6
Electronics						
Arrow Electronics	15%	4.4%	3.8%	6.8	13.0%	10.3
Avnet	13%	4.2%	3.7%	7.9	12.9%	11.6
Electrocomponents	51%	9.2%	8.8%	2.5	17.0%	16.4
Information technology						
Ingram Micro	5%	1.3%	1.2%	11.1	11.5%	13.54
Bell Microproducts	7%	0.8%	0.1%	9.3	0.6%	N/A
Synnex	5%	1.5%	1.3%	10.2	14.3%	11.67
ScanSource	11%	3.8%	3.5%	6.5	15.9%	19.97
Tech Data	5%	0.0%	-0.2%	13.1	-2.2%	21.33
Pharmaceuticals & healthcare products						
Henry Schein	29%	5.9%	5.7%	6.3	15.4%	23.67
AmerisourceBergen Corp	4%	1.2%	1.2%	15.5	18.1%	16.43
McKesson Corp	5%	1.4%	1.4%	10.9	16.1%	20.56
Cardinal Health	6%	1.6%	1.4%	11.1	11.5%	26.75
Office supplies and business products						
United Stationers	17%	5.2%	4.8%	5.6	23.5%	13.04
Corporate Express	30%	4.0%	2.5%	8.5	5.7%	16.39
Multi-sector						
Genuine Parts Co	31%	7.6%	7.4%	3.2	25.3%	16.27

Figure 2.2 Illustrative distributor business performance by selected industry sector

Many companies use a mix of distribution models in order to cover the market completely and to reach the different customer segments for which their ranges of products are intended. Operating with multiple distribution models and multiple channels creates the potential for channel conflict, where two or more channel players are taking the same product into the same customer. This is not always a bad thing (think of different retailers all offering Heinz baked beans for sale), but the multiplicity of channels can mean that some channels are given an unintentional advantage or that some are 'freeloading' on the work of others; this can be very damaging to your ability to get your products to market. For example, the specialist hi-fi shop that invests in specialist sound studios and trained sales people to show the advantages of your brand of audio equipment will not be too impressed if the customer can walk around the corner to a Costco discount warehouse and pick it up for 30 per cent cheaper. While managing channel strategy and addressing channel conflict are outside the scope of this book, a solid understanding of the different economics of the two types of channel player will ensure an objective approach to the challenges.

Business models are key to value propositions

Although every supplier would like to think its products and services are world-beaters that virtually sell themselves, there are very few brands or products that ever achieve this status and those that do quickly find the competition catching up. As a result it is rarely convincing to tell the intermediaries in a channel that your product has terrific customer benefits. The channel will regard your product's customer appeal as only one aspect of its business proposition, ie one that will shape its likely rate of sale. It will want to know all about its margin, what it will cost to sell and support, its probable life cycle, the likely level of returns and warranty claims, the level of your promotional spend to build demand (both direct to the consumer and through them), stocking requirements, the opportunity to sell related products and services, and many other specific aspects of the business model. It is the composition of all the elements of a commercial relationship that determines whether a supplier can command advantage in the distribution system.

Take, for example, the suppliers of oil lubricants such as BP Castrol or Shell Lubricants. They both sell what are essentially the same products, the oils used in oil changes for cars, marine engines and industrial and agricultural engines. Certainly each company will provide detailed scientific justification of the technical superiority of its brands. But as a customer, do you really have a preference for which brand of oil is used in your car's annual service (Ferrari owners excepted!)? Quite. So how do Shell and BP Castrol persuade their dealers and distributors to take their products to market? The answer lies in understanding the business models of these dealers. Many of these dealers are small independent garages with limited cash resources. The oil suppliers compete to offer finance for major equipment purchases such as hydraulic hoists or diagnostic computers or even the storage facilities for their new and drained oil supplies in return for a multi-year commitment to buy their particular brand. Their value proposition to the dealers has everything to do with the business model and nothing to do with lubricants.

Here's another striking example. Manufacturers looking to get their products into catalogue retailers know that the costs of producing and printing the catalogue are a large up-front investment for the retailer, with upwards of a million copies of a several-hundred-page catalogue printed one or more times a year. Offering these retailers a retrospective rebate for achieving sales targets at the end of a season is hardly going to convince the category buyer that your company is serious about taking a major spread in the relevant section of the catalogue. You may well find yourself holding the door open for your competitor on your way out. Smart suppliers will recognize the opportunity to help the category buyers to manage their printing costs and offer up-front funding to buy premium space and placement. Easily said, but many companies used to dealing with traditional retailers find it difficult to adjust their standard marketing funding models to deliver this, unless they have developed a good understanding of their channel's business model at the highest levels of their management hierarchy.

If your role involves building business through your channel partners, it is critical to understand how their business model works to be able to communicate the value in your company's value proposition. You need to know what levers in the channel's business model are available to you and how to connect your proposition to those levers. As we have shown in the examples above, these levers can come from almost any aspect of the channel's business, not just the margins or rate of sale of your products. But this is only half the story; you also need to look inside your own business model and identify unique strengths that your competitors cannot match and then find ways to turn these into compelling value propositions for your channels.

For example, if you are a market share leader, you should be looking for fixed-cost investments that you can spread over your higher unit volumes to give you a lower cost per unit. This might be in the form of a national media campaign that drives traffic or sales-leads to your channel partners, or a supply chain initiative that increases the responsiveness of your logistics capability to fluctuations in demand experienced by the channel.

In the United States, the major grocery chains will major on Coca-Cola instead of Pepsi for the big holidays because they know that Coke can replenish the stores three times a day and they cannot afford to run out of stocks on 4 July or the Super Bowl. Pepsi cannot match this, and no amount of additional discounting or rebates on each unit sold will win this business back. By owning all the major holidays, Coke dominates the category. In this way Coke has used its unique strengths to the detriment of its competition.

The successful suppliers will go further and understand the 'business model inside' or how the business model for their products and services look inside their channel's business model. They will know whether they are a drag on their channel's business or an enabler on all the key measures such as margins, volumes, stock levels, credit allowances and so on. As we show in the chapters on each type of distribution business model, there are many measures that can be used and it is important to identify the measures that matter, not just for the generic business type, but for the specific partner you are pitching to.

A structured approach to positioning your value proposition

A key thrust of this chapter has been that as a supplier you need to understand the business models of your downstream (ie nearer to the customer) channel partners in order to develop and communicate a compelling value proposition – just as the final tier needs to understand its customer's business in order to make the most effective offer. You need to adopt a structured approach to positioning your value proposition to ensure that you apply a well-grounded and logical approach to gaining advantage.

Figure 2.3 sets out the key steps in the process and the important questions that need to be tackled. Note how it requires you to consider what the competition is doing as well as identify your own strengths in developing the proposition which best positions you in terms of the channel's objectives.

Many suppliers require that their partner account managers establish themselves as trusted business advisers to their key distribution partners. They are expected to develop the relationship to the level of a strategic partnership with significant interdependencies. This imperative demands excel-

Structured approach to positioning your value proposition

Analyse channel's business model	Identify own unique strengths	Identify opportunities	Develop and sell value proposition
• What are the channel's business objectives? • What are its primary business measures? • What is the channel's core business strategy? • How well is the channel performing? • What are its greatest threats and weaknesses?	• What are your unique assets and strengths? • How can these be deployed to the channel's benefit?	• How can you help the channel achieve its objectives? • What is the competition doing? • What gaps exist in the market? • How can your position be improved?	• What are the core thrusts of your value proposition? • What channel business measures does it impact? • What are its unique advantages for the channel over the competition?

Figure 2.3 Structured approach to positioning your value proposition

lent understanding and insight into the business model of their key partner. With this foundation the account manager can recommend unique investments that his or her company should make to further differentiate their value proposition.

Those partner account managers who work with the broad mass of channel partners in a particular segment need to understand the fundamentals of the business model of the particular type of channel partner with which they work. This is essential to their ability to sell in new products, programmes and terms and conditions. We have found that channels in every type of industry respond very positively to the supplier that has invested in understanding their business. They will share information more openly if they believe the supplier will add value to their business as a result.

This business model insight needs to be applied throughout the supplier's organization, not just at the frontline, for maximum competitive advantage. In every industry examples abound of programmes and promotions that were conceived in innocence of the channel's business model and then amazement is expressed when the channel fails to take advantage. Even worse, the channel may take the programme even though it harms its business because it fears the impact on its supplier relationship if it refuses. An obvious example is the type of end-of-quarter, 'channel stuffing' incentives which encourage dealers to take large amounts of product into stock in order to help the supplier to achieve its quarter-end targets. We show in Chapter 4 why this is so disastrous for the supplier as well as the channel, which often ends up having to discount heavily to clear the over-stock, diluting margins to the point that they may not even cover the extra cost of financing, stocking, damage, etc. And this is before taking into account the distortion of their trading practices, impact on positioning and all the longer-term implications of pushing these bulges through the channel's business. This type of error could be reduced if product and programme managers as well as senior management understood the implications of their actions, through a solid understanding of the business models of the channels through which they go to market.

Be careful with comparisons

We use a lot of examples in this book, including real financial and business measures. You will inevitably find yourself comparing these to the measures in your own business or that of your partners, so please heed this health warning: Be Very Careful – use comparisons to raise questions, not to provide answers!

Despite the best efforts of the accounting profession, there is still much more scope for accounting for the same thing in different ways that you might imagine. And because businesses are so different, it simply isn't possible to tie down one way for everyone to keep score consistently (which is one reason why financial analysts are paid so highly to interpret the accounts of public companies even though they are the most regulated of all published accounts). This means that when you compare the numbers and measures of two businesses, you are rarely comparing like with like.

For example, take two companies which have had identical trading years with identical resources and both have finished the year with rather too much inventory, which is now obsolete. Company A is very prudent (run by an accountant) and as soon as a product spends more than three months in the warehouse, its value is written down to half its cost and after five months it is written down to zero value. Company B is rather more optimistic (run by a marketer) and waits 6 months before writing down a product's value by a third, 12 months for another third and 18 months before it finally writes the value down to zero. These are judgements and both are acceptable under accounting rules (providing always that the inventory is never valued higher than the price it would command in the market), but will produce very different financial results: Company A will report much reduced profits as the value of the write-downs is taken against profit and will have a smaller balance sheet, compared to Company B at the end of the current year. However, next year the situation may be reversed as these products are cleared out and Company A can make a reasonable profit against its written-down inventory and Company B takes the hit on its more fully valued inventory.

This simple example shows the danger of comparing different companies in the same business, and the problem is compounded when different companies operate in different businesses or with a different mix of different businesses. For example, comparing Tesco and Sainsbury would be problematic because although both are grocers based in the UK, Tesco has expanded significantly overseas with large operations in Thailand, Eastern Europe and elsewhere, whereas Sainsbury has not. Similarly Tesco has a large internet/home delivery business but Sainsbury does not and Tesco has a larger non-food business than Sainsbury. Not only are these two companies made up of different blends of business models, but Tesco may have depressed its current performance profile by investing heavily in start-up activities that will pay off in future periods. Simply comparing the numbers without this insight as to what is going on inside these businesses might lead to some very unfortunate conclusions as to which might make the better retail partner. The real lesson is to be armed with as much understanding as possible about the underlying business when attempting to interpret the business and financial measures.

Even making year-on-year comparisons for the same business is not always straightforward, though it is much more likely to be consistent than inter-company comparisons. Changes in management teams often result in a different attitude to risk and exercising judgement – just look at what happens when a new chief executive is appointed: so often there is a 'kitchen sink' approach to revisiting previous judgements and the first period's results contain an enormous write-down of values, clearing the decks for the future years' results to show an improvement. Comparing year-on-year results in this context would be a minefield. Other factors that can cause disruption include changes of ownership, where the new parent company's accounting policies are applied, though if these are different the previous year's results (one year only) will be restated under the new policies.

The golden rule is to use financials, benchmarks and comparisons to help you ask smart questions, not to jump to conclusions. The rest of this book should help you to ask the right questions and enable you to understand and even anticipate the answers, so that you can improve your performance through better distribution business models.

Part 2

Distributors and wholesalers

3

The role of the distributor

Distributors/wholesalers

For the purposes of this book, we will consider distributors and wholesalers to be the same, and certainly in terms of business model, they are the same. We regard the distributor as an intermediary that services other intermediaries, as for example the cash and carry serving small independent retailers, or the builders' merchant serving people in jobbing trades such as plumbers, builders, etc, or the broadline distributors found serving thousands of computer or electronic dealers. This means that distributors as we are defining them are to be found only in two-tier (or three-tier) distribution models and it is worth considering their role in terms of both their customers and their suppliers.

Customer role – core functions

For their customers, distributors fulfil a number of core roles, all of which are aspects of being a one-stop shop. For the most part their customers are smaller, independent traders, dealers, retailers and so on. As such, these customers cannot afford the complexity and cost of sourcing their stocks and supplies from the hundreds of suppliers whose products are integral to their own offer to end-customers. It is more efficient for these final-tier players to be able to go to a limited number of distributors with whom they can establish trading relationships that meet most or all of their needs. And for the distributors, there are a number of services they can provide which leverage their own scale advantages either as an integral part of their core offering or as discrete services which their customers can opt to use (Figure 3.1).

Note that the **one-stop shop** does not necessarily mean that the customer is buying hundreds of different items at the same time. In fact across a surprisingly wide number of industries, the average number of different line items bought at a single time or on a single invoice is around two (ie bricks and plaster, not two bricks). It really means that the customer expects to be able to go to the distributor for anything and buy it without needing to wait or to place it on back order. The customer is likely to shop around for price and availability, trading off convenience and cost. In some industries the distributor's day is characterized by providing price and availability answers to enquiries in the morning and then taking and fulfilling orders throughout the afternoon, building up to a peak at the end of the day. Core to the distributor's role is the ability to provide products on demand, saving or minimizing the stocking burden on the part of its customers. Typically the distributor will offer many thousands of SKUs (stock-keeping units) to be able to promise universal availability of virtually every 'standard' and many not-so-standard products. For example, automotive parts distribu-

Typical core offering	Typical optional services
• One-stop shop – range and availability	• Sourcing of products • Back-to-back ordering • Simplified supply logistics
• Bulk breaking	• Consignment stocking • Repackaging
• Credit	• Extended credit, project finance
• First-level technical support (pre-sales)	• Second-level technical support (post-sales) – effectively acting as an outsourced provider of support • Technical training
• Logistics – delivery	• Logistics – drop shipment to ultimate customer
• Order consolidation	• Project management – coordinating the supply of several suppliers and shipping to multiple locations
• Product information collateral	• Marketing services – effectively acting as an outsourced provider

Figure 3.1 Typical core offering and optional services offered by distributors to their customers

tors hold many thousands of individual parts ready for 24-hour delivery to garages and workshops servicing and repairing customers' cars, some of which can have been out of production for many years.

Implicit in the distributor's offer is also a value proposition that has value to both the distributor's customer and supplier – **breaking bulk**. Most distributors break bulk to quantities nearer that required by the end-customer, such as case-quantities for wine and spirits in alcoholic drink distribution. Many distributors do very little genuine 'wholesaling', ie in large volumes, but sell in ones and twos, as their customers effectively trade back-to-back in the volumes required by individual end-customers. This does vary by industry sector, but as dealers and traders do not wish to carry stocks of anything but the most essential supplies, they regard the ability to buy in retail quantities to be an essential aspect of the distributor's offer.

The provision of **credit** is a core benefit enabling customers to be able to supply, install, or fit the products without having to finance their entire work-in-progress and end-customer receivables. This liquidity is often multiplied in a market with traders and dealers sourcing from three or more distributors to maximize the credit facilities available to them. The distributor uses its local market and trading knowledge to set sensible credit limits and can spread the risk of any bad debts over thousands of trading relationships.

Most distributors provide some level of **technical support**, usually on a pre-sale (and therefore free) basis. This is an integral part of the selling-in process, especially for new products and technical innovations, and varies from simple 'does this do the job or work with other components in a system?' enquiries to ensure the right product is supplied through to what can be quite sophisticated configuration activities in the high end of technology-based industries. This role may extend to include post-sale support in a troubleshooting mode to resolve mis-supply or configuration issues. As an extension of this selling-in to the final tier of the channel, distributors will often provide **product marketing collateral** for the trade to use in selling-in new products to the end-customer and support the overall marketing communication process.

Different industries and markets will have different norms for the provision of delivery **logistics**. In some industries, distributors may provide this free, in others distributors may charge on orders below a minimum amount and in others distributors may expect the customer to collect. Where a distributor is out of stock or does not carry a particular item, it will order it from the supplier and then ship it out to the customer when it arrives. Typically as industries mature, costs become more transparent and so delivery charges will be shown separately from the core product price.

Depending on the situation, it is often hard for the distributor to recover some or all of these costs. Additional charges for small order supplements, etc, are often well below the actual costs of the delivery. Distributors rarely know the true cost to serve and their shipping charge supplements tend to be arbitrary and designed not to alienate customers. Closely related to this is **order consolidation**, enabling customers to minimize their delivery costs by waiting until an entire order of different products from different suppliers is ready to ship.

All the elements above (with the possible exception of delivery charges) are built into the price paid by the customer for the product. All the additional optional services that can be offered go beyond this core proposition and therefore are charged in addition to the product price – either as a service charge on a fee basis or as an addition to the transaction cost per item. These services typically emerge as an industry matures and the margin on the core value proposition becomes increasingly squeezed and the distributor needs to find new sources of profitability. The same competitive pressures apply to the final tiers, who look to eliminate any activities that are not core to their differentiation and turn to the distributor to provide these functions on an outsourced basis, taking advantage of their scale and depth of capabilities. These can be related to product supply such as **consignment stocking** (see panel) of specialist products or the **project management** of complex multiple shipments across multiple suppliers to multiple locations or logistics as in **drop shipments**, where the distributor delivers direct to the end-customer, on behalf of the final tier. This can be enhanced to include packaging and delivery notes that appear to be from the final-tier player and even invoicing, all saving costly handling events and activity in the value chain. Providing the distributor is efficient, savings can be shared between the distributor, the final-tier player and the customer (through lower prices).

Consignment stock

In developing markets, where finance and distributor capital are tight, consignment stock is often used to finance market expansion and penetration. For example, in the years immediately after the fall of the Berlin Wall, many companies scrabbled to secure market share in a 'land-grab' situation. Many US and European companies used consignment stock to finance distributors, fill shelves and block access to competition. BAT, for example, took the risk of setting up a consignment stock for its distributor, Brodokomerc, in Croatia. This risk, given the unstable nature of the market, was doubly surprising as the agreement to operate a consignment stock did not make any reference as to whom was liable for any bad debt that might arise! This is a good example of taking a risk-positive approach to securing market access in the early stages of market development.

Bespoke services that are not directly attached to transactions include **sourcing** of new suppliers or products and outsourced marketing, where the distributor acts as the **marketing services** supplier to the final-tier players who do not want to in-source this activity. This enables the final tier to run more intensive marketing activities at key points in the year without bearing an overhead cost at other times. They are also able to access a depth of specialist marketing skills they could never justify on their level of sales. In technical sectors this can blur with the provision of second-level and post-sales **technical support** which again the final tier may not be able to afford in-house but can subcontract to the distributor.

Supplier role

Distributors can play a wide variety of roles for suppliers as we describe below, depending on the maturity of the product category, product life-cycle stage, market share of the supplier and density of the final tier in the distribution system. But in every case, the distributor's primary role is as a route to market for the supplier and its effectiveness will be critical to the supplier seeking to reach a segment or the entire market.

Alternative models

This range of distributor types can be characterized in terms of their business model (Figure 3.2):

■ **Value added distributors** – these distributors are focused on products where there is limited distribution, ie very few or only one distributor

Spectrum of distributors defined by business model

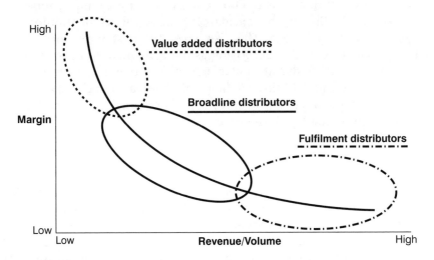

Figure 3.2 Spectrum of distributors defined by business model

operates in the market. This could be for reasons of a small market size, or that the suppliers are new into the market or the technology of the products is at an early stage of the adoption life cycle. In each case, the supplier is looking to the distributor to be highly proactive in recruiting and developing the often specialist final-tier players who can reach the right segments in the market. Market development is their core offering to the supplier. The distributor is tasked with building the demand for the product through marketing and proactive sales activities which can include extensive training for the final-tier channel players, co-selling and the provision of extensive pre-sales technical support. To be able to do all this, the distributor needs to invest its own time and resources in fully mastering the product from a technical and marketing perspective. All this work does not come cheap, so the distributor expects to earn a rich margin to compensate for its investment in each sale and for the fact that initially sales will be relatively low in volume.

■ **Broadline distributors** – as indicated by their name, these distributors provide the mainstream market coverage, both in terms of the product range they carry and the proportion of the market they service. Market access is their core offering to the supplier, covering most or all of the channels a supplier needs to reach through established trading relationships and with long-standing marketing and communications tools (catalogues, mailers, websites) with proven response rates. There will usually be several distributors competing in the market, creating a more price-competitive environment, leading to lower margins on product sales. Suppliers can expect to pay for placement in the marketing tools or for running sales promotions as these costs cannot be absorbed by the normal trading margin. As a result market share leaders tend to be better served by the broadliner as their scale of business ensures high visibility and share of mind among the distributor's sales and marketing teams. Some brands, however, will go further and may seek greater influence over the distributor's resources – such as by financing a dedicated product manager. Smaller suppliers tend to have to work hard to ensure there is sufficient focus on their products and may have to offer one distributor in the market exclusive distribution rights in order not to dilute their focus. As markets mature, consolidation among broadliners reduces the number of distributors available to suppliers, increasing the distributors' power in extracting significant discounts and rebates from the supplier (at industry conferences it's interesting to observe whether the distributors are paying court to the leading suppliers or the other way around!).

■ **Fulfilment distributors** – these distributors operate in markets where products are 'bought' rather than 'sold', such as aftermarket products and consumables. No marketing is involved in respect of the products, and sales are driven by price, availability and convenience. In effect these distributors are logistics engines for the supplier, who will have to make all the running to create brand awareness and preference in the end-customer market. Margins are very low, so the distributor runs a high-volume, highly efficient operation, doing all it can to eliminate unnecessary activities and complexity. The distributor needs massive volume at these tiny margins to be able to cover its infrastructure and operating costs. Orders are increasingly received through the website rather than the call centre and warehouses are highly automated centralized operations. How do these distributors differ from the pure logistics companies such as Fedex or UPS? In two major ways: first, they bear a stocking risk, balancing demand and supply through their inventory management skills; and second, they bear the credit risk, leveraging their local market expertise. Suppliers may compensate fulfilment distributors either through the trading margin or, more recently, by negotiating a fee per transaction as the cost of distribution tends to be the same regardless of the selling price. This ensures that smaller-ticket items are not subsidized by big-ticket items as would happen through a trading margin.

Supplier role – core functions

Given the description of the different distributor models above, it can be seen there are two core functions provided by distributors to suppliers, demand generation and supply fulfilment. Additional functions include providing market information and serving as an outsourced front office, representing the supplier in a territory, or outsourced service and support function, providing warranty and technical backup and support services to the final tier or even end-customer in certain circumstances.

As suppliers increasingly move to focus on their core activities, they have turned to distributors as the logical partners to whom non-differentiating activities can be outsourced. As these activities themselves have varying investment, cost and margin profiles, distributors are segmenting their businesses to offer specialized services from discrete divisions. This enables them to align their pricing and business models and avoid unplanned cross-subsidization of services and to be more competitive. The nature of these services varies by industry, but some typical examples are given in Figure 3.3.

Note that many of the activities listed under Typical Core Offering will be charged for in addition to the trading margin or distributor discount, especially the provision of sell-out information and participation in sales spiffs (short-term promotions involving incentives for the sales staff) and marketing collateral and catalogues. In many distributors the marketing function is a profit centre, attracting marketing development funds from its suppliers by offering innovative marketing tools and activities.

Depending on the product or the territory, the distributor may play an active role in **demand generation**, actively building up awareness and selling capability amongst its customers, who in turn promote sales among the end-customers. Typically, suppliers negotiate targets for sales levels for a year and reward distributors with either higher levels of discount related to volumes or pay for results through rebates or other incentives for passing the target.

Suppliers can have a range of products requiring distribution that can range in number from a few tens of SKUs up to many thousands. Typically the sales volumes of these products are subject to Pareto's law, ie 20 per cent of the SKUs account for 80 per cent of the revenues. For reasons of margin and customer service, the supplier expects the distributor to carry the full range, or a significant proportion of it, to ensure **supply fulfilment**. Contracts may specify the inventory holding requirements of each class of product, or there may be a fee or incentive for stocking a proportion of the range. In many cases, it is in the distributor's interest to hold some inven-

Typical core offering	Typical specialized services

• Demand generation
 – Channel recruitment
 – Channel accounts and database
 – Marketing fund deployment
 – Special pricing management
 – Teleweb outbound and inbound sales
 – Regular marketing mailings
 – 'Spiff' sales promotions
 – Channel conferences
 – Channel training
 – Channel financing through credit
    provision
 – In-market product management
 – Frontline technical support
	• Demand generation
	 – Channel account management
	 – Programme management
	 – Co-op fund management
	 – Special channel financing and credit
	    offerings
	 – End-customer marketing and lead-
	    generation programmes
	 – Conference and exhibition services

• Supply fulfilment – Bulk breaking – Outbound logistics – Reverse logistics – Channel credit risk	• Supply fulfilment – Consignment stocking – Vendor managed inventories – Vendor stock warehousing
• Market information – Sales out reporting – Channel intelligence	• Market information – Channel research – End-customer research
• Outsourced services	• Outsourced services – Warranty management – Break-fix operations – Second-level and post-sales technical support – In-market representation – Trademark registration and protection

Figure 3.3 Typical core offering and optional services offered by distributors to vendors

tory as the uncompensated costs of handling a back order for a one-off SKU can outweigh the costs of stocking.

By acting as the supplier to potentially thousands of local trade customers, the distributor takes the **credit risk** on these sales, requiring it to have excellent credit control and credit insight to minimize the exposure and cost of bad debts. This is of real value to the supplier who would otherwise bear the cost of the credit management function as well as the bad debt risk.

To manage their channels, suppliers need good information about their distributors' sales and inventory levels and are prepared to pay to get it. This is either built into the margin allowed or is an explicit element of the discount. The latter approach enables a supplier to withdraw the margin in the event of a particular distributor failing to provide information of appropriate quality or in the right format. In mature industries, this is typically provided on a weekly or even daily basis through EDI links or internet-based automatic reporting. This **market information** may be augmented by other data such as competitor activity, customer recruitment reports, lost sales reports and so on.

Information sources

Distributors in many cases are not only sources of information, but may even regard such market information as their differentiator or value to the supplier. Fallouts with distributors may leave supposedly strong brands with no alternative routes to the consumer. For one major oil company operating throughout Europe, its knowledge of many of its international distributors was limited to little more than the tonnage delivered to each of them. Recognizing the weakness of its position, it took steps to address the situation by investing heavily in understanding the business model and modus operandi of its distributors in order to increase not only its market knowledge, but the effectiveness and efficiency of compensation paid to each distributor.

The distributor also acts to a greater or lesser degree as an **outsourced front office** for the supplier, providing the channel development function – recruiting new partners, the supplier's local or territory representative and providing services such as warranty or pre- and post-sales support. All these functions are determined by contract and can be the subject of intense negotiation, the outcome of which usually reflects the relative balance of power between the supplier and the distributor. The agreed levels of distributor compensation are paid either through the margin allowed through discounts or as specific activity-based fees. In some cases the fee will be partially or wholly dependent upon customer feedback on service levels and quality.

4

How the distributor business model works

Role defines business model

The roles fulfilled by the distributor for both customer and supplier define the business model of the distributor and its key characteristics.

The first of these is that the distributor's business model is capital intensive, driven by the need to hold stock and finance trade customer credit, less any supplier credit received. Second, as essentially a high-volume, low-value-add business, the distributor trades on thin margins, and thus needs to be a low-overhead business. This is a challenging model, requiring the ability to manage both profitability and asset efficiency or productivity. Let's look a set of typical distributor financial statements to see this in action (Figure 4.1).

The first thing to note is that the balance sheet, on the right, is dominated by three numbers:

- **inventory** (products held for resale);
- **accounts receivable** (from customers for sales made on credit);
- **accounts payable** (to suppliers for products bought on credit).

These three items are the constituent elements of working capital (inventory plus accounts receivable less accounts payable). A balance sheet shows

ABC Co distributor financials

	$m				$m
Sales	19,316		**Fixed assets**		**423**
Cost of sales	18,308		**Current assets**		
Gross profit	**1,008**		Inventory	1,408	
Overheads	952		Accounts receivable	1,897	
Operating profit	**56**		Cash	401	
Interest	12		**Total current assets**		**3,706**
Profit before taxation	**44**		**Current liabilities**		
Taxation	16		Accounts payable	1,550	
Profit after taxation	**28**		Other	764	
			Total current liabilities		**2,314**
			Net current assets		**1,392**
			Long-term liabilities		59
			Net assets		**1,756**
			Shareholders funds		**1,756**
Income statement			**Balance sheet**		

Figure 4.1 ABC Co distributor financials

the situation at a moment in time, so it is effectively showing us a snapshot of the working capital cycle frozen in action. The other items such as **fixed assets** (land, buildings, warehousing systems, IT systems, etc) and **other** balances are relatively immaterial. It is mainly the net total of the working capital items that determines how much capital the distributor needs to raise to finance its business. It's a fine balancing act; too little and the distributor runs out of inventory ('stock-outs') or cannot pay its suppliers in time while waiting for payments from its customers; too much capital and the cost of the capital required drags down the profitability of the business.

Profit is a very small number between two very big numbers

Looking at the income statement on the left we can get a sense of just how tight the margins can be in some sectors of distribution. The gross margin is the difference between the price the distributor pays for its products to suppliers (= **cost of sales**) and price it gets for them when sold to customers (= **sales**). It's a very small number between two very big ones. And the distributor has to pay for all its overheads and interest out of this margin, leaving whatever is left over as its **net profit**. And that's an even smaller number compared to the two big numbers, sales and cost of sales. After tax is deducted (assuming there is a profit), whatever is left is available to be paid out as a dividend or retained in the balance sheet to finance a bigger working-capital balance (needed if the distributor intends to grow in the next trading period).

It gets even more interesting when you compare the gross profit made in the year of $1,008m in our example with the working capital of $1,775m (= $1,408m + $1,897m – $1,550m). This means that our distributor has tied up over 1.75 billion dollars for a year to earn just over a billion dollars in gross profit... and 44 million dollars in net profit. Seems like a lot to lay out for not much return. The slightest hiccup in buying, say, some products that need to be written down in value because they don't sell, or incurring a few bad debts, would have hit profits and turned even that profit into a loss.

Managing working capital is a balancing act

This balancing of the profitability and working capital profile of the product range is at the heart of the distributor's business model. Each of the types of distributor profiled earlier (value added, broadline and fulfilment) has a balance that is right in the context of its value proposition and business model. All of them are striving to get higher margins and reduce their working capital while offering the best range of products and in-stock availability to their customers in the market. The role of product managers in the distributor is critical and their incentives should be tied to *both* margin and working capital (or at least inventory) management.

The smart distributor knows that margin management is critical to its success, using a portfolio approach to blend fast-turning, low-margin products with slower-turning but higher-margin products. Even tiny improvements in margin make for a big impact in the operating profit. The challenge is to balance the product range and stocking depth with what customers are demanding and the suppliers are insisting on with what makes sense financially. The 80:20 rule applies everywhere in distribution, with 20 per cent of the products accounting for 80 per cent of the volumes, but a *different* 20 per cent may account for 80 per cent of the profits. To make things more complex, distributors are vulnerable to offers from suppliers to take lorry loads of extra stock into their warehouses for an additional discount (usually near the end of a quarter or a supplier's financial year). These discounts initially appear attractive, but as the deal is being offered to all the distributors in the market, any cost advantage often ends up being passed on to the customer as a discount incentive to ensure the extra stock moves out of the warehouse. The net result is happy customers and suppliers but often not much more profit for the distributors, with the extra sales putting more pressure on their infrastructure. However, the distributors cannot afford to be out of line with the market on high-volume items so often feel they have no choice but to take the extra discount available (and extra volumes) in order to protect their market positioning and customer base.

Controlling overheads is equally important, with many of the costs being essentially fixed in nature, ie they do not vary directly in line with sales volumes. Distributors looking for growth need to time their investments in additional capacity carefully to avoid getting too far ahead of the curve and pushing up the cost base before sales have grown to cover it. This can be trickier for IT systems, which seem to take years to deliver their promised productivity, than for warehouses, which can be thrown up in less than a year. Increasingly, distributors are looking for ways to make more of their costs variable by outsourcing elements of their essential infrastructure, including transport, warehousing and even sales call centres. Each of these involves tough trade-offs between the benefits of improved cost flexibility and lower costs and the risks of loss of control and potential impact on customer satisfaction. Another challenge is whether to put more sales through web portals, reducing costs of order taking but losing the chance to up-sell or cross-sell the customer on a call or the opportunity to respond to a competitor's pricing to keep a valued customer.

For distributors, working capital management is all about recognizing that they are dealing with a finite and expensive resource – capital. Money tied up in product A is not available to invest in stocking product Z. Credit extended to (or stretched by) one customer cannot be used until the debt is paid. Supplier credit limits, once used, need to be paid off before more products can be ordered in. In order to grow, the distributor needs to increase its working capital to match the bigger trading volumes or accelerate the cycle of cash to cash: money paid out to suppliers for inventories which are sold to customers on credit who eventually pay for them. Distributors that fail to plan for growth find that their cash situation deteriorates rapidly despite sales and profits growing healthily. Often called 'overtrading', it has been the cause of more distributors getting into trouble than falling sales and the speed at which it happens is startling. Taking ABC Co's financial statements as shown above, a 20 per cent growth in sales volumes would require a similar increase in working capital, which in cash terms means $355m (ie $1,775 × 20%), almost eliminating its cash balances of $401m and leaving it with just $46m. Another 20 per cent the following year would require an overdraft of nearly $400m (ie after a further $355 × 120% = $426m has left the building). So in just two years, ABC Co would have traded its way from a cash balance of $400m to an overdraft of the same amount. Even if ABC Co applies all its after-tax profits to funding working capital, these would make barely a dent in the overdraft: $28m × 1.2 in year one equals $33m, plus $33m × 1.2 in year 2 equals $40m, making a total of $77m. This is less than 10 per cent of the $800m change in the cash balance, and assumes no cash is used to replace fixed assets or repay long-term liabilities, etc.

To increase its capital the distributor has to retain more profits (assuming it's earned any), borrow more or go back to its shareholders and ask for more capital to be invested. Both borrowers and investors will ask tough questions about the business plan and the distributor's ability to service the investment (pay the interest or dividends) and either repay the principal borrowed or grow the capital value of the business for shareholders. Any investor will want to know what sort of return he or she will get on his or her investment. In our example above, the net profit of $44m is the return generated in a year on capital invested of $1,756m which is a return of about 2.5 per cent, ie some way short of the rate available by leaving the cash in the bank. And ABC Co is unlikely in purely financial terms to command a high price for its original investors if it were to be sold with that level of profitability. (It may secure a premium for some strategic market positioning.)

The alternative is to accelerate the working capital cycle, which means tightening customer credit, reducing stocking levels or asking suppliers for extended credit terms or credit limits. Each of these has implications for the distributor's key trading relationships and may conflict with its growth ambitions.

All in all, the distributor is faced with a challenging business model, one that requires exceptional day-to-day management control as well as a clear business strategy and well-defined market positioning.

The measures that matter and how to manage with them

The measures that matter in a distributor reflect the way the business model works, with margins, working capital management and productivity measures (combining margin and working capital management) being especially powerful. We have devoted a chapter to each of these types of measure (Chapter 5 – Margins and profitability, Chapter 6 – Working capital and Chapter 7 – Productivity), explaining how and why distributors should use these types of measure to manage their businesses. In Chapter 8 we show how to assess sustainability – the long-term business health – of a distributor and set out a recommended template or dashboard for monitoring the entire business. Finally in Chapter 9 we focus on the challenge of managing growth and show how to define the safe level of growth for a distributor without overtrading.

5

Margins and profitability

Multiple margins

The first point to note about margins is that although the basic concept of the margin is to measure the profit of the business, there are as many ways to calculate a margin as there are distributors, certainly when measured on an internal basis. Even with national and international accounting standards, there is still plenty of room for the exercise of judgement as to what can and can't be included in a margin calculation. So never assume that you can compare margins between distributors (or any business) without first asking what is and is not included. Even the most qualified of accountants would have no hesitation in asking 'how are you calculating your margins?', so neither should you. Let's start with the basic types of margin and what they tell you.

Gross margin and value add

The **gross margin** is a measure of the distributor's value added as it is the purest measure of the difference between the price paid to suppliers and the price obtained from customers.

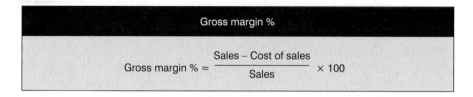

Figure 5.1 Gross margin %

The higher the margin, the greater the value added by the distributor. In our example distributor, ABC Co, the gross margin is $1,008m/$19,316m × 100 which equals 5.22 per cent. There are several things to note for even this simple measure:

■ Neither sales nor cost of sales should include VAT or sales taxes.
■ Cost of sales (sometimes called cost of goods sold) includes all costs incurred in getting the product to its state and condition necessary for sale. So it will include any shipping inbound costs but *not* costs incurred in shipping the product to the customer.
■ Cost of sales includes any work done on the product such as testing, processing, configuration, assembly and packaging. If these costs are internal to the distributor, they should include a fair allocation of labour and overhead costs.
■ Any discounts, rebates or other price reductions received from suppliers should reduce cost of sales, and therefore increase gross margins.
■ The cost of writing down inventories for obsolescence, shrinkage or stock losses, deterioration and so on is added to cost of sales, reducing margins as soon as the loss is recognized.
■ Costs of selling the product or sales commissions are not included in cost of sales but discounts given to customers are deducted from sales.
■ Prompt payment discounts received from suppliers are generally not deducted from cost of sales nor those granted to customers deducted from sales. However, in some industries these discounts are so significant that they have become part of the normal discounting mechanism used by suppliers and are deducted to present a fair picture.

Note also that the gross margin is the gross profit expressed as a percentage of sales. If it were expressed as a percentage of cost of sales it would be a mark-up (in our example the mark-up is 5.51 per cent, ie $1,008m/$18,308m). It is not uncommon in talking with distributors to find the terms gross margin and mark-up used interchangeably, and incorrectly, so do not assume that the term has been used correctly – ask the basis of the margins you are being presented with.

Gross margins can be applied to the entire business, as we have just done for ABC Co, as well as to individual SKUs, product lines, product categories, suppliers, business divisions, customers and customer segments. It does not matter whether it is calculated for a year or for a day's trading, so long as the sales and cost of sales are for the same period.

One point to watch is that percentages can be used or interpreted in misleading ways because they convey no sense of the size of business done. For example, which is better: a gross margin of 12 per cent or one of 7 per cent? Well, if the 12 per cent margin was earned on product A with sales of $1,000 and the 7 per cent margin earned on product B with sales of $5,000, the distributor would have earned a gross profit (or 'money margin') of only $120 on product A but $350 on product B. This might seem obvious, but it is a key point that can be overlooked. It is important because most distributors' overhead costs are usually fairly fixed so they need to earn a fixed amount of gross profit before the business can earn an operating profit. In managing their business model, distributors need to beware of incentivizing their product managers just on gross margins expressed as a percentage as the profit measure, as the chart shown in Figure 5.2 illustrates.

Dropping the market leader to focus on the new entrant could wipe out gross profits of $500,000 which sales of the other brands would be very

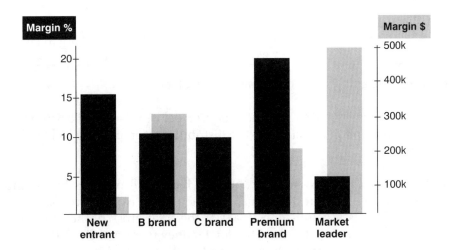

Figure 5.2 Comparison of gross margin % and gross margin $ earned on different brands

unlikely to replace, as relatively few customers would be switch-sold. There is more than one global distributor that in seeking to increase its gross margins has focused on products with higher margins at the expense of its high-volume, low-margin products. This has led to lower overall gross profits, and in one case caused operating losses for several months before it was able to turn the situation around.

Margin mix or blended margin

For distributors handling the brand leaders in a market, the margins will tend to be lower, but the volumes higher if they are getting their fair share of the brand's market-leading volumes. Attempting to increase margins by dropping the top brands damages not only gross profits but also the distributor's market credibility if customers expect to find the major brands stocked at their usual distributor. The answer lies in managing the **margin mix** or **blended margin**.

Consider the example shown in Figure 5.3.

Product	Sales price	Cost price	Gross margin	Gross profit per unit	Volume	Sales revenue	Gross profit
A	$500	$450	10.0%	$50	100	$50,000	$5,000
B	$400	$352	12.0%	$48	50	$20,000	$2,400
C	$350	$322	8.0%	$28	200	$70,000	$5,600
D	$300	$279	7.0%	$21	500	$150,000	$10,500
E	$180	$168	7.0%	$12	950	$171,000	$11,400
Total			7.6%			$461,000	$34,900

Figure 5.3 Example of blended margin calculation

The blended margin of these products is 7.6 per cent (= $34,900/$461,000). What are the options available to the distributor for improving its blended margin?

■ Reduce sales of products D and E, which have margins below the blended margin, but this would put the money margin at risk. These two products account for $21,900 of the total gross profit or money margin, almost two-thirds of the total money margin of $34,900.
■ Increase sales of products A, B and C, which would increase overall gross profits as well as strengthening the blended margin.

- Add a higher margin product into the mix, which would dilute the impact of the existing products in the blended margin, and increase the blended margin so long as the new product's gross margin was higher than 7.6%.
- Increase sales prices of any of the products or negotiate better discounts from the suppliers.

In practice, many distributors can often increase prices for products that are lower volume, because they do not represent price-benchmarking items. One famous example from the IT sector is that the distributor can make such a high gross margin on the carrying case compared to the laptop computer that it makes more money margin on the case! Even within product categories, there will be SKUs that are less price sensitive than others and these can be eased upwards without impacting sales volumes. Smart differential pricing within a category and across categories is termed **portfolio pricing**, enabling the distributor to achieve its targeted blended margin by continually tuning its pricing and making more effort to cross-sell from its high-volume products which are priced to drive volume and meet customer demand.

Making some minor improvements to the pricing and volumes of products A, B and C in our example could achieve a new blended margin of 8.7 per cent, up from 7.6 per cent (Figure 5.4). Note that not only has the gross margin percentage increased, but revenues are up by 8 per cent and the money margin is up by almost 25 per cent. Unfortunately, it sometimes takes a crisis before a distributor can be persuaded to make these types of moves with its pricing strategy, but there is much to be gained by experimenting with price changes and finding out which products will bear higher prices and which will not. The rewards available justify taking some carefully controlled risks and, where volumes are adversely affected, prices can be quickly adjusted back again. Good product managers should be able to identify most of the safe products and SKUs that can bear price

Product	Sales price	Cost price	Gross margin	Gross profit per unit	Volume	Sales revenue	Gross profit
A	$525	$450	14.0%	$75	120	$63,000	$9,000
B	$420	$352	16.0%	$68	70	$29,400	$4,760
C	$355	$322	9.0%	$33	240	$85,200	$7,920
D	$300	$279	7.0%	$21	500	$150,000	$10,500
E	$180	$168	7.0%	$12	950	$171,000	$11,400
Total			8.7%			$498,600	$43,580

Figure 5.4 New blended margin calculation

increases but it requires excellent coordination with the sales teams to make sure that the cross-selling is driven through to maintain and build volumes in the right SKUs.

Sales management is a key discipline in distributors' margin management and one that needs constant attention and monitoring. In most distributors, there are multiple discounts that can be applied by a sales person to allow for the size of the order, the loyalty or spending power of the customer, the need to defend against specific competitors or to support current promotions. Wily sales people can usually find a way to play these rules to the customer's maximum advantage to ensure they maximize their sales. The distributor's sales people don't see an additional 1 or 2 per cent discount as a big hit to their margin objectives. The result of this mindset is potentially very damaging to the economics of the distributor's business model. Take the extra 1 per cent discount given away and put it into context. For a distributor making, say, 8 per cent gross margin and 1 per cent net margin on sales, that extra discount knocks the gross margin down to 7 per cent and wipes out the net margin. As highlighted earlier, profit is a small number between two very big ones, so a small reduction in the sales line (without any impact on cost of sales) becomes a very big hit on the profit line – in our example 100 per cent of the net profit! Sales people need to have this in the front of their mind when negotiating the last few points to clinch a sale.

One way distributors attempt to manage this is to ensure that the absolute floor or 'low ball' on pricing is still profitable, so that even the most aggressive sales people cannot discount their way into a loss. In countless distributors examined, the effect of this is to produce a gross margin percentage–volume chart that looks like Figure 5.5.

This chart shows the volume of sales closed at each level of gross margin in bands of a half per cent, so for example $300,000 of sales were closed at between 4.5 and 5 per cent gross margin. The 'low ball' is the lowest gross margin at which the sales team can make a sale by applying all the discounts allowed according to internal rules. This margin should be possible only when selling to the distributor's best customer, buying its on-offer products in a single large order and claiming that it can get a better price from the competition... obviously a fairly rare situation. But look at what the analysis (taken from a real case) shows. More business is done at this 'minimum' margin (ie maximum discount level) than at any other. Rather than being a floor, the low ball has become a leaning-post propping up the majority of the sales. What does this do to the blended margin? It pulls it right down to around 4.5 per cent. And even worse, there is something over $100,000 of sales closed *below* the low ball, something that shouldn't be

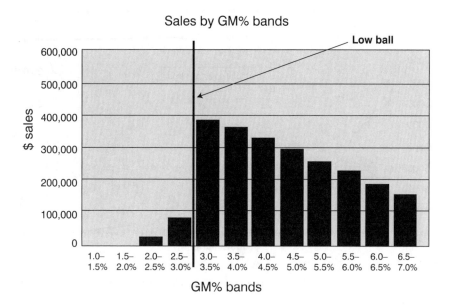

Figure 5.5 Illustration of sales volume by margin where there is a 'low ball'

possible under the distributor's own rules. The lesson is clear; sales people will find ways over, under and through any rules controlling discounts if there is a sale to be made. Regular analysis of this type is needed to track the situation and to take control.

Interestingly, the far right of the chart – out of sight in the figure above – will often show a few pockets of business closed at very high gross margins. Investigation of these sales, in terms of which products have been sold to which customers, can uncover some interesting niche opportunities that are worth developing into bigger business activity. Indeed, taking a customer perspective often throws up a picture of opportunities to improve the way discounts are applied to improve margins. Figure 5.6 shows customers ranked from left to right by sales volumes (left-hand axis) and the margins earned from them (right-hand axis).

Applying the normal rules of giving better discounts to the best customers would suggest the margin curve ought to slope smoothly up to the right in a mirror image of the sales curve. Instead, what we find (taken from a real case) is that there are some customers at the far right-hand side with the smallest level of business delivering margins as low as the distributor's best customers. Some of these dips may be caused by the particular

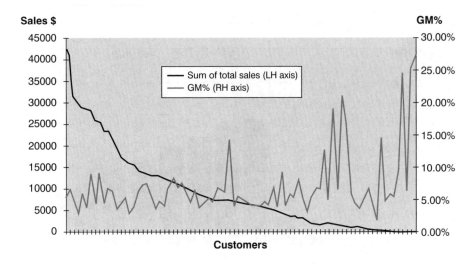

Figure 5.6 Illustrative distribution of gross margin % by customers' sales revenues

products bought, but on investigation, the random pattern of the margins owed much more to the random pattern of customer discounts awarded by the sales team. It also suggested that the distributor was not doing enough to take care of its best customers.

Contribution margin

So far we have focused on the gross margin, but how do you account for the fact that some products require a lot more pre-sales support, take more time to sell to customers, require special handling or attract a higher level of returns involving expensive reverse logistics? Or that some customers demand more account management, require shipments to go to multiple drop-off points, quibble over every invoice and take twice the credit period to pay? These customers may deliver the same gross margins as ones that don't behave in this way but they certainly don't deliver the same level of profitability for the distributor. The measure that reveals the impact of these types of factor on profitability is **contribution margin** (Figure 5.7).

This margin deducts variable costs as well as cost of sales so that it reflects all the factors illustrated above. There is no definitive list of the items that make up variable costs, so the contribution margin is not one that can be

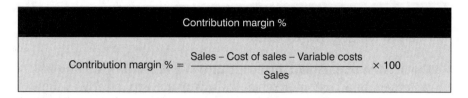

Figure 5.7 Contribution margin %

compared between distributors. It is up to the individual distributor to decide which costs it deducts in striking the contribution margin. In some distributors they will strike a series of contribution margins, working down the profit and loss account to bring in additional factors and costs and savings ('contribution margin 1, contribution margin 2, contribution margin 3'), which will be used for different analyses. In order to allocate costs to the specific product or customer, distributors use some form of allocation algorithm or mechanism, which means that the contribution margins are less accurate than the gross margin. For example, it may be easy to allocate the sales commissions paid to the sales team and the rebates and allowances provided by suppliers to specific products, but it may be harder to allocate the pre-sales or returns costs.

Earlier we highlighted the fact that market-leading brands tend to have lower gross margins, but equally they require less marketing and selling activity on the part of the distributor than a new brand for which the distributor is building up a market presence. The contribution margin is one way to quantify this impact if it includes some allocation of sales and marketing costs. Good distributors run frequent contribution analyses of different cuts of their business, by product category, by supplier, by customer or customer segment. Typically these analyses show that the best performers are earning contributions 20 per cent higher than average and the worst 20 per cent below. This is a significant range (ie 40 per cent) and smart distributors use this insight to make decisions about the mix of products, suppliers and customers in their business and identify the opportunities to fine-tune the contributions earned.

It is vital for a distributor to have a **customer view** of its business and to understand the economics of its different customers and customer segments.

Fire the biggest customer

The need to understand the economics of a distributor's different customers and customer segments was made very clearly in the case of one distributor which in sales terms was successful but was struggling to make an operating profit. Its cash flow was sinking to the point that action was needed to save the business.

Analysing the contribution by customer showed that the distributor's biggest customer, who accounted for over 25 per cent of its sales, was in fact making a negative contribution. In other words, the distributor was paying for the privilege of serving its biggest customer – not a healthy way to run the business.

Action was taken to identify the cost drivers that were hitting the contribution (extended credit, multiple ship-to points, pre-sales support) and the customer invited to change its demands or to accept that it should pay for them. These were tough negotiations but the distributor management team's backbone was stiffened by the thought that failure to confront the situation would leave them without a viable business. The customer refused to accept new terms so the distributor bit the bullet and terminated the trading relationship. The sales, management and other resources in the distributor that been focused on its previous biggest customer were rapidly redeployed to build up other, more profitable customers and find new ones. Within a month, the distributor's profitability improved and cash flowed back into the business. To put the icing on the cake, its fired customer returned with requests to supply (lower-volume and higher-margin) products that it had been struggling to source reliably elsewhere, making it now one of the distributor's more profitable customers. It was a salutary lesson, but it had taken a cash flow crisis before the management team were prepared to undertake the right action.

All too often the situation is left to continue because the distributor does not do the analysis or is afraid to lose the business by getting tough with costly customers. Rigorous analysis shows just how expensive this approach can be and highlights that the best customers are often subsidizing the worst customers, putting long-term success at risk.

The differential costs of serving customers can be classified under a number of headings:

- **Marketing-driven costs**
  - Relationship management
  - Allowances
  - Programmes (eg loyalty programmes)
- **Sales-driven costs**
  - Discounts/rebates
  - Promotions
  - Sales person time required
  - Sales cycle times and conversion rates
  - Sales channel used
- **Transaction-driven costs**
  - Order complexity
  - Size of order
- **Logistics-driven costs**
  - Shop-to points
  - Returns
- **Inventory-driven costs**
  - Inventory levels
  - Product mix required
- **Finance-driven costs**
  - Credit limits
  - Credit period taken

Mapping these graphically would look like Figure 5.8, giving a complete profile of the **cost to serve** of one customer or customer segment.

Comparing these charts between customers (or between customer segments) will reveal which costs are the most differentiated and thus should be tackled. Customers with a high cost to serve can be incentivized to reduce the costs they impose on the distributor, eg offering a discount for moving from dedicated to non-dedicated sales people or, better yet, ordering online. Alternatively, discounts could be offered for less frequent but larger average orders. Clearly these discounts need to be less than the costs already incurred, but customers will change behaviour for surprisingly small incentives or, if preferred, penalties. Most distributors will either set a minimum order size or charge extra for multiple ship-to points.

One word of caution: some distributors have got carried away with analysis and installed full-blown activity-based-costing (ABC) systems to allocate every cost in the business. The test to apply is: are you able to measure

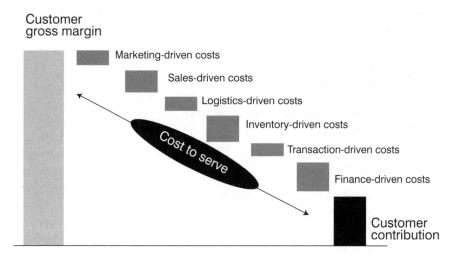

Figure 5.8 Cost to serve profile of one customer or customer segment

the cost driver – for example the number of ship-to points – and does it vary significantly by customer or product? If you cannot answer yes to both, then do not bother allocating the cost. It wastes your time and adds complexity and confusion rather than clarity and insight.

The contribution margin takes account of the variable costs in the cost structure, leaving the **fixed costs**, which need to be less than the contribution if the business is to make a net profit. Fixed costs are defined as costs that do not vary directly with unit volume. They aren't really fixed, of course, but in the short term they are relatively fixed and certainly are not affected by incremental sales. They tend to be related to infrastructure such as warehouses and storage racking or the IT systems, call centres and payroll. Distributors monitor their cost structures by comparing either individual elements or the total to their sales. In our ABC Co example, overheads are $952m/$19,316m or 4.9 per cent. Over time, as the distributor grows, it would expect this percentage to go down as it gains the benefits of economies of scale. In some industries that are experiencing declining average selling prices (ASPs), such as in the high-technology or telecommunications sectors, at times falling by up to 40 per cent over a year, stable revenue will hide a significant increase in volumes, putting the cost structure under pressure. The extra activity will mean more orders, more picking and packing, more invoicing, etc, but for the same amount of revenue. Distributors faced with this challenge try to up-sell their customers (encourage them to buy bigger-ticket items) or increase the cross-sell rate (number of customers who buy additional products) to counteract the effect of falling prices. Two key measures used by distributors to track their effectiveness is the **average order size** and the **average cost of processing an order**. Both of these are key profit drivers, with even small increases in average order size or small decreases in costs per order processed having a big positive impact on the bottom line.

Net margin and operating margin

The best measure of a distributor's overall profitability is **net margin** as this shows the level of profit made from the business as a percentage of sales. As with gross margins, care needs to be taken as to exactly which net margin is being used. As there are several profit lines struck in the profit and loss account (operating profit, net margin before tax, net margin after tax), so each of these can be used to calculate a net margin. Internally, management teams will focus on **operating margin** as they may feel that the interest costs, which are ignored in this margin, are not their responsibility because the capital structure of the business is given to them. However, the executive team may focus on the pre-tax **net margin** and benchmark this against other competitors or industry norms. Tax is ignored in this margin as the vagaries of the tax system, timing of allowances, use of brought-forward losses or group tax reliefs may distort the picture and are not really a measure of the business's performance. All of these margins are calculated as a percentage of sales (Figure 5.9).

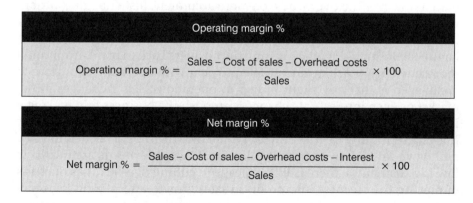

Figure 5.9 Operating margin % and net margin %

In our ABC Co example the operating margin is:

Operating profit of $56m/Sales of $19,316m which equals 0.28%

and the net margin is:

Net profit before tax of $44m/Sales of $19,316m which equals 0.23%

Where the distributor is part of a corporate group, the corporate management will focus on the pre-tax net margin as the measure of the operational management's profitability performance. Tax management will be a group-level responsibility. In some corporate groups the treasury function is also centralized, which effectively removes responsibility for the funding structure of the business from operational management. However, the cost of capital achieved by the treasury function should be applied to the capital employed in the business by each operation. Distributors are capital-intensive businesses and controlling the capital requirements is very much an operational management issue. We would be very wary of any distributor management team that only focused on the operating margin and absolved themselves from the interest charge and net margin before tax lines. Certainly changes in the cost of capital and interest rates will be a factor in the level of interest costs, but a much bigger factor will be the amount of capital required and this is very much in the hands of the operational management team, as we will see in the next chapter.

ABC Co is effectively trading at break-even with an operating margin of 0.28 per cent and a net margin of 0.23 per cent. Break-even means that the volume passing through the business is generating just enough gross margin to cover the overheads (or, more accurately, just enough contribution margin to cover the fixed costs) and so is making neither a profit nor a loss. Taken in isolation, this is not good. But if the previous year's results have been loss making, then getting the business back to break-even could represent a major achievement. The problem with operating at or close to break-even is that any slight hiccup in operations, slight changes in the market or even interest rate changes can push the business into making a loss. It is a precarious position to be in and, without profits, the business is not generating any cash with which to finance the capital needed to grow and move up and away from break-even. Given overheads are relatively low in a distributor, there is little mileage in cutting overheads as the basis of moving the business into profit, so sales growth and margin improvement are the only real strategies to move above break-even. ABC faces a tough challenge in the next year.

Investors in an independent distributor will use the net margin after tax as their key measure, as they can only participate in these distributable profits after deduction of tax. They will expect management to include the minimization of tax costs as part of their overall fiduciary duty to the shareholders. And, as investors, they will be comparing the after-tax returns on their investment in the distributor to other investment opportunities.

As we have shown, the net margin is usually a very small percentage of sales and can be significantly influenced by changes in the gross margin. Distributors' overheads are relatively stable and, being a small percentage of sales, fluctuations in the cost structure do not have such a dramatic impact on the net margin. Over the longer term, management are expected to ensure that net margins are improved by ensuring that sales growth feeds through to the gross margin at a faster rate than the overheads. This is more easily achieved in mature sectors where prices are relatively stable, but can be extremely challenging in fast-growing and technology industries where average sales prices continually move downwards.

6

Working capital

Working capital management

Working capital is an excellent descriptive term for the capital tied up in the trading cycle of a distributor. It represents the capital needed to fund the cash-to-cash cycle, ie the time taken from cash leaving the business to pay suppliers until it comes back in from customers when they pay for their products after the period of credit given to them and includes the time the products spend in inventory in between. The shorter the cash-to-cash cycle, the less working capital a distributor will need. It is, however, a confusing term because 'capital' is normally a term applied to a *source* of funds and in this context it is describing an *application* of funds.

Managing the three components of the working capital cycle is of paramount importance to a distributor, both individually and as a system, and the whole emphasis is on time. The speed with which a distributor can turn its working capital back into cash having made a margin on the products passing through its hands determines how much cash it needs to have tied up. So all the measures of working capital management convert the financial amounts into days – how many days the inventory will be on the company's books, how many days it is taking for the customers to settle their debts and how long the distributor is taking to pay its suppliers. Put all these together and you know how many days it takes for the distributor to turn its cash through the working capital cycle (Figure 6.1).

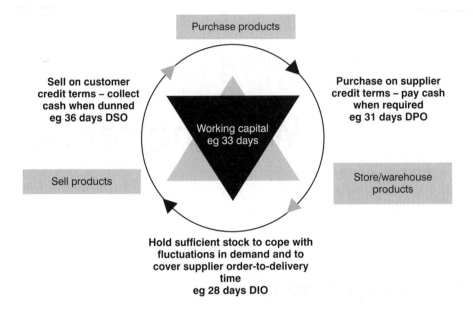

Figure 6.1 The working capital cycle

Supplier credit

Taking the components in turn, the time taken to pay the suppliers is known as **days payable outstanding (DPO)** or sometimes 'supplier days' or 'creditor days'. It is calculated by working out the average accounts payables balance divided by cost of sales as a fraction of the year (Figure 6.2).

Technically, accounts payable are the result of making purchases on credit, so the calculation should use accounts payable divided by purchases. However, the purchases number is not disclosed in published accounts, so cost of sales is often used as an approximation. In practice, as

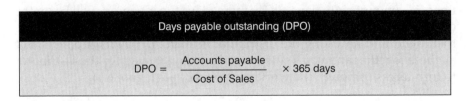

Figure 6.2 Days payable outstanding (DPO)

long as inventory levels are not volatile, there will be very little difference between purchases and cost of sales. In our ABC Co example, DPO is:

Payables of $1,550m/Cost of sales of $18,308m × 365 days to give 31 days

How do you interpret this? Usually by comparing it to standard supplier terms, which are typically 30 days, or by making comparisons to prior periods to see whether the distributor is stretching its supplier credit. In this case, ABC Co seems to be paying its suppliers almost exactly on standard terms, though of course this is an average number and within it there will be a range of payment terms taken. Some suppliers offer attractive prompt payment discount incentives that justify early payment by the distributor (reducing its DPO) and some suppliers will be so dependent upon the distributor for market access that they will cede generous payment terms and credit limits up to 90 days or even beyond. Regional variations will also apply, with longer credit terms generally applying in southern Europe, for example. Distributors use all the usual strategies of querying items or demanding credit notes before paying invoices in order to legitimately delay payment beyond the official credit terms, and the actual DPO will be the outcome of the power struggle between the accounting departments of the distributor and its suppliers.

Should you take the prompt payment discount incentive from the supplier?

Many suppliers will offer credit terms along the lines of '2 per cent 15, net 45', which means that should you choose to pay them within 15 days you will be given a 2 per cent discount off the invoice value, but otherwise you must pay the full amount within 45 days. Is this a good deal and should you take it?

At first glance, it appears that you are being offered a good deal as you can earn 2 per cent for paying 30 days early, which equates to an annual rate of interest of 24.3 per cent (2% × 365/30), which is probably better than the rate you are paying on any loans or overdrafts. However, there are two other factors that you should consider: the market and the impact on working capital.

In terms of the market, this prompt payment discount may in fact be a disguised trade discount if all your competitors are taking it and using it to lower their prices to the final-tier trade players. In effect, you have no choice but to pay up early and take the prompt payment discount in order to be able to offer competitive prices yourself. Where this is the case, we have seen distributors account for the discount as part of their gross margin because they consider they have no option and so cannot treat it as a financing issue, but simply a pricing issue.

In terms of working capital, by paying early you are effectively sucking 30 days of working capital out of your business and, if you are capital constrained, this could have a much higher cost than you might realize. Effectively you are constraining the sales levels of your business by 30 days' worth of trading. What contribution margin could you earn on that? If you are earning, say, a 10 per cent contribution margin on sales of that supplier's products of $3.65m, then another 30 days' sales would generate a contribution of $30,000 ($3.65m × 30/365 × 10%). The annual value of the prompt payment discount is $65,700 ($3.65m × 90% × 2%), so it would still be worth taking the prompt payment incentive. But if your contribution margin is 20 per cent, look again... the value of 30 days' lost sales is $60,000 and the annual value of the prompt payment discount is $58,400 ($3.65m × 80% × 2%), so the lost sales are worth more, although with such a small difference other factors may come into it.

Inventory

Once purchased, the products go into the distributor's inventory waiting to be sold to customers. The time spent in inventory is known as **inventory days** or **days inventory outstanding (DIO)** and is calculated in a similar way (Figure 6.3).

Note that cost of sales is used, as both inventory and cost of sales are valued at cost (sales would include a margin on the product and so would distort our calculation). In our example ABC Co, inventory days is:

Inventory of $1,408m/Cost of sales of $18,308m × 365 days to give 28 days

This means that on average the inventory is spending just under a month in the distributor's warehouse. Is this good or bad? Well, it depends on the nature of the products. If they are strawberries or cream cakes, this is very bad indeed! If they are electronic components or computer products, this would probably be acceptable though risky, as prices seem to fall rapidly in that sector. And if they are steel or brass bars, tubes, pipe connectors etc, then this is probably acceptable. The reason any distributor holds inventory is to be able to offer instant availability when customers enquire. If demand is relatively stable and suppliers can be counted on to deliver reliably within a few days of orders being placed, the distributor need hold only enough inventory to cover sales in the order-to-delivery period plus a safety buffer, a total of, say, 10 days' worth of inventory. However, delivery is an expensive activity for suppliers so they will want to deliver in bulk to minimize their costs and pass on the cost of breaking the bulk (and holding it) to the distributor. If the products move in large volumes, this will not inflate the inventory levels, but for slower-moving items, the distributor will find itself with three months or longer of inventory of these products.

It is a vital lesson to remember that averages can hide a wide range, so ABC Co's average of 28 days' inventory can include products that spend a few days in inventory right up to some that will be in inventory for over a year. Many distributors operate sophisticated product management systems to control their inventory levels and match depth of stock to the volume shifted. To determine target inventory levels, all of these systems employ some key parameters such as volume (or 'run rate' or 'rate of sale'), marketing support for the product, volatility of demand, order-to-delivery time from suppliers, minimum order quantities and reliability of supply. An additional factor that can be taken into account is where the product is in its life cycle. Early on in the life cycle a distributor may 'take a position' in the product to ensure it has plenty of availability for when demand kicks in, and towards the end of the life cycle, may run down inventories to ensure it is not caught with obsolete product when it is superseded.

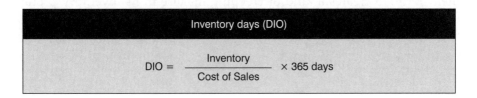

Figure 6.3 Inventory days or days inventory outstanding (DIO)

Typically the inventory will be stratified into an A to E classification with 'A's being fast-moving products with daily or twice-weekly replenishment, allowing stocks to be kept in single figures in terms of days of inventory. 'B's will be slightly slower-moving products with possibly weekly or 10-day replenishment and so on. The 'E's will be service parts and spares that the distributor stocks as a service to its customers (and for which it should earn a high margin as compensation for the value of this service). One of the many balancing acts the distributor has to manage is the mix of products across the A to E range as this will be the way that it can manage its inventory days to minimize its investment and minimize the risk of stock-outs. Another complexity is seasonality, with distributors needing to increase stocks ahead of the peak season and ensure that they exit the season with stocks run down to lower levels. In judging the inventory days, it is important to bear in mind the date of the balance sheet in relation to the seasonal profile. Usually distributors' financial year ends are set just after the peak season has ended to enable them to present balance sheets with low inventory days, which is a sign of good management.

Some distributors narrow the bandwidth of their business model, for example stocking only the fast-moving products in their industry and avoiding the riskier, slower-moving products. In office products there are distributors selling only the paper, printer supplies and consumables products, who seek to compete on price against the one-stop-shop convenience of the broadline, catalogue-based distributors. These specialist distributors work with thinner margins, but do not incur the costs of inventory write-downs or big warehouses and complex systems and they can capitalize on volume discounts and logistics efficiency incentives from their suppliers.

Even with sophisticated inventory management systems, Pareto's law bites hard in inventory, with 20 per cent of the products accounting for 80 per cent of the volume. This can mean that the majority of the inventory is held in the 80 per cent of the products that account for only 20 per cent of the sales. In the next chapter on productivity measures you will learn how to judge whether a product justifies its inventory investment. For many distributors the effect of constantly adding new products and suppliers to their portfolio creates a kind of creeping malaise in its inventory profile that only a periodic audit can address, to help reduce the inventory days.

Drivers of stock levels

Stock levels of companies are not only set by 'industry norms' but are often influence by cultural differences and market maturity. In some countries, such as Turkey and to a lesser extent Greece, historic high inflation and currency devaluation have had a great bearing on how inventory was viewed. Even today in Turkey, long after the worst of the hyperinflation has gone, Turkish distributors hold considerably more stock than, say, their German or British equivalents. In the automotive lubricant and chemicals industry it is not uncommon for distributors to hold six to nine months' stock, whereas in the UK a similar distributor of similar products will typically hold six weeks to two months.

Market maturity often brings increased pressure on business to control costs in the face of squeezed margins. As price pressure and competition grows, companies respond by driving down the most visible business cost-driver, stock levels. This reduction is supported by the investment of suppliers in ever more sophisticated supply chain technology that give the security and service previously only deliverable with high stock levels. Stock levels in many mature sectors are now around half what they were only 10 years ago, with the consequent saving in cost, but increased risk of business disruption if transport logistics are affected by weather, strikes or unforeseen changes in demand (such as when a product is suddenly put under the spotlight as when Delia Smith exhorted the use of cranberries on her cooking programme, broadcast nationally – the shops were emptied within hours).

Customer credit

Products leave inventory when they are sold to customers on credit, creating a receivable balance. The time customers take to pay is called **days sales outstanding (DSO)** or 'customer days' or 'debtor days'. It is calculated by working out the average accounts receivable balance divided by sales as a fraction of the year (Figure 6.4).

Days sales outstanding (DSO)

$$DSO = \frac{Accounts\ receivable}{Sales} \times 365\ days$$

Figure 6.4 Days sales outstanding (DSO)

Note that sales is used as both accounts receivable and sales are valued at sales prices. In our example ABC Co DSO is:

Accounts receivable of $1,897m/Sales of $19,316m × 365 days to give 36 days

This means that, on average, customers are taking just over five weeks to pay for their products. As with DPO, this number should be compared to the terms that apply, in this case the standard customer credit terms. In practice, different customers may be offered different terms depending on their importance, track record, credit-worthiness and market practice. Some customers may have to pay cash with order, so a proportion of sales won't generate any accounts receivable. But if the normal terms are 30 days then ABC Co is doing a pretty good job in getting the money in, given that at any point in time a certain proportion of its invoices will be the subject of disputes and so on. As with DPO, it is useful to track DSO over time to make sure that the credit control function is not slipping or that there has not been some shift in the overall mix of credit arrangements that is giving rise to an increase in the distributor's investment in customer credit.

DSO in seasonal businesses

In some sectors where sales vary significantly by month, such as fashion or garden products, a more accurate way to calculate DSO is the 'count back' method. An example illustrates this:

Receivables at 31 December: $480,000
Monthly sales: December $385,000 31 days in month
November $325,000 30 days in month

The receivables balance is assumed to be built up from all of December's sales (31 days), which leaves $95,000 (ie $480,000 – $385,000) that came from November's sales. This represents 9 days of November's sales, calculated as follows: $95,000/$325,000 × 30 days. So the total DSO is 40 days, ie 31 days from December plus 9 days from November.

Working capital cycle

Putting these three elements together gives the **working capital days**: ie inventory days plus DSO less DPO. In the case of ABC Co, its working capital days equals inventory days of 28 days plus DSO of 36 days less DPO of 31 days to give 33 days. This means that ABC Co takes 33 days to cycle its cash through working capital and back into cash again. Another way to think about this is in terms of how fast it is turning over its working capital a year (Figure 6.5). In the case of ABC Co this is 365 days/33 days which is 11 times per year.

The faster the capital turns, the less cash is needed to finance the working capital cycle and the more efficient is the distributor. Small improvements in the elements of working capital can lead to a significant change in the overall efficiency of the distributor and reduce the cash needed to finance the business. See the box (Unlocking the cash) to show how this works.

It was mentioned earlier that some distributors operate a narrow-band-width business model to keep inventories low. We have seen distributors that exploit their focus on high volumes with a few suppliers to negotiate extended trading terms up to 60 or even 75 days' credit. This enables them to operate with negative working capital: inventory days of 20 plus DSO of

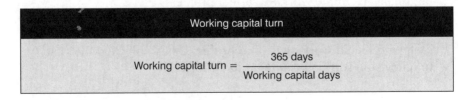

Figure 6.5 Working capital turn

35 days less DSO of 75 days gives working capital of *minus* 20 days. What does this mean? It means that the distributor has 20 days of sales worth of cash in its business, sometimes termed a 'cash float'. The bigger the business grows, the more cash it holds in its bank accounts. By putting the cash on long-term deposit and earning a decent rate of interest, the distributor can either make a super-profit or cut its prices to increase its competitiveness and attract more business. This option is available to any distributor that has the clout to negotiate advantageous trading terms and as a result use its suppliers to effectively finance its inventories and customer credit. As we have seen, the lower the working capital balance, the more efficient the distributor and the more it can grow without needing additional finance.

Unlocking the cash

Take a distributor with sales of $20m and cost of sales of $19m with the starting and improved working capital profiles shown in Figure 6.6. By improving each working capital element by 5 days, the reduction in working capital is 15 days (down from 60 to 45 days). This means that the investment in working capital falls from $3.25m to $2.45m, an improvement of $0.8m. This is very significant in a business with sales of $20m.

Working capital	Starting profile		Improved profile	
	Days	$ value	Days	$ value
DIO	40	2.08m	35	1.82m
DSO	45	2.47m	40	2.19m
DPO	−25	−1.30m	−30	−1.56m
WC days	60	3.25m	45	2.45m
WC turn	6 times per year		8 times per year	

Figure 6.6 Example working capital profiles

If this distributor is looking to grow but has been strapped for cash with its old working capital profile, it has unlocked the cash to reinvest in working capital at its faster cycle:

$0.8m free cash × 8 turns per year => $6.4m extra, taking sales up to $26.4m

This is a growth rate of nearly 40 per cent and all this expansion can be financed without extra capital or loans.
If the distributor was not looking to grow but trying to avoid a cash flow crisis, the cash freed up would appear in its bank accounts within 45 days, keeping the bank at bay!

The ability to manage working capital efficiently is a core competence for any distributor. As we have seen, it has a fundamental impact on the amount of capital needed in the business and thus the distributor's ability to finance its own growth without needing to raise more capital or increase borrowings. Typically in a distributor, the day-to-day management of the three key measures we have covered in this chapter are the responsibility of different departments or functions. DSO is managed by the credit control team, DPO by the bought ledger or purchasing team and DIO by the product managers. Each of these roles can be incentivized to improve the performance of these measures, though care should be exercised to avoid the law of unintended consequences. None of these measures should be driven beyond a certain limit or range. For example, attempting to drive down DSO to the formal credit terms would wipe out a lot of the distributor's business as large and loyal customers would resent such aggressive dunning behaviour and move their accounts. However, an incentive to keep DSO within management's view of an acceptable benchmark can be effective if applied by a smart and commercially aware credit team manager. The same applies to DPO, where some key suppliers should be paid on time, every time, but not all suppliers are equal and renegotiating extended terms from lesser suppliers may prove beneficial. We will look at the way product managers should be targeted in the next chapter as they need to balance the 'earn and turn' priorities across their portfolio in tandem.

However, all the working capital measures are framed by the strategic choices made by the distributor's management team. The markets and customer segments chosen to be served will determine both product requirements and typical DSO terms. For example, many distributors aim to serve the largest and most successful final-tier trade players. But here the competition is often the most intensive so there may be an unwillingness to exercise credit control too aggressively for fear or losing these premium customers. However, those distributors that focus on the 'B' and 'C' players may find that they can earn better margins and effectively charge higher prices to those players to whom no other source of credit supply is available. With this positioning will come the ability to apply assertive credit control practices reducing DSOs (and reducing bad debt risks). Other distributors may choose to serve final-tier players servicing the public sector and the provision of liquidity to the channel may be a competitive weapon. But it will mean that the DSO will be much higher than for those players servicing the commercial sector. It may also impact DIO as the public sector often makes demands for supply availability. In a similar way, the strategic choices as to whether to distribute only well-known major brands or to focus on new and emerging brands will determine the length of credit a distributor can secure from its supplier base.

7

Productivity

Earn and turn

So far we have looked at measures that help distributors to manage the profitability and working capital aspects of their business separately, but there are a number of powerful measures that combine both aspects in one metric. These measures, sometimes called **productivity measures**, combine both the 'earn' and the 'turn' aspects of the business as well as of individual products, categories, suppliers or customers.

The simplest of these measures is **gross margin return on inventory investment (GMROII)** (Figure 7.1). This measure, which can be expressed as either a money amount, or as a percentage if multiplied by 100, shows the amount of gross profit earned per year per dollar invested in inventory. In the case of ABC Co GMROII is:

Gross profit of $1,008m/Inventory of $1,408m = $0.72 per $ or 72%

This needs context to be interpreted, for example the industry sector average, but by most benchmarks this is likely to be low as we have already earlier indicated that the gross margin (earn) was low and the inventory turn was average. Some examples will bring this to life (Figure 7.2).

Product A has generated $1 of gross profit for every $1 invested in inventory for the year. It has achieved this with a gross margin ('Earn') of 10 per cent and a sales-to-inventory ratio ('Turn') of 10 times per year. Distributors refer to this as a GMROII of a hundred and, as a very rough rule of thumb across most industries, a product needs a GMROII of 100 to justify its place

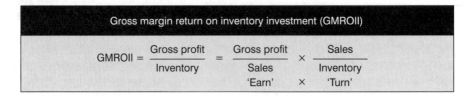

$$\text{GMROII} = \frac{\text{Gross profit}}{\text{Inventory}} = \underbrace{\frac{\text{Gross profit}}{\text{Sales}}}_{\text{'Earn'}} \times \underbrace{\frac{\text{Sales}}{\text{Inventory}}}_{\text{'Turn'}}$$

Gross margin return on inventory investment (GMROII)

Figure 7.1 Gross margin return on inventory investment (GMROII)

Eg	Sales	Gross profit	Inventory	'Earn'	'Turn'	GRMOII %	GMROII $
A	15,000	1,500	1,500	10%	10x	100%	$1.00
B	25,000	1,250	1,250	5%	20x	100%	$1.00
C	20,000	2,400	1,667	12%	12x	144%	$1.44
D	25,000	2,500	1,500	10%	17x	170%	$1.70

Figure 7.2 Example product 'Earn' and 'Turn' combinations

from a financial perspective. Products can have very different profiles with the same GMROII. Compare product B to product A: its margin is half that of product A at a lowly 5 per cent, but it earns that 20 times a year to deliver the same return on inventory investment. All distributors have products with a range of profiles from low-earn, high-turn products like product B to high-earn, low-turn products. Note how relatively small improvements in both factors multiply up to deliver a very attractive GMROII as in the case of product C compared to product A. Product C has a slightly better margin and slightly better turn to give a GMROII that is close to 50 per cent better. This is significant because it means that the distributor has earned considerably more gross profit with product C than product A, an increase that will have a much bigger impact on the bottom-line operating profit. Against that, it's possible that, as product C is turning faster than product A, it is driving more transaction activity, but then it's spending less time in the warehouse.

Most distributors have a natural rhythm to the business and 80 per cent of their products will fit within a reasonable range of earns and turns. Products outside this range have a distorting effect on the whole business model and make it harder for managers to tune the business. Distributors can increase their productivity and capital efficiency by setting a minimum threshold for GMROII and either eliminating all products that fall below it or changing one of their earn or turn characteristics. By definition, such products have low margins and low turns, but product managers tend to trot out arguments for retaining these below par products such as 'it completes the range' or it is necessary to continue to list the product for 'credibility in the category'. This may be so, but it is no justification to make a low margin on a low-turning product. If it is retained in the category for reasons of category credibility or customer service, it is fair to ask for the service to be paid for through the margin. Generally it is easier and cheaper to improve the margin on these types of product by increasing prices than it is to accelerate turns by increasing rate of sale.

The reason GMROII is such a powerful measure is that it can be applied up and down the business, from an individual SKU to the product line group, the category, the vendor and so on, right up to the business as a whole. It is an ideal performance measure for product managers as it encompasses both dimensions of their role in a single, intuitive measure and, by splitting out the 'earn and turn' dimensions, it is easy to identify what action is required to improve business performance. It is often used as the measure on which to target and incentivize product managers.

Contribution margin return on inventory investment

One refinement that should be adopted, if all possible, is to replace the *gross margin* with the *contribution margin* to establish **contribution margin return on inventory investment (CMROII)** (Figure 7.3). This provides a more effective measure for the same reasons that the contribution margin is a more effective measure than a gross margin, ie it allows for all the costs and allowances that are directly attributable to the product. In general, managers should use contribution margins and profits instead of gross margins and profits when making decisions such as which products to promote over others, or in allocating scarce working capital resources across categories and product lines.

Continuing with the theme of using a product's earn and turn characteristics, product managers can profile their entire portfolio against the category averages using volumes and contribution margins (Figure 7.4).

In this chart (taken from a real case, but simplified), each dot represents a single product SKU. The axes are positioned at the category averages. Those products with above-average contribution margins and sales volumes are termed *winners* for obvious reasons and there will tend to be relatively few products that exhibit this high-earn, high-turn profile.

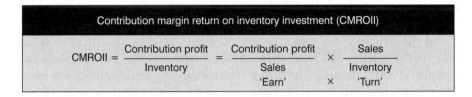

Figure 7.3 Contribution margin return on inventory investment (CMROII)

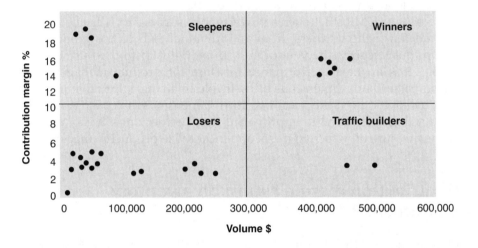

Figure 7.4 Product portfolio profiled in terms of 'Earn' and 'Turn' characteristics

Products with a low-earn, high-turn profile are termed *traffic builders* as these tend to be the strong brands that customers buy in volumes but which distributors know they need to discount aggressively in order to compete in the market and use as a price positioning signal.

The most interesting products are the *sleepers*, which generate high contribution margins but sell in relatively low volumes. Some of these may be the service-type items which are bought rather than sold. However, there may be products here which are perhaps early in the life cycle (and less prevalent in the market) and would respond to sales stimulation efforts. It is likely that the suppliers of these products will share the aim of accelerating sales growth and make a financial contribution to sales and marketing efforts, protecting the distributor's own contribution margin. The real opportunities lie in finding ways to connect the traffic builders to the sleepers, as there is usually a very poor connect rate. An analysis of sales invoices or sales by customer will show the connect rate. Given that the average number of sales lines on a distributor's sales invoice (ie the number of different SKUs) is less than two in many industries, it is easy to see that the connect rate will be low. Where distributors have put real incentive and education into the sales force to improve connect rates, they have seen dramatic improvements in profitability as traffic builders are leveraged effectively.

The final group of products are termed *losers* as these drag down overall business performance with low volumes and low contribution. Product managers should review these products at least every quarter and either raise their prices (and contribution) or remove them from the category to free up cash for higher-performance products. Simply removing these products will have a marked impact on average contribution earned. See the case study below for an example of how one distributor applied this approach to its business management.

Active portfolio management

In one distributor, portfolio analysis was turned into an active management discipline, with the segments termed BMWs (winners), Fords (traffic builders), Ferraris (sleepers) and Ladas (losers) with matching green, blue, red and grey colours to pep up the interest and attention of the sales force and product mangers. As customers requested products, the order system's colour coding highlighted the segment of the product and stimulated a conversation to either change the customer's preference or cross-sell another higher-contribution product in addition.

Customers' recent purchasing history was also analysed to identify those whose contribution was below average. Account management campaigns were run to understand the full needs of high-volume customers and ensure that they were aware of the full range of products available. The order entry system was programmed to highlight low-volume customers whose purchases were exclusively traffic builders. When these customers called to enquire about prices and availability, they were aggressively cross-sold other winners and sleepers. If this failed to make an impact on their purchasing profile, prices on traffic builders to these customers were marked higher. The distributor took the view that if

the customer was only buying its traffic builders, then the customer was going elsewhere for the rest of its business and should
not be retained.

Over the course of around six months, the distributor was able
to improve its contribution margin by over 30 per cent and reduce
working capital by 20 per cent while increasing sales. It took a
combination of incentives and training for both the sales force
and the product managers to drive home the changed approach as
well as some minor IT programming. The return on these investments was excellent.

Returns on working capital

The two productivity measures, GMROII and CMROII, are powerful because
they can be used within the business, but they take into account only the
inventory component of working capital. In order to optimize the business
model, measures are needed which include the other two elements of
working capital, accounts receivable and accounts payable (Figure 7.5).

In the case of ABC Co distributor GMROWC is:

Gross profit of $1,008m/Working capital of $1,755m = 57.43%

This would generally be regarded as a very average performance, like its
GMROII measure, but possibly improved by its good management of
DSO.

This is probably the best measure for product managers, but it does
require good IT systems to be able to allocate all the working capital ele-

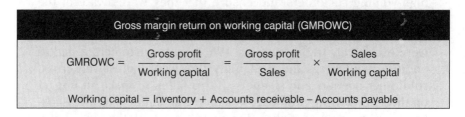

Figure 7.5 Gross margin return on working capital (GMROWC)

ments to the category. In the absence of this, some spreadsheet work done on a periodic basis will reveal the productivity of one category in comparison to others. Working capital is always scarce in a distributor and should be allocated to those products and categories that can generate the best return. Tracking GMROWC performance for a category over time is an excellent way to target and incentivize product managers' performance as it requires them to fine-tune the balance of earn and turn characteristics of the possibly hundreds of products in the category. As with any percentage or ratio measure, GMROWC does not indicate the scale of the business so it should be used in combination with sales volumes and dollar values.

The final version of this measure is contribution margin return on working capital (CMROWC), which replaces the gross profit with the contribution profit but is the same in all other respects (Figure 7.6).

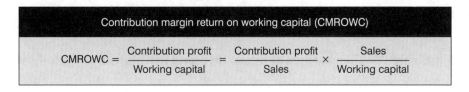

Figure 7.6 Contribution margin return on working capital (CMROWC)

The CMROWC measure is probably the single best indicator of a distributor's performance in the short term as it includes all the costs and allowances directly related to products and customers and the complete working capital cycle. It is also possibly the best guide to supplier productivity as it builds in all dimensions of its economic performance.

Return on brand investment – another name for CMROWC

Some distributors and their suppliers use the term 'return on brand investment' instead of CMROWC as a rather more snappy term. Using the same framework, they can compare results for one brand inside distributors (or within just one distributor), which can be very revealing (Figures 7.7, 7.8, 7.9 and 7.10).

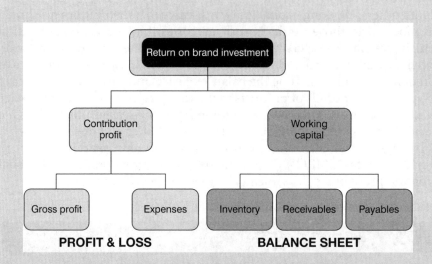

Figure 7.7 Components of return on brand investment

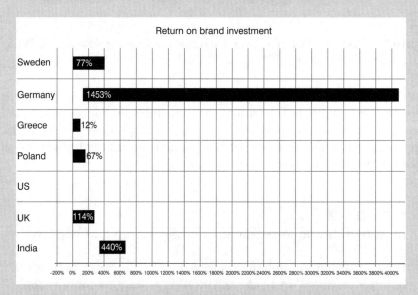

Figure 7.8 Example of return on brand investment by country

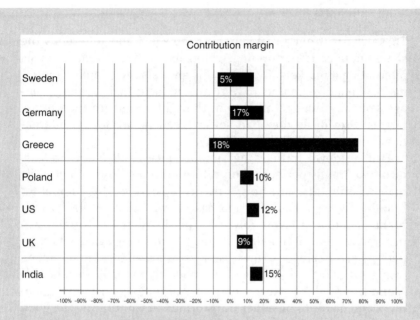

Figure 7.9 Example of contribution margin by country

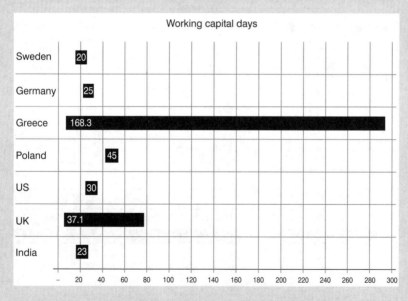

Figure 7.10 Example of working capital turn by country

These charts (from a real supplier) show just how differently the same supplier is performing within its main distributors in its international markets. By doing this analysis the supplier's international management team were able to focus their account managers on the ground on addressing the right issues with appropriate targets. Previously they had set one benchmark for all international markets with little credibility.

Drilling down further, the supplier investigated how well its own two brands performed on return on brand investment in its main distributors and how these compared to the competitor brands (Figure 7.11). The analysis showed that, while its own brands compared favourably with the distributor's overall business measures, the supplier was underperforming against its competitors in the category. Further analysis showed that the supplier's own average hid a disparate performance between its own brands A and B. Brand A is clearly underperforming against any benchmark and needs to be either transformed or withdrawn. The good

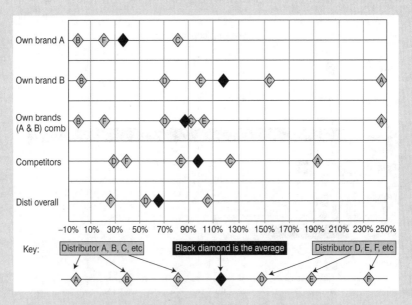

Figure 7.11 Example of return on brand investment benchmarked against competitors

news is that Brand B outperforms against the competition and can be used to anchor the relationship with the distributors while Brand A is sorted out. In this real example, the supplier was the first to run this type of analysis and was able to convince its distributors to act on its recommendations. Many of the distributors had not been aware of how the different brands they distributed performed for them and were very impressed by a supplier that was able to show them how to improve their own business performance.

8

Sustainability

Sustainability – longer-term business health

Given that the distributor's business model is predominantly tied up in moving products through working capital as fast and profitably as possible, we have focused on the measures that help monitor those aspects of business performance. In the shorter term, this is all that really matters, but it is also important to monitor the other, longer-term aspects of the business, which include fixed assets and long-term liabilities such as loans and the capital structure of the business. These factors matter when it comes to measuring the management team's performance in delivering good returns on the assets they are accountable for or on the capital with which they are entrusted.

Return on net assets and return on capital employed

There are two measures that are similar and are often used to track the business's overall performance: return on net assets (RONA) and return on capital employed (ROCE). We will look at RONA first (Figure 8.1).

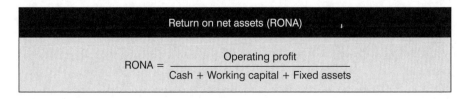

Return on net assets (RONA)

$$RONA = \frac{Operating\ profit}{Cash + Working\ capital + Fixed\ assets}$$

Figure 8.1 Return on net assets (RONA)

RONA measures the return on the assets employed in the business, so is useful when applied to the distributor's business units, subsidiaries or divisions where assets can be clearly allocated as well as to the overall business. In the case of ABC Co the RONA is:

$$\frac{\text{Operating profit of \$56m}}{(\text{Cash of \$401m} + \text{WC of \$1,755m} + \text{FA of \$423m})} = 2.2\%$$

This would be regarded as a woeful performance, delivering a return of just over 2 per cent on net assets of over $2.5billion. Either the management is asleep on the job or there is something seriously wrong with the business model. It may be that competition has found ways to drive down costs or is much more efficient in its management of working capital and it would be instructive to compare its earn and turn characteristics with competitors to see where the disadvantage is greatest.

Let's see if their use of capital is any better, using ROCE (Figure 8.2).

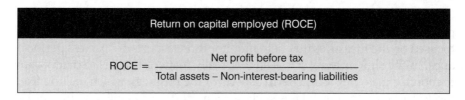

Figure 8.2 Return on capital employed (ROCE)

ROCE for ABC Co is:

$$\frac{\text{Net profit before tax of \$44m}}{\text{Shareholders funds of \$1,756m}} = 2.5\%$$

This is slightly better, but this is the return that investors would compare to other investment opportunities and, in most economies, this return would be well below that available from simply putting the money on deposit.

Return on invested capital

Now it gets more complex. Some of the world's largest and most sophisticated distributors use **return on invested capital (ROIC)** as a purer measure
for management targets and incentives. This measure focuses on the operating components of the business model and relates them to the relevant
portion of shareholders funds (Figure 8.3). Note that the top line is operating profit after tax (sometimes called *net operating profit after tax* or NOPAT),
which means that although it uses an after-tax profit number, it should not
have had interest deducted.

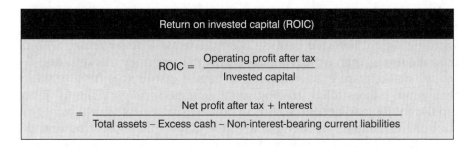

Figure 8.3 Return on invested capital (ROIC)

Here's what this looks like for ABC Co:

$$\text{Operating profit after tax} = \frac{\text{Net profit after tax of \$28} + \text{Interest of \$12m}}{} = \$40\text{m}$$

$$\text{Invested capital} = \begin{array}{c}\text{Total assets of \$4,129m} \\ \text{(being \$423m Fixed assets} \\ + \$3,706\text{m Current assets)} \\ - \text{Excess cash of \$401m} \\ - \text{Non-interest-bearing liabilities} \\ \text{of \$2,314m}\end{array} = \$1,414\text{m}$$

This gives an *ROIC* of \$40m/\$1,414m = 2.8 per cent.

How do you interpret this number, which certainly looks a lot better than
the RONA or ROCE returns? The test of ROIC is whether it is higher than
the weighted average cost of capital (WACC), because this determines

whether the management team have created any value with the invested capital allocated to it for the year. Think of WACC as interest paid on the capital invested at a rate that's adjusted for the risk in the business (it's more complex than that because the capital will be a mix of equity and debt and WACC calculations are a somewhat technical specialty. The WACC for a start-up with a new business model would be higher than for a long-established distributor with a proven business model with the same mix of debt and equity). So the following applies:

$$\text{ROIC} > \text{WACC} \Rightarrow \text{Management has created value}$$

$$\text{ROIC} < \text{WACC} \Rightarrow \text{Management has destroyed value}$$

In other words, management has to demonstrate that it should be entrusted with the capital invested because it can generate a better return with its business model than by leaving the capital in the money markets. And the money markets are exactly where the largest distributors have to go for their multi-billion-dollar funding requirements, through rights issues to tap the equity markets or the issue of bonds to raise debt. As we saw at the start of this chapter, distributors are generally capital absorbing and the bigger the distributor, the bigger the capital requirement. So it makes good sense for the executive team of the distributor to ensure that their management direct reports in charge of the operating subsidiaries in each of the markets in which it operates should be measured and rewarded on their ability to drive ROIC upwards.

The argument for adopting ROIC is just as applicable for smaller distributors, regardless of whether they are publicly accountable, quoted companies or privately owned companies or subsidiaries. In all sizes and types of distributor the management team should be rewarded for creating value above the cost of capital allocated to its business. However, care should be exercised in the way management teams are incentivized, as ROIC is vulnerable to short-term optimization. An unbalanced focus can encourage management to ignore growth possibilities and damage long-term value creation. And as we have highlighted before, it is a percentage measure which means that it ignores the scale of the business and dollar dimension of the value created or destroyed.

Value creation

The concept of value creation is powerful and quite intuitive (though the maths behind some of the calculations can be somewhat technical). It requires that management teams have to make not just a profit, but a profit in excess of the cost of the capital they used to make that profit. As we have seen with ROIC, it is possible to determine whether a management team is creating or destroying value in comparison to its WACC.

The **value creation (VC)** measure (otherwise known as economic value added or EVA) uses this concept but establishes a dollar value, which is more intuitive than a percentage and reflects the scale of the business. And it has the advantage that it can be applied in managing components of the business, as we shall see later on. Let's start with the basic value creation measure (Figure 8.4).

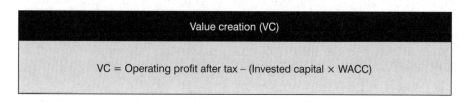

Figure 8.4 Value creation (VC)

To calculate value creation for ABC Co we need to know its WACC, something that is usually possible only for quoted companies, but these public rates can be used as a guideline for private companies (possibly with an uplift for additional risk). Taking a WACC of 6.2 per cent for the sector average, and the values for operating profit after tax and invested capital calculated earlier, gives:

$$\begin{array}{c} \text{Operating profit after tax of \$40m} \\ - \text{(Invested capital of \$1,414m} \times 6.2\%) \end{array} = \text{Value destruction of \$48m}$$

This is not an enormous sum given the scale of the business (with sales of almost $20 billion) but it is a negative number, which means that some value has been destroyed, ie the management has been unable to generate a profit in excess of the opportunity cost of the capital invested, a result which is consistent with that which the RONA, ROCE and ROIC measures would have suggested.

There is much evidence to show that VC is the performance measure most closely linked with the creation of shareholder wealth over time. It can be used as a measure for targeting and rewarding managers within the business and indeed it provides a single framework for measuring and guiding the performance of managers in functional areas as well. With a good training programme and useful tools, managers can understand how to use VC in their everyday decision making as they understand how each part of the business model influences whether value is created or destroyed using the value creation 'tree', which links all the elements we have covered. The VC tree is like a map of the business model showing how all the different dynamics interact. Every decision taken within the business will impact how the business performs and the VC tree shows how these effects cascade up the tree to impact the value created or destroyed.

Figure 8.5 shows the value creation tree for ABC Co. To the right of the each of the profit numbers is their related margin as a per cent of revenue (eg gross margin of 5.2 per cent is next to $1,008m). To the right of each of the working capital elements is their equivalent in days (eg DSO of 36 days is next to $1,897m). The best way to understand the value of this VC tree layout is to watch the impact of changes dynamically ripple through to ROIC and VC. If we look at how ABC Co has performed in the following year (year 2), we can compare the two years and see the changes.

In year 2 ABC Co managed to grow the business in a tough market so its aggressive discounting shows up in a lower gross margin. However, on the plus side the management team achieved tight overhead control and some small improvements in working capital management.

Figure 8.6 shows the balance sheet and profit and loss account in the traditional format. What has happened to the key measures of the business? Do these changes mean that the business has created or destroyed value in year 2 (Figure 8.7)?

Starting from the top of the tree, we can see that ABC Co has in fact managed to create $2m of value compared to destroying value to the extent of $48m in year 1. While this is a small amount in the context of the scale of the business, it is a considerable improvement. Which changes have contributed to this achievement? Working down the tree, ROIC has made a dramatic improvement from a paltry 2.8 per cent to 6.4 per cent (which is higher than WACC, hence value is created). This is the result of doubling the NOPAT from 0.2 per cent to 0.4 per cent on a reduced invested capital base. By working on both elements simultaneously, the management team have effectively multiplied improvements in the business model. Had they only managed to improve NOPAT on the same invested capital base, ROIC would have been 5.5 per cent, which is still below WACC and ABC Co would have suffered another year of destroying value.

This is a critical lesson; management had to fine-tune its performance in *both* profitability and the management of capital to create value. Improving either side of the business model on its own would not have been sufficient.

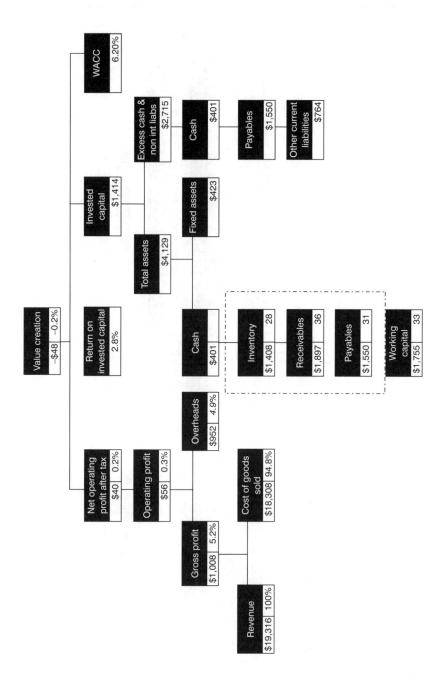

Figure 8.5 Value creation tree for ABC Co – year 1

Income statement

	Year 1 $'000	Year 2 $'000
Sales	19,316	21,054
Cost of sales	18,308	19,901
Gross profit	**1,008**	**1,154**
Overheads	952	1,028
Operating profit	**56**	**125**
Interest	12	22
Profit before taxation	**44**	**103**
Taxation	16	38
Profit after taxation	**28**	**66**

Balance sheet

	Year 1 $'000	Year 2 $'000
Fixed assets	423	456
Current assets		
Inventory	1,408	1,492
Accounts receivable	1,897	2,011
Cash	401	232
Total current assets	**3,706**	**3,735**
Current liabilities		
Accounts payables	1,550	1,690
Other	764	855
Total current liabilities	**2,314**	**2,545**
Net current assets	**1,392**	**1,191**
Long-term liabilities	59	75
Net assets	**1,756**	**1,572**
Shareholders funds	**1,756**	**1,822**

Figure 8.6 ABC Co balance sheet and profit and loss account

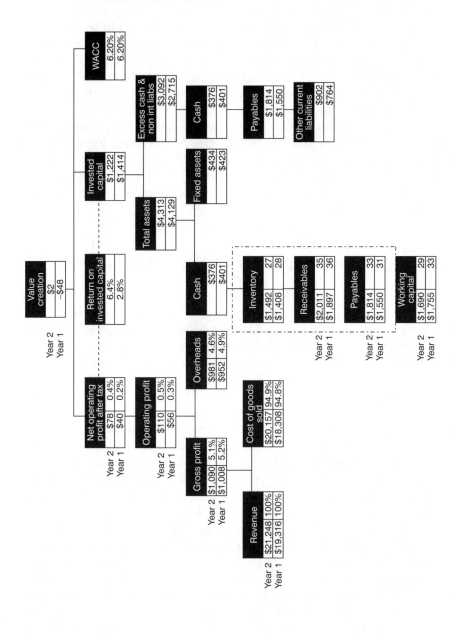

Figure 8.7 Value creation tree for ABC Co – years 1 and 2

The key to reducing invested capital has been the improvement in DPO or payables days. The extra two days on average that ABC Co is taking to pay its suppliers has shifted the burden of financing the extra working capital from the shareholders to the suppliers. (Note that this could be the result of negotiating better terms or shifting the supplier mix, rather than merely becoming a slow payer.) In addition the one-day improvement in each of inventory days and DSO or customer days has reduced the total working capital needed, so there has been an overall improvement in working capital of four days. Is four days really all that significant? Well, in this distributor's case, it's worth about $230m, which accounts for most of the reduction in invested capital. This shows the power of the logic of using invested capital in these measures, because although ABC has actually grown its net assets year on year in the balance sheet, the capital invested in the trading operation has gone down, thanks to management's skilful handling of its business model.

Managing value creation on an operational basis

Value creation is an excellent overall measure, but how can managers working at an operational level relate to it? At a very basic level, every manager should be able to consider the implications of his or her decisions in terms of the income statement and balance sheet dimensions that drive value creation. Senior management has a key role here in communicating down and across the organization the major value drivers on which it wants operational management to focus.

However, more sophisticated suppliers and distributors are looking at value creation at an individual customer level. And distributors are looking at the value created in their own business by the major suppliers whose products they distribute. Most businesses can measure customer (or supplier) profitability at a gross margin level and many go further to contribution margin. Some businesses now are allocating their major working capital assets and liabilities across customers and even including the impact on their fixed assets, such as distribution systems and factory utilization (for example, a customer that places orders in line with forecasts will drive efficiency through the factory compared to one that fluctuates wildly, distorting factory production). By factoring all these elements into a value creation measure, and applying the cost of capital inside your own business, it is possible to look at whether an individual customer (or supplier) is creating or destroying value. Figure 8.8 shows a real example from a distributor's analysis of its customers.

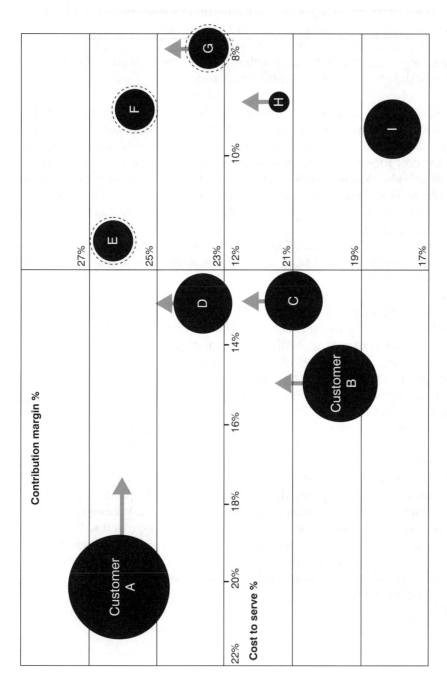

Figure 8.8 Illustrative analysis of value created by different customers mapped on axes of contribution margin and cost to serve

The size of each circle represents the amount of value created and each has been positioned on the axes of Contribution margin and Cost to serve as these represent the two primary value drivers. The arrows and dotted circles represent the distributor's objectives for each account. The implications of the analysis shown on the chart are:

- Account A is creating the most value, through its substantial contribution margin, which is more than covering its high cost to serve. The account team looking after this account will be tasked with addressing the cost-to-serve drivers next year and moving the account to the right, which should increase the value created for the distributor. By sharing the rewards generated, both customer and distributor will benefit.
- Account B by contrast is creating value through its low cost to serve, but needs to improve the contribution margin generated.
- Accounts E, F and G are all in excellent positions, high contribution, low cost to serve, and just need to be grown, with G possibly moving up its contribution.

Each account team will be tasked with drilling down further to understand the factors driving the position and size of their account's circle on the chart and then to partner with their account to improve in the direction required. Regular meetings of all account teams together will be useful to share best practices and insights that all accounts can share. This type of analysis may look difficult, time consuming and expensive to commission, but in fact this is usually only true the first time it is done. Once the cost and revenue allocation algorithms have been developed and the data feeds from the company's information systems established, the analysis models can be run pretty much at any time. It probably does not make sense to run the analysis more frequently than quarterly as the types of changes needed to make an impact can be significant and take multiple quarters to plan and implement. Clearly a distributor managing its strategic relationships using value creation is going to be at a competitive advantage as it will be taking the conversation to real value drivers that both sides can benefit from improving. This is quite a different game from the traditional confrontational approach where both sides are fighting over the same, possibly shrinking margins.

9

Managing growth

Growth dynamics

Managing growth in distributors is a demanding management challenge because the hundreds of buying, pricing, selling and stocking decisions taken every day affect the margins and costs reflected in the profit and loss account. As we have seen, there is very little room for slippage – a couple of points off the margin and a couple more points on the costs and the profit turns into a loss. The market context plays a big part in the challenges of managing growth, because it's one thing to grow with the market but quite another to fight for market share against the competition in order to grow faster than the market. The challenge is even more severe if attempting to grow in a shrinking market.

Overcoming these challenges requires some form of competitive advantage such as product exclusivity, more (or more effective) advertising and promotion or better prices, service, availability or more responsive delivery speeds. Each of these competitive advantages comes at a cost, so what are the advantages of growth that more than compensate for these costs? What economies of scale can the distributor gain? There are two major benefits available: cost structure efficiencies and working capital efficiencies. But there is also a limit; growth means that increased working capital is required, and that absorbs cash. How fast can a distributor grow before it overtrades and runs out of cash? We start with working out the limits and then explore how to realize the economies of scale.

Internally financed growth rate formula

We have already seen how the size of the distributor's business and the efficiency of its working capital management determine how much cash is needed to fund the business. The same principles apply in determining how much growth a distributor can finance from its own internal resources – called its potential growth capacity (Figure 9.1).

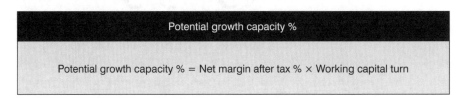

Potential growth capacity %

Potential growth capacity % = Net margin after tax % × Working capital turn

Figure 9.1 Potential growth capacity % – internally financed growth rate

In other words, assuming the distributor is trying to maximize its growth, it will apply all the profits it generates to funding its increased working capital requirements. This assumes that no dividends are paid out of the after-tax profit, but that everything is retained and therefore added to retained earnings in the balance sheet as additional shareholder funds. The distributor can of course choose to apply the capital in other ways, such as buying fixed assets, but we are looking for the theoretical maximum growth rate here. This means that all the increased capital is invested in working capital to support the increased sales. The working capital turn is the number of times the capital is used each year (ie sales divided by working capital), so multiplying the extra capital by the working capital turn gives the extra sales that are possible.

Applying the formula to ABC Co (year 1) gives the following:

$$\frac{\text{Net margin after tax of } 0.15\%}{\times \text{ WC turn of 11 times}} = 1.6\%$$

This means that ABC Co can grow at 1.6 per cent in year 2 with its own resources and with the same business model. If it grows faster than that, it will run down its cash balances and push them into overdraft or will need to increase its third-party borrowings, or a combination of the two. We know that sales in year 2 were actually 9 per cent bigger than year 1, so how did ABC Co achieve this? It did two things:

1. It improved its working capital turn from 11 to 12.6 (ie 365 days/29 days). This slightly increases the growth capacity to 1.9% (ie the net margin of 0.15% × 12.6 turns).
2. It allowed its cash balances to be reduced (and absorbed into working capital) from $401m down to $232m. This difference of $169m is partly used to increase fixed assets (net of the increase in long-term liabilities) and the rest – $152m – is also cycled through the working capital turn 12.6 times to fund a sales increase of $1,915m or 9% of year 1 sales.

In other words, because its potential growth capacity was so low at the end of year 1, ABC Co has had to run its cash reserves down in order to fund the growth it achieved. This will be fine for a couple of years but no distributor has inexhaustible supplies of cash in its balance sheet. It will run into the buffers after another couple of years and that source of growth funding will no longer be available to it. In many industries, the bigger distributors have become public companies with access to the capital markets to fund both their organic growth and their acquisitions to bolt on growth. The price of tapping the capital markets is the high cost of adhering to listing requirements and the extraordinary level of public (ie analyst) scrutiny, which demands the highest standards of management to optimize the business model. The returns generated by ABC Co would not pass muster, with its returns on capital (ROIC) below its cost of capital (WACC) and its ROCE below that generally available from putting the funds in the bank. If ABC Co wants to grow in the next several years, it needs to continue improving its business model, especially its net profitability.

Perhaps growth will bring its own profitability rewards as economies of scale kick in…

Economies of scale – profitability

There is considerable evidence that the activities of a distributor benefit from economies of scale as the fixed costs become spread over a larger volume of business. Some of the costs of a distributor vary directly with sales – what accountants term **variable costs** – that is, costs such as sales commissions. However, most costs are **fixed costs**, which is really an accountants' misnomer for **stepped costs**. Virtually all the IT systems, warehousing, logistics, product management and marketing costs are costs that increase in steps as investments in additional capacity are made. The key to realizing economies of scale is to make sure that capacity is fully utilized before incurring the additional costs of increasing it. Even a delay of six months in stepping up capacity is six months of operating at or near to maximum capacity which is where the economies of scale lie.

Take a look at the chart shown in Figure 9.2, which shows fixed costs stepping up as volume increases compared to the smooth increase in contribution from revenues after deducting variable costs. The interaction of these two profiles is the generation of alternate net losses and net profits as the contribution moves above fixed costs and then is overtaken as fixed costs step up again. This example, which is a simplified version of a real distributor's experience, suggests a business model that is fluctuating above and below break-even. Every time the business looks as if it has moved into profit by growing revenues, management invests in increasing capacity that incurs another set of fixed costs which swing the operation back into a loss. Look at what could happen if management were to operate the business with a delayed investment strategy, as in the chart shown in Figure 9.3.

Apart from the initial period, the business model remains in profit with the same stepped increases in fixed costs. The key to this strategy is delaying making the investments that increase fixed costs until *after* revenue growth has pushed up the contribution to above the new level of fixed costs. This means that the business may need to operate under stress for a while as it runs at close to capacity for a number of months (or years), but management needs to see this as the way to generate the returns on previ-

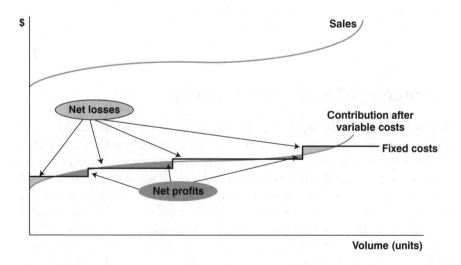

Figure 9.2 Profile of how contribution margin and fixed costs interact as sales increase

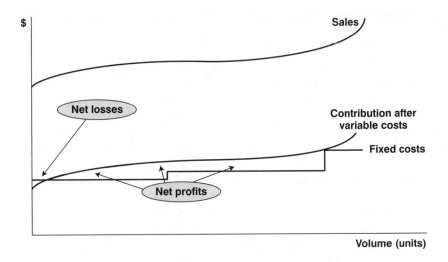

Figure 9.3 Profile of how contribution margin and fixed costs interact with delayed investment strategy

ous investments. Most management teams naturally tend to focus on the future, building the business case for growth and increased investment. But in distributors, management teams need to be just as focused on the past, ensuring that they deliver on past promises of improved returns. This is a vital strategy in the low-net-margin business model that typifies most distributors. We have seen net profitability jump dramatically from less than 1 per cent of sales to over 2.25 per cent of sales through the disciplined operation of the delayed investment strategy.

It requires management to have a good strategic sense of how fast the market is changing, sound forecasting of the speed at which the distributor can grow and a steady nerve to get the balance right. Taking this strategy too far could put a distributor at a competitive disadvantage through under-investment that might take years to recover from because of the negative effects on customer experiences. Probably the hardest area in which to get the balance right is in committing to major IT system upgrades with their long lead-times, complex implementations and initial negative impacts on productivity. In some cases, we have seen more changes of position among the top three or four distribution players in a market caused by their relative successes (and failures) with complex integrated system implementations than by any difference in their price/availability/service-level propositions.

Interestingly, management teams find that they can learn some useful lessons from operating their business under the stress of working at or near full capacity. They find out which members of their teams thrive under high pressure and which wilt and let performance suffer. Often, valuable innovations are developed to enable the business to go the extra mile with the current resources and capacity; inventory turns a little faster, resources are allocated more carefully to optimum suppliers or product categories or customers, and poor-performing products and categories are terminated earlier. We have seen processes become more streamlined by the order processing, warehousing and product management teams as they work to cut out activities that waste their own time, in efforts to relieve pressure on themselves.

But management needs to be able to recognize the symptoms of burnout and ensure that the new investment or additional capacity is on stream before the pressures turn high performance into reverse. In addition, management needs to judge how much effort the investment is going to require in terms of change management. We mentioned earlier the impact that systems implementations can have and these often impose huge burdens on process teams when they are implemented or upgraded. The benefits of these investments often lie in the fact that they require fundamental changes in processes, with steep learning curves, accompanied by shifts in the burden of work from back office to front office teams. Changing systems and processes while operating at full capacity is not to be recommended and can be compared to changing the engines on a 747 while in mid-flight!

Indeed, managing growth dynamics can be seen as a continuous exercise in change management and it is often the 'softer', human aspects of change that are the hardest to get right. One of the critical success factors in managing change is to inculcate a solid understanding of the business model and the planned impact of changes among the people directly affected. We have seen too many instances of teams undergoing significant changes in their roles and working practices without any real understanding of the objective. Equally we have seen the real benefits of involving these same people in exploring ways to achieve the step change in performance required and gaining both commitment to the change and the additional insights and innovations that could come only from those people that have first-hand experience. People are invariably the critical factor in realizing economies of scale and giving them an informed role in achieving business improvements will usually achieve more than simply 'managing by the numbers'.

Economies of scale – working capital management

There are some significant advantages to working capital management in operating a larger-scale operation. In inventory, buffer stocks can become a smaller proportion of the inventory-holding requirement as the larger distributor benefits from priority in stock replenishment from its suppliers. For the A and B lines (the high-volume lines), orders from large distributors will comprise one or more truckloads, which make for easier and faster scheduling for suppliers than part truckloads. These factors combine to enable the larger distributor to run at higher sales to inventory ratios, which is another way of saying that it can operate at higher inventory turn ratios for the same or lower risk of stock-outs.

In managing all the elements of working capital, increased scale increases the likelihood that investments in IT and operating systems can be made to pay out. For example, it is only the largest distributors that can generate a return on 'warehouse in the dark' operations. These are highly automated facilities where the physical placing and retrieval of product is handled by robots (ie with no need to have the lights on) governed by sophisticated algorithms that decide where to put each SKU according to the frequency and volumes of orders to be picked. These systems constantly appraise when it is worth moving SKU items around as demand for them rises and falls, and can rely on computer memory rather than a systematic system for layout organization. (Imagine the chaos if 30 pickers were working in a warehouse that is reorganized several times a week – but this is effectively what a robotic system can do.) Other systems can be deployed to increase the efficiency of credit control, credit management and billing to improve the management of accounts receivable. Equivalent systems can improve the management of payables balances, ensuring that all credit notes are claimed, vendor credit balances are maximized and promotions are exploited to the full.

These systems are expensive capital investments that can only be justified if amortized across hundreds of millions of dollars worth of business but can generate significant efficiencies in working capital turns. Such systems do not completely replace the need for human judgement and management experience. We have seen several instances where the lack of these human skills has negated the benefits of some major investments. For example, the power of these systems can tempt the distributor to increase the number of vendors, product lines and SKUs in its efforts to promote growth. However, each additional SKU brings a dimension of cost and working capital that dilutes the overall efficiency of the distributor's business model. In our turnaround projects, one of the first areas in which we can find quick wins is to eliminate the bottom 10 per cent of products and vendors. This can release working capital and other resources that would be more effectively redeployed to the 'sleepers' and 'winners' discussed earlier.

The number of locations at which a distributor holds inventory is another factor which can undermine financial scale. Each separate inventory location multiplies the number of buffer stocks required and can render the biggest distributor little more efficient than the local player of equivalent size. There is a constant shift in the balance of costs between shipping and storage, reflected in the trend to centralize or localize distribution operations at any one time. This is a complex calculation, but the distributor seeking to grow should be wary of using additional locations as a key plank in its growth strategy. We would need compelling evidence that sales could not be serviced from a central location before allowing an additional stocking point to be added to a distributor's operations. Vendors are wise to the costs they incur of serving multiple ship-to points and will penalize a distributor financially if it has to drop to more than one distribution location.

Risks of growth – diseconomies of scale

Growth brings its own complexities, which can become diseconomies of scale. These are related to the coordination and control of an operation that is handling millions or even billions of individual transactions. Complexity can hide the issues in the distributor that are holding it back. Answers to key questions such as which customers and which products are delivering the best returns become elusive, hidden in the mass of data and information about thousands of products and customers. Layers of managers are needed to coordinate teams within acceptable spans of control. Each additional SKU, product, product line, supplier, customer, customer segment, service offering and location adds another dimension of complexity as well as incremental growth.

Managers of distributors that have grown successfully keep their focus on the basics of the business model. They use the measures we have covered in this part of the book and they make sure that each of their subordinates understands how his or her actions can affect the performance of the business model. Success in distribution comes from understanding the dynamics of running a business in which profit is a small number between two very large numbers and that managing both earn and turn is equally important.

10

How to sell to distributors

What we mean by selling to distributors

This chapter heading is a bit of a misnomer. 'Selling to distributors' really refers to the process by which a supplier secures a listing with a distributor such that the distributor will act as a route to market, providing reach and access to the final tier of trade or resellers that supply the end-user market. This is a process you may think of as 'sell through' rather than 'sell to'. In fact, the supplier wants more than this. It wants the distributor to focus on its products and actively promote their sale through whatever combination of market education, product management, marketing, promotion and competitive selling is required. The supplier may also want the distributor to take on one or more of the activities listed in Chapter 3 on its behalf. And the supplier will want to nurture and build the relationship with the distributor over time to increase sales, which is really more account managing than selling. But as well as a handy shorthand, 'selling' is not a bad mindset to adopt in thinking about how to persuade the distributor of the merits of your product or offering in terms of its business case. And that requires you to think widely about all the aspects of the commercial relationship you want to build as a supplier in partnership with your distributor.

To the distributor, the supplier and its products are not remotely interesting in or of themselves. The distributor sees them simply as a means to its strategic and commercial ends, which we know are earning and turning products to create value. The salient attributes of the product as the end customer sees them are only of relevance to the distributor in persuading it that your end-customer demand will be higher than for your competitors' equivalent products. In other words, the better mousetrap is only better to the distributor if that means customers are going to be demanding it from the distributor's trade resellers. But if you don't have the best mousetrap, you can still be the distributor's preferred mousetrap supplier if you can convince the distributor that it will make the most money doing business with you. This might be because, as the supplier, you are prepared to spend more on stimulating customer awareness and brand preference to drive higher revenues, or you are prepared to allow the distributor to make a higher gross margin, or maybe fund a dedicated sales person on its team. Perhaps you'll allocate consignment inventory or extended credit terms so that the distributor doesn't need to invest in working capital for your products, or you'll grant it an exclusive distribution deal so that it doesn't have to compete with other distributors. Perhaps you only go to market through 'the trade' and don't have a direct sales force competing for the same business and creating channel conflict. And perhaps you'll commit to this model so that the distributor knows that any investment it makes in you will be protected. Any and all of these could be very powerful in persuading the distributor to stock and promote your particular brand and products. But they all come at a cost to you as the supplier. You need to make sure that every cent you invest in the relationship is valued by the distributor. And this is where the sales mentality kicks in. Remember you are selling a commercial relationship; you are selling your channel value proposition, you are not selling your products.

The sales process

All good sales people start with the customer. They take the time and effort to find out the customer's needs. What are their business objectives? Which objective is the greatest challenge to them? What are their points of pain? What threats and weaknesses do they face (and do they recognize them)? These questions are just as valid when you are looking to win or build your business with a distributor. They form the first stage of your sales process (Figure 10.1).

It is essential to understand and **analyse your intended distributor partner's strategy**. You must be able to position your relationship in that context, showing how you are going to help it achieve its objectives. We

Figure 10.1 Distributor engagement sales process

have seen countless suppliers waste their time by failing to grasp this simple point and act on it, for example:

■ suppliers basing their pitches on enabling the distributor to broaden its range just as the distributor declares its intent to rationalize its ranges and offer best-of-breed to its customers;
■ other suppliers focusing on sales volumes (of their low-margin products) when the distributor is struggling to get above break-even;
■ suppliers failing to mention the potential of their higher-end products to sweeten margins;
■ suppliers only mentioning in passing the enormous end-user marketing campaign they are about to unleash;
■ distributors with capital constraints looking to grow and failing to understand that the supplier is offering extended credit as part of the standard terms and conditions;
■ suppliers burying distributor-friendly terms such as price protection (protects the distributor in the event of the supplier reducing the prices in its price list) in fast-moving industries in the small print of their contracts.

Most distributors are happy to share their intentions and the strategy by which they plan to achieve them. Good questioning (classic sales technique) by the supplier will uncover where the distributor feels vulnerable or under pressure: which customers are switching business to other distributors, which categories are not growing as fast as required, which are not delivering the margins expected, which markets the distributor plans to attack or develop next. You may also learn which existing suppliers are damaging their relationship with the distributor by increasing channel conflict (by selling direct, for example) or adding new distributors in the same territory.

In the late eighties, the Edrington Group (then Robertson and Baxter) sought to find a distributor for its premium Scotch single malt brand, Glengoyne, in France. Edrington knew that Taittinger, a major Champagne house and distributor of wines and spirits, had recently lost the distribution for Glenmorangie. For Taittinger, Glengoyne would be a *margin generator* and a valuable addition to the catalogue. However, Edrington was not the only suitor of the distribution power of Taittinger, and needed to be sure it could win over other contenders. The Edrington Group quickly learnt that what Taittinger lacked and desired most of all was an upmarket Scotch blend as their own private-label brand that would be a *cash generator* for the company. At that time, private-label suppliers were mostly producers of low-quality cheap supermarket brands and could not deliver the quality Taittinger required. The Edrington Group quickly developed a proposal to supply Taittinger with Defender Scotch, a quality product, as part of a comprehensive distribution rights proposal that included Taittinger distributing the Glengoyne malt, which was accepted.

The Edrington Group had successfully analysed the distributor's strategy and needs, identified the opportunity to tie Taittinger to the company, developed the strategy to produce Defender and sold Taittinger a business proposal based on its total business needs rather than the narrow item, price and volume discussion on the Glengoyne malt.

The insight gained from the strategic dialogue should serve as the bedrock of your response. You now know how to position your own strategy and make the connections in terms of markets, opportunities and shared goals. You should think of the business objectives of the distributor as the coat pegs on which to hang your bespoke business case. Each objective represents a potential **opportunity** for you to do business together. What investments are you making or actions are you taking that will address these opportunities and how do these create value for the distributor? Are you opening up new market spaces, developing new types of channel, generating new service opportunities? Are you generating additional market pull that will increase volumes or promoting some form of differentiation that will improve margins? Can you offer a more attractive distribution strategy (fewer distributors) than your competitors? Will you be reducing the inventories needed or lowering the cost-to-sell for the distributor? All of these are potentially of interest to the distributor, but hold them up against the coat pegs of the distributor's objectives and make sure they are relevant.

For those opportunities that measure up, **develop the strategy and tactics** of your relationship plan. This is the bit that most suppliers do well. It is important to make sure that it is obvious how the strategy and tactics advance the distributor's objectives. This is the bit that most suppliers do badly. We hear all about what they are going to do, less about how it delivers the distributor's objectives.

Now you are ready to **prepare and pitch your business case**. This includes both the strategic and commercial dimensions. Even the most tactical distributors needs to know if they are looking at you as someone bringing them a deal or someone with whom they can partner over a sustained period to achieve their objectives. Show the distributor that you know which of its business objectives you can help it with and on which of its business measures you can help it move the needle. Use the distributor's business model as a checklist in your preparation, and mark up the impact of your proposals, for example as shown in Figure 10.2.

Note that there are eight measures that the supplier is claiming will be improved for the distributor by adding its product line. Using all of these in the pitch would swamp the conversation with accounting jargon. Select the one or two measures that the distributor's management team themselves focus on to make the most compelling case. ABC Co's management team would be impressed by a supplier showing how it could improve return on invested capital, their priority measure, especially if that was the key measure in their bonus plan...

At one time, the Uniroyal tyre brand was distributed in Italy by a network of 22 regional distributors. Uniroyal was a premium brand competing with Pirelli and Michelin, while other, less well-known brands made up the sales in the mid and price-fighter segments. As all distributors were multi-brand, they needed well-known brands to complement their offering in the bottom two segments. Uniroyal management recognized an opportunity to secure a disproportionate share of the distributor's time, energy

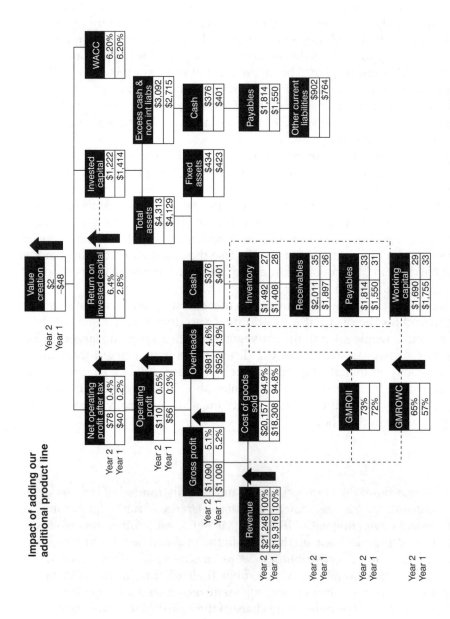

Figure 10.2 Example impact on a distributor's business model of adding an additional product line

and resources. They sourced a cheap no-name brand and badged it as Uniroyal to sell to the distributors, shutting out competition from the low-price, high-volume end of the market. Although the margins on these products were very much lower than could be expected on the Uniroyal brand, the company gained a bigger share of the distributors' revenues, strengthened their position in distribution and protected their higher-margin products.

Managing the account relationship

Most distributors expect to sustain long-term relationships with their suppliers. They recognize that there is a high cost to them of switching key suppliers and will only fire a supplier if things have really broken down, both commercially and in terms of relationship management. However, there is a world of a difference between being a key strategic partner, leveraging the full capability of the distributor's market access, and being just a makeweight supplier barely commanding the attention of the category manager. Some suppliers can command distribution attention simply by virtue of their market share, but without active account management, even the most strategic supplier can waste the potential of the relationship. Smaller suppliers can differentiate themselves significantly by the quality of their account management. This involves many skills, including the many dimensions of multi-level selling, relationship building and so on, which you can read about in other books. The key differentiator though is a laser-like intensity on the commercial dynamics of the relationship based on understanding the key measures that matter for the distributor and fed by good visibility of how these measures are performing on a day-to-day basis.

Let's take an example to illustrate what can be done. Imagine you are an account manager representing Megabrands, a widgets manufacturer, and you are in a tough conversation with National Distico, the dominant distributor in your home market. Here's the situation:

■ The product manager in National Distico tells you that her gross margin objective is 11%. She also lets slip that the margin on the widget accessories sub-line is 15%, but these account for only 10% of her sales.
■ She is about to stop selling your 4 mm widget (one of three brands stocked) because they provide only a 7% gross margin. You think the

margin on the competitors' 4 mms is 12% (one of these brands is almost exclusive to this account).

■ You suspect that 6 mm widgets account for about a fifth of sales at a margin of around 11% and 8 mm widgets represent around 20% of sales at an average margin of 13%, the rest being 4 mms.

■ You know that Megabrands has about two-thirds of each of the widget product lines in National Distico. Apart from the 4 mms, you believe Megabrands' margins are similar to the other brands sold by National Distico.

You must develop **arguments** to persuade her not to take your 4 mms out of her warehouse and propose **actions** to help her meet her gross margin objective to achieve a win–win outcome. Let's start by mapping out the numbers we have into a coherent picture of the category (Figure 10.3).

Product lines	Sales mix	GM%	GM '$'
Widget accessories	10%	15.00%	150
4 mm widgets – Megabrands		7.00%	
4 mm widgets – Competitors		12.00%	
6 mm widgets	20%	11.00%	220
8 mm widgets	20%	13.00%	260
Total	100%		

Figure 10.3 Megabrands' current position in National Distico's widget category

Now we work out that the sales mix for the 4 mm widgets must be 50 per cent in total (100 per cent less the total of the other product lines), and we know that Megabrands is about two-thirds of the 4 mm product line, so we can deduce that Megabrands 4 mms are 33 per cent of the total category and the competitors 4 mms are 17 per cent. We can now extend the sales mix and the margins for each product line to calculate the money margin – shown as GM '$' – and from this the current blended margin for the category as a whole. For completeness, we can also calculate the final column, the margin mix, which shows how much of the money margin comes from each product line (Figure 10.4).

Now we can see that our product manager does have a legitimate issue in that her category is running a blended margin of 10.65 per cent against the target of 11 per cent. Our first challenge is to protect our position by making telling **arguments**. These might include:

Product lines	Sales mix	GM%	GM '$'	Margin mix
Widget accessories	10%	15.00%	150	14%
4 mm widgets – Megabrands	33%	7.00%	231	22%
4 mm widgets – Competitors	17%	12.00%	204	19%
6 mm widgets	20%	11.00%	220	21%
8 mm widgets	20%	13.00%	260	24%
Total	100%	10.65%	1065	100%

Figure 10.4 Current margin mix (or blended margin) of National Distico's widget category

■ The loss of money margin because Megabrands' 4 mms account for 22% of the total money margin made by the category.
■ It is unlikely that the competitors will replace Megabrands as one of the competitors is exclusive to National Distico and therefore unlikely to be so well known among the trade customers, so something up to 33% of the total sales in the category could be lost (being Megabrands 4 mms sales).
■ The loss of this amount of sales could put volume discounts from Megabrands at risk, reducing further the contribution margin, or downgrade National Disitico's priority as a Megabrands account, losing status in channel programmes, marketing funding, etc.

It would be a brave product manager that could ignore these arguments and still go ahead and exclude Megabrands' 4 mm widgets from the category. There's every chance that we can save the line. Note that these arguments are built on the other measures that matter to the distributor (sales, contribution margins, money margins), but we still have not delivered on the one measure that matters to the product manager, the gross margin. By examining the financial profile of the category, some actions suggest themselves:

■ Increasing cross-sales from the widgets to the widget accessories, because the gross margin of 15% is above that earned by any other product line in the category. An incentive to the sales team to lift the connect rate from the current 10% to, say, 15% would have the impact shown in Figure 10.5, taking the blended margin up to 10.9%.
■ Increasing the proportion of the sales to the 6 mm and 8 mm widgets as a 'sell-up' campaign would tip the category over the 11% gross margin target. This would also likely increase total sales and money margins as the bigger widgets will have a higher unit price than the 4 mm widgets.

■ Finally, introducing a new product line with a gross margin higher than the sales it displaces in the sales mix (note the sales mix must always add up to 100%) would also accelerate the improvement in the category blended margin.

Product lines	Sales mix	GM%	GM '$'	Margin mix
Widget accessories	15%	15.00%	225	21%
4 mm widgets – Megabrands	31%	7.00%	217	20%
4 mm widgets – Competitors	16%	12.00%	192	18%
6 mm widgets	19%	11.00%	209	19%
8 mm widgets	19%	13.00%	247	22%
Total	100%	10.90%	1090	100%

Figure 10.5 Margin mix (or blended margin) of National Distico's widget category resulting from Megabrands' proposed actions

So by astute use of the category economics, Megabrands can change the situation around from facing losing its biggest-selling line in National Distico to persuading National to keep the range intact and possibly expanding it with the introduction of additional lines! The only cost may be sharing in funding some of the incentives need to change sales behaviour in the ways proposed.

You can see from this example that analysing the situation is critical to success. Our heroic account manager has made compelling arguments to the distributor for being retained. Even though the arguments did not solve the problem for the distributor, they demonstrated that the action proposed by the distributor (removing or de-emphasizing the supplier) would make things worse. This would buy time and maybe even force the distributor to put pressure on other suppliers. It is the actions proposed that solve the problem. This is real account management, finding the win–win, coming up with actions that deliver benefits to both parties. Note that the measures that matter here can be different, as they often are, and the skill is finding the actions that deliver on both parties' agendas (or coat pegs).

Managing the relationship with a distributor is a portfolio management challenge. Some products or product lines will deliver volumes, others growth and yet others high margins (see winners, losers, sleepers and traffic builders). The key is to position products to deliver the measures that they are capable of impacting positively. You will never get a high-market-share product to deliver good gross margins because it will be widely distributed and frequently used to signal the distributor's own price positioning (ie that it is price competitive). However, it will draw traffic and, by working together, you can develop strategies for improving the connect rate to higher-margin products (be open-minded to building traffic for a non-competing complementary supplier if necessary).

Some rules of thumb for making compelling business cases

There is no substitute for tailoring your business arguments to the unique situation facing your distributor and your own position. However, there are some rules of thumb that can give you a head start.

If you are a market-share leader

Being a market-share leader can apply to either the supplier as a brand or a particular product or product line. There are a number of elements to the business case that normally apply in this situation:

■ **Focus on the GM$s** that a market share leader will generate, even on the relatively low GM%, from its high level of unit sales. Make the case that these 'bankable' GM$s are valuable in covering a significant proportion of the distributor's fixed overheads. This argument may not cut much ice with the category buyer whose performance measures include hitting a target GM%. But as a market share leader you should have a relationship higher up the distributor's management structure where there will be recognition that this is a valid argument. Figure 10.6 shows a graphic illustration of this business case argument.

■ **Switch the focus from gross margins to contribution margins** (% and $s). As a major brand in the category, the cost of selling your product will be lower than for a less well-known brand. The trade channels will be benefiting from your end-customer marketing activity and ordering familiar products from the distributor, which requires very little sales time and marketing effort on its part. This should be reflected in the notional contribution margin if not actually in the way any one distributor actually measures its contribution margins.

Similarly, the larger volumes of well-known brands and products typically have a lower cost-to-ship from a logistics perspective and incur lower rates of return and associated (expensive) reverse logistics costs.

And the same business argument extends to pre- and post-support, with few if any demands being made by the trade channels for help on products with which they are very familiar. Even the costs of new product introductions will be amortized over the higher volumes, reducing the cost-to-sell per unit to negligible costs.

■ **Switch the focus from return on sales to return on asset/capital**. The high volumes of market leaders usually means that their asset turns are good, giving them above-average returns on working capital. This is the critical combined measure of 'earn and turn' for any distributor. Those products that dominate their revenues in a category need to deliver on these returns on asset/capital measures for the distributor. Many distributors set some form of turn target on their category managers, and more are now setting targets using the return on working capital measure.

These three elements will form the backbone of your business case with a distributor, so before you go in to make you case you need to do your

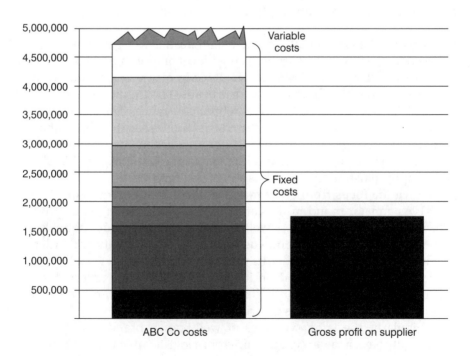

Figure 10.6 Illustrative vendor gross profit contribution to covering a distributor's fixed costs

homework. Analyse just how your portfolio of products is performing across both the measures the distributor uses today and the ones that you want it to recognize. Be able to answer for yourself questions such as:

■ In each category, are our products pulling up or dragging down the key measures?
■ Overall, is our brand a puller or a dragger on the distributor's business model?
■ What is the value of the GM$ (or contribution$) that our brand is generating for the distributor, and what proportion of its fixed overhead costs does this represent?
■ Can we show that the contribution from our products is comparatively better than our gross margins?
■ What evidence can we provide of the level of connected sales and margins generated from the traffic generated by our brand?
■ How fast are our products moving through the distributor? Can we show an above-average rate of return on working capital?
■ Which are our 'problem' measures and which our 'star' measures?
■ Which measures matter to our distributor's senior and junior management?

If you are a smaller vendor or new entrant in a category

Smaller vendors often struggle to get attention from the senior management of the distributor, so they need to concentrate on the category manager and show just how good a job they can do of hitting the measures that matter at this level:

■ **Focus on the GM%.** Typically as a smaller supplier, your products will be less widely distributed and you will be looking to the one or few distributors appointed to be doing more to create a market for your products. Your distributors' category managers will be struggling to hit their GM% targets, and one possible way to achieve them is to increase the proportion of sales of higher margin products... such as yours. Few distributors are proactive in this regard and active account management will be well received if it drives up margins by putting some of your key products in the spotlight. Even the limited amount of marketing dollars you will be able to apply will have an impact if tightly targeted on the highest-margin products in your range, building revenues for you.

Most categories will have one or two market share leaders on which the distributor makes very small margins, so it looks to its third and fourth brands to make up the margin it seeks. To do this, the distributor needs to sell these second-tier brands in sufficient volumes to be able to move the blended margin for the category. This is your opportunity. Emphasize the degree to which you have given the distributor (actual or near) exclusivity on your products so it will benefit directly from all your end-user and final-tier marketing spend. Build up the support for switch-selling the top-tier brands and provide the evidence that your products are just as low cost to sell and support. If you are very small, you may need to focus on one part of the final-tier channel and concentrate your marketing (and direct the distributor's efforts) to gain traction.

■ **Emphasize the growth rate, especially in percentage terms**. All category managers look for growth in their category and, coming off a small base, it will be easier for you to demonstrate relatively high growth rates.

■ **Highlight the connect rate opportunities**. Most distributors make more money on the accessories than they do on the core products that they attach to. But how many accessories do they sell per core product? Often less than one in fifty. Certainly not all deals will be for end-users who require accessories, but we have seen many distributors uncover and exploit some very profitable connect rate opportunities. Your role is to help the distributor see the potential of connecting your products to the traffic builders and build some sales force and trade channel incentives around these proposals.

Summary

Distributors are a key link in the route to market for many sectors. Although they seem to fulfil only a few basic functions, breaking bulk, providing credit and offering one-stop convenience to the trade channels, their pervasive presence in emerging and mature markets is testament to the value they deliver.

The distributor business model is highly challenging to get right, with its very small margins on massive volumes across tens of thousands of individual SKUs, each requiring decisions on stocking levels and reorder quantities. On top of that, the distributor has to ensure it sells only to creditworthy customers and then get them to pay on time. It has to find products that the trade channels want and then extract the best possible terms out of its suppliers, ensuring that its marketing and sales costs are predominantly covered by marketing funds from these suppliers. And by doing all this, the distributor has to create more value than that its investors would have earned in an investment of equivalent risk.

Traditionally, distributor management controls the business by breaking the business model down into its 'earn' and 'turn' elements, but it is the combination measures (such as GMROII and GMROWC) that reveal the true financial productivity of products, categories and customer segments. More sophisticated managers are now applying the principles of value creation both to measure and to motivate their teams to focus on the levers of value in the business.

Suppliers looking to engage effectively with distributors need to develop a thorough insight into their partner's strategy and recognize that they are selling a complete business model. It has to be a model that creates positive forces on the distributor's economics. The successful supplier will be able to analyse where it can deliver commercial advantage to the distributor and make the business case for commanding more of the distributor's resources. The prize for those suppliers that get it right is a cost-effective route to market that can build and sustain profitable market share across a large number of trade channels.

Part 3

Final-tier trade channel players

11

The roles of the final-tier trade channel players

The final-tier trade channel players

Although the generic term of 'final-tier trade channel players' used for this part of the book may not mean anything to you, this part focuses on the players that interact with the end customer. This can be in any capacity, including straightforward product supply such as dealers or retailers as well as the whole array of service-related players who install, set up or integrate products for the end customer. And it includes the players who don't touch the product at all but can have a major influence on the customer's choice, such as architects who specify the fittings in a new house or building, or the accountant who recommends the bookkeeping package a small business should use.

Every industry uses its own language to label its different types of player, reflecting tradition, the role or simply industry jargon. Figure 11.1 shows just a small selection by industry of the types of player we are covering in this section, which may help you to recognize the players you are interested in.

Industry	Final-tier trade channels	Typical activities
Automotive – cars, spare parts, consumables (oil, screen wash), tyres, accessories, cleaners, etc)	Dealers	Sell, service and support cars, bikes, vans, trucks
	Workshops	Service and repair cars, bikes, vans, trucks
	Specialist repair shops	Supply and fit tyres, exhausts, brakes, clutches, etc
	Accessory shops and retail motor factors	Supply (and possibly fit) spare parts, accessories and consumables
	Garage forecourts	Supply consumables, some generic parts and cleaners
Information technology and telecommunications – hardware, software, components, switches, etc	Resellers, dealers, corporate resellers, independent software vendors (sell hardware on which their software runs)	Sell and support computers, software, telephones, etc
	Value-added dealers, value-added resellers, solution providers, service providers	Install, set up, configure IT and telecoms systems, possibly using their own specialized software or solutions
	System integrators	Specify, design, install and integrate complex IT and/or telecoms solutions
Building and construction – windows, pipes, taps, switches, boilers, radiators, burglar alarms, wood, paint, glass, tools, specialist clothing, etc	General tradespeople (such as plumbers, carpenters, decorators, glaziers, electricians, heating engineers, etc)	Supply and fit new or replacement products or systems, service and repair existing installations
	Specialist tradespeople (such as window installers, kitchen fitters, alarm installers, etc)	Design, install and integrate windows, kitchens, alarm systems, etc
	DIY superstores	Supply wide range of products
	Hardware or specialist stores	Advise and supply products, can sometimes provide or broker installation services

Figure 11.1 Types of final-tier trade channel player by industry

You can see even from this limited selection that there is a huge range of types of players and that they can range in size from a single one-person independent trader through small and medium-sized businesses up to global enterprises. Despite this large degree of variation, there is surprisingly a high degree of commonality in terms of the roles or activities that types of partners fulfil in the value chain. As a result of this commonality, their business models also reflect some standard characteristics.

There are bound to be some players that are extremely specialist, but you will find that their business is simply a very pure version of the one of the models we will explore in this part of the book. Many of the players in any industry are, to some degree, hybrids, often as a result of customer demand or expectation. For example, shops selling car hi-fi systems and car alarms have found that they need to operate a service bay (usually round the back of the store) to fit systems into customers' cars to be able to sell these after-market products. Most customers simply do not have the time, skills, tools and expertise to do the job, so unless the shop is prepared to start levering out door trims, their hi-fis and alarm systems are going to remain on the shelves. The same is true in the business world, where many businesses do not have, and do not want to have, the specialist skills to install and configure new IT or telephony systems.

In our increasingly connected and complex world, this need to customize, install and integrate products is a major driver of the role of final-tier trade channels, whether selling to consumers or to businesses. Once installed, these products and systems need maintaining, servicing, repairing and upgrading. Very few products, beyond fast-moving consumer goods, can be sold as stand-alone items. In a world of fast-changing technology, it makes no sense to develop or own the relevant skills in-house. Not only is the need for these skills highly intermittent, it is expensive to ensure skills are always bang up to date. A dedicated installer whose business is focused entirely on this type of work is going to have (it hopes) a steady demand for its skills and can therefore afford to invest in keeping them at the cutting edge. The smart installer will also develop techniques and proprietary tools that enable it to do the job quickly and safely and work to predictable estimates, enabling it to accurately price projects in advance, knowing the margins for error and profit.

The one type of final-tier partner business model that we are going to leave to the next part of this book is that of the retailer. Retailers are sufficiently specialized in their operation and different from the players whose role involves some element of service that we will deal with it in Part 4. Note though that many final-tier trade channels may include an element of retailing in their hybrid business model. And many retailers offer services, so usually they are operating hybrid models.

The common thing we have established about the final-tier trade channels is that they play a vital enabling role in the sales process by virtue of their skills and expertise in making the product work for the end customer. This means that these players deliver value both upstream to the vendor of the products and downstream to the end customer, which should make for an attractive business model, something we shall examine in Chapter 12. First though, we need to understand their role in more detail, so that, no matter which industry, you can identify the implications for either managing or working with these businesses.

The possible roles of final-tier trade channel players

One of the interesting things about the final-tier channel players is that they can be different things to different people. For example, to a small or medium-sized business customer (let's call them 'Acme Widgets'), its IT provider ('Advanced Computing Co') may be a solution provider. Advanced Computing Co helps to work out what combination of servers, computers, storage, switches and other hardware Acme needs to run its office, network, e-mail, accounting systems, management applications and so on. Each time Microsoft upgrades its operating system, Advanced will advise Acme on whether it makes sense to upgrade, and then installs and integrates the systems to work seamlessly. Advanced may also provide day-to day support and troubleshooting. It possibly won the relationship with Acme in the first place because it offers a specialist production control software that is built on Oracle's database product. So Advance Computing Co is simultaneously:

- a **customer advocate** to Acme Widgets;
- a **solution provider** to Acme Widgets;
- a **service provider** to Acme Widgets;
- a **reseller** for various hardware suppliers like Hewlett-Packard, IBM, Cisco;
- a **value added reseller** for Microsoft;
- an **independent software vendor** for Oracle;
- an **influencing partner** for the accounting software supplier.

In another example, Mr and Mrs Smith decide to do a loft conversion at the top of the house to create an extra bedroom with en-suite shower room.

They contract with Easy Lofts to do the job for them and indicate the shower and bathroom fittings that they prefer. Easy Lofts draws up a loft design and does the plans for the project. It orders in the three special loft windows, heating pipes and radiators, and subcontracts the bathroom installation to a specialist fitter, Pipes and Co. Pipes and Co points out to Mr and Mrs Smith that their first choice of fittings isn't really suitable for the loft conversion and recommends an alternative that they accept. It also recommends the extractor fan and trunking required by building regulations that are installed by Easy Lofts.

So Easy Lofts has been:

■ a **master contractor** for Mr and Mrs Smith;
■ a **specifier** for the windows, pipes and radiator vendors;
■ a **trade installer or reseller** for the windows, pipes and radiator vendors;
■ a **master contractor** to Pipes and Co;
■ a **trade reseller** of the timber, plasterboard, floorboards, plaster, paint, etc.

And Pipes and Co has been:

■ a **specifier** for the shower and bathroom fittings;
■ a **trade installer or reseller** for the shower and bathroom fittings;
■ an **influencer** for the extractor fan and trunking vendors.

And in the background there are one or more local builders' merchants who supplied the timber, plasterboard, floorboards, plaster, paint, etc, and the shower and bathroom fittings as **first-tier distributors** for the suppliers of these products.

In order to cut through the complexity caused by the myriad of different labels used in each industry, we are going to suggest some generic roles that you should be able to recognize and apply, no matter what terminology your particular industry uses. We believe that there are five discrete roles (see Figure 11.2) that final-tier trade channel partners can chose to fulfil.

These roles are:

■ **Extension of a vendor** – essentially some form of outsourced capability, usually handling logistics or back office processes. The recent growth in offshoring has increased the range and depth of the activities that partners can undertake. The partner can take on some of the business risk

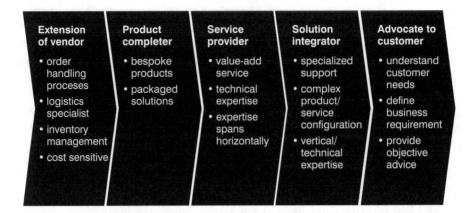

Figure 11.2 Roles for final-tier trade channel players

in the activity, such as providing financial credit insurance for large capital purchases, or simply be paid a fee for operational activities such as for freight forwarding or logistics.

■ **Product completer** – providing some degree of customization of the supplier's product for individual customers or for whole customer segments. This can be a very extensive role when the supplier is a component supplier, in which case the supplier is sometimes termed an original equipment manufacturer (OEM). For example, where Brembo braking systems are installed into Ferrari cars, Ferrari is the product completer for OEM Brembo. Alternatively, the product completer role can be as simple as opening the box and adding the local type of power supply cable and local language manuals, before shipping to the end customer.

■ **Service provider** – providing any of a huge range of services such as design, pre-sales support, post-sales support, installation, on-site configuration, maintenance, financing and so on. Depending on the product, the service provided can be minimal, such as helping to select the right product for the customer's needs, through to fundamental such as constructing the conservatory base for the prefabricated windows and doors provided by the conservatory supplier. We tend to characterize the service provider in 'horizontal' terms, that is, its skills and capabilities are related to the product rather than the customer. This is in contrast to the…

■ **Solution integrator** – which applies customer insight (vertical skills) and knowledge to render a solution fit for the unique needs of the customer. A large solution integrator can cover a wide range of customer types, perhaps with different divisions or sections within its business, whereas a small solution integrator may specialize in just one type of customer. The critical difference between the service provider and the solution integrator is their orientation, with the latter often helping the customer to make several products and services work as a seamless whole (think of a master contractor commissioning a new production line in a customer's existing factory) in comparison to the service providers ensuring that their particular products work (the electricians installing the control systems and the riggers setting up the conveyor belts and operations stations). The service provider has to make the product work to the specifications agreed; the solution integrator has to make the whole solution work for the end customer.

■ **Advocate to customer** – is the role that has a bigger impact the more its skills and knowledge are needed to specify and select solutions. These are players whose roles have become highly specialized and as a result are needed only intermittently. Examples of this role include the independent financial adviser, which helps its customers choose the best life insurance and pension plans to meet financial objectives and risk tolerances; the strategy consultancy that helps its customers select the best information technology systems to support its strategy; the doctor who prescribes the best pharmaceutical remedy for an ailment; and the accountants who recommend the best accounting package for use by its small business customers.

You will have detected that there is shift in orientation across these roles, from completely supplier orientated at the extension of a vendor end through to completely customer orientated at the customer advocate end. And as we will see in the next chapters, this has a very big bearing on the business models associated with these roles. You can think of these roles being defined in terms of the knowledge value chain or core competencies (Figure 11.3).

In most sectors, partners can fulfil several of these roles seamlessly and in some cases may fulfil all but one of the roles – it would be too great a conflict of interest to encompass both ends of this value chain in the one player. Most often the divide comes: 1) between the product completer and service provider, where the service provider role is essentially 'on the customer's side'; or 2) between the service provider and the solution integrator, where the service provider role is 'on the supplier's side'.

Note that even in the first of these situations, such as, say, an automotive workshop (like Halfords), where the service provider is working to give

These roles…

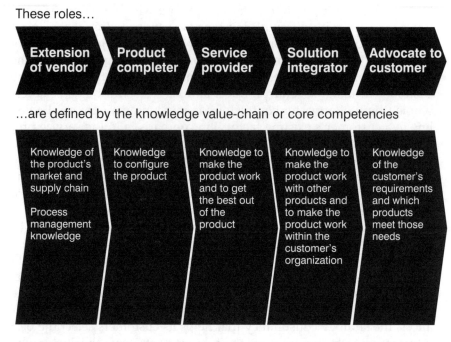

…are defined by the knowledge value-chain or core competencies

Figure 11.3 Final tier roles defined in terms of the knowledge value chain or core competencies

the customer the right parts at the right price, it is very much in the parts suppliers' interests to train and support the service provider in the correct installation of their products. The smart supplier would want to make sure that the service provider understands its product range and how its products are differentiated from those of its competitors. It may even want to offer the non-brand-specific training needed to become a competent mechanic in an attempt to win share of mind and, with it, share of recommendation. Taking this to an extreme, look at how the big pharmaceutical companies seek to influence prescribing doctors (GPs) with seminars on the latest techniques in treating, say, cardio-vascular thrombosis… that just happen to be held in Disneyland, Florida. Strict ethical controls have been introduced to ensure that the 'channel partner' does not cross sides from customer/patient to supplier.

Matching channel roles to channel players

As we explore each role, you will probably find that you can quickly map the roles to the types of partner in your industry. Often, in industries that are consolidating or changing structure rapidly you will find a mix of partners playing multiple roles competing with partners that have chosen to fulfil only one role. In more mature industries, the players settle into well-established roles that everyone understands until there is some form of technological, political, economic or legal shock that upsets the landscape. For example, in the household appliances market the structure usually looks something like Figure 11.4.

Consumers thinking of remodelling their kitchens would make a considered purchase, taking inputs from a variety of sources, before ordering the products of their choice from a retailer. When the products are delivered to the consumer's house, a kitchen fitter is employed to install them and ensure they are integrated into the kitchen. Behind the scenes, various supply chain logistics players have moved the products from the factories to the retailers, possibly through distributors.

However, recently in the United States and in a few European markets, the mass-merchandise retailers have made moves to capture more of the margin available from providing services. They have set up websites offering an online or in-store kitchen design service and take on full responsibil-

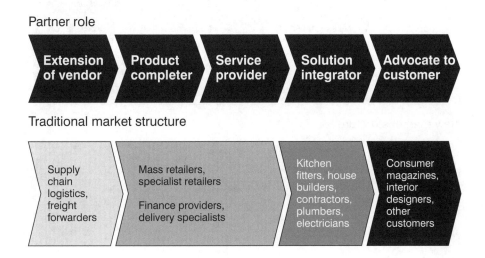

Figure 11.4 Traditional final tier roles in the household appliances market

ity for the entire installation and integration, making their role look more like the new market structure at the bottom of Figure 11.5.

By offering a range of possible designs and styles as well as a wide range of domestic appliance suppliers and price points, the retailer holds itself out as a credible customer advocate. And by taking on the full installation role, the retailer integrates the solution, providing all necessary services, including financing options if required. Of course the consumer still has the choice of going it alone, but to a segment of time-poor, cash-rich customers, the convenience outweighs any restriction on choice and possibly any price premium for the full 'turn-key' process. It remains to be seen whether the demand from this segment can cover the costs incurred by the retailer in setting up the processes and infrastructure needed to pull this off as a credible and effective customer offer.

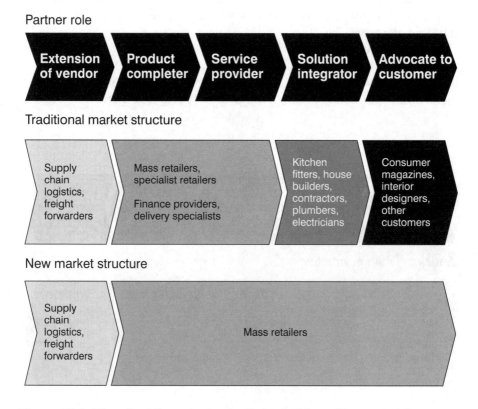

Figure 11.5 New final tier roles in the household appliances market

Be prepared to find the customer fulfilling some of the partner roles. This is especially frequent in the business-to-business context. For example, in the small and medium business sector, very few information systems are properly integrated. Customers have to work out for themselves what systems they need and muddle along with what they are given, but rarely get the best out of what they pay for. Some computer dealers have recognized the opportunity and positioned themselves to fulfil the customer advocate and solution integrator roles, usually by selecting a particular segment of customers in which they can specialize and become expert. The two market structures look something like those shown in Figure 11.6.

In many industries, channel players have had to 'switch sides' (from the supplier side to the customer side) like this in order to survive as the industry has matured. In new and emerging sectors, suppliers need to build their routes to market and will compensate the channel handsomely for

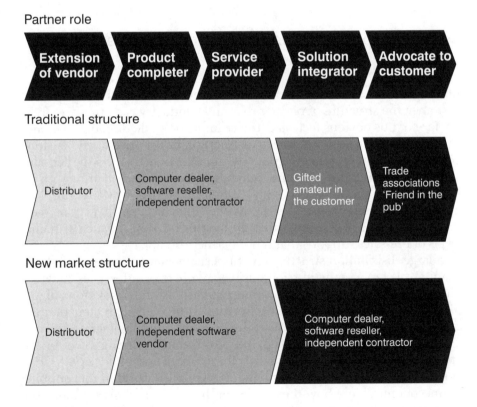

Figure 11.6 Traditional and new final tier roles in the computer products market

doing the work of unlocking the demand of end customers. This naturally tends to create a channel full of service providers who are 'on the supplier's side' and who look to the supplier for their compensation. As the sector grows and matures, two things happen: the number of service providers multiplies and customers start demanding a lot more integration in exchange for their custom. The service provider finds it is stuck in the middle, with declining margins for what have become almost commodity services and suffering from a lack of ability to compete for the higher-end work demanded by customers. The service provider either has to become the price-leader in commodity services (through scale efficiencies) or 'switch sides' and become specialist enough to be able to command compensation from the customer for higher-value-added integration work, ie become solution integrators. Compensation becomes highly or entirely customer determined through negotiation of the scope of the work and the degree of expertise required.

Different roles command different compensation models

Although ultimately all trade channel compensation is paid for by the end customer, the structure of partner roles in an industry can appear to fly in the face of this obvious fact. Take the example of 'trade discount', where a supplier gives the trade channel a discount off its list price to end customers. This discount is often governed by conditions set by the supplier, such as extra discounts for volumes purchased by the trade partner, or for accredited qualifications in highly technical categories. Many suppliers operate a 'Preferred Partner Programme' in which partners that meet certain criteria have access to direct and indirect discounts (such as higher levels of pre-sales support) that other partners do not.

In large distribution structures, with perhaps many thousands of trade channel players competing for business with few differences between them, these trade discounts become the basis of differentiation. Bigger players with bigger trade discounts (secured through their greater volumes) can afford to pass part of their discount on to the end customer – known as 'passing it to the street' – and win business through offering lower prices. Smaller players are unable to match these prices and either cry 'foul' in every conversation with the supplier or eventually abandon that supplier as uneconomic. Note how the whole emphasis of this compensation conversation is between the trade player and the supplier. Where are the customers in all this? How does their point of view get heard? Sometimes the customers can exacerbate the problem by conducting the entire pre-purchase process (called pre-sales by the trade channel, of course) with a smaller player, who is perhaps more expert on the customers' particular needs, and then complete the process by placing their business with the cheapest (larger) bidder, who has turned up late but offered cheap pricing as its trump card.

Suppliers have found that this situation, if left unchecked, will damage their distribution network by eliminating all but a few price-led partners. Their ability to launch new products and install their products into specialist segments of the market is destroyed by this. Their response has been either to make it harder for the trade channel to pass its discount on to the street or to move away from volume and recognize accredited skills and competencies as the basis of discounts.

The typical approach to making the trade discount 'stick' in the channel has been to make part or all of the discount uncertain, so the trade cannot afford to give too much away in case it doesn't earn it in the first place. Sometimes called 'black box' discounts, there are all sorts of ways suppliers have found to create uncertainty:

- Giving the trade channel discount in the form of a rebate or 'back-end margin' rather than built into the price as 'front-end margin'. The rebate has to be earned based on hitting some targets during a period (annual, half yearly, quarterly, etc), so unless the target is achieved the trade player cannot be sure it has earned the rebate. These targets can be sales volumes, but can also be end-customer satisfaction scores or quality ratings. The targets need to be renegotiated each period, which creates an account management burden for the supplier. The types of target can also be varied each period to create more uncertainty across periods. The downside is that 'order, counter-order leads to disorder' and the channel disengages through being driven first one way then another.
- Awarding bonuses after the end of a trading period. These bonuses can be pre-announced with a scheme of rules, or simply announced after the end of the period as a 'reward' for exceptional performance. Care must be taken not to become too predictable or else the trade will start factoring the expected bonus back into its street prices. The bonus can be related to the supplier's own performance, which will have affected the size of the 'pot' available to share out, as well as that of the channel's, which determines each member's share of the 'pot'.
- Ranking partners based on performance in a period and giving different discounts to the different tiers. Performance can be defined in many

ways other than sales volumes, such as accounts opened or quality and customer satisfaction ratings. Partners will not know until after the trading period into which tier they have qualified, so cannot afford to give away the higher-level discounts.
- A mix of these different elements, though undue complexity will cause the trade players to switch off and become unmotivated to sell that supplier's products.

The accreditation approach can apply in both low-tech and high-tech industries. In low-tech sectors, the accreditation can apply to factors such as compliance with operating guidelines, health and safety compliance, basic technical qualifications, adherence to trade association business practices, etc. Even the most basic of products will benefit from the sales and installation teams being trained in how to sell and install the product, so accreditation can be as simple as the number of people who have attended the supplier's product training. In high-tech sectors, the need for accreditation is more obvious. Cisco led the way in the IT sector in the 1990s by allowing its smallest partners to secure the biggest trade discounts provided they had the required number of qualified engineers to qualify under its tiered partner programme. This meant that the big players no longer had any price advantage and it enabled Cisco to promote its trade channel as the one best qualified to serve customers' networking needs.

The alternative approach to 'black box discounts' is to pay for functions or activities performed by the final tier. At a very basic level, this may simply be in the form of the supplier paying an extra half or one per cent discount for receiving 'sell out' data, telling it in some prescribed level of detail about the sales actually made to the end customer. In some sectors, this approach has evolved to cover many functions and levels of performance in a blend with more traditional discount structures as shown in the box.

Fee for function

For many years a major film and home entertainment distributor had compensated its channel partners in Germany, the UK and Spain by giving discounts and rebates based entirely on sales volumes. These were either in the form of on-invoice discounts or applied as month-end, quarter-end and annual rebates. Although the distributor had tried to persuade its channel partners to carry out a series of activities to the best of their ability, it had no mechanism for recognizing and rewarding such performance.

The distributor took the bold move to change its approach and decided to re-allocate the available compensation by paying partners for discrete activities based on the partners' ability to deliver on four dimensions: Ranging, In-store, Consumer touch and Efficiency in addition to the basic compensation model (Figure 11.7):

■ Although volume targets remained, they would be flexible to reflect individual partners' performance rather being a set unearned percentage.
■ Other elements such as the partners' merchandising, display of products and point-of-sale displays would be rewarded on a fee for function **basis.**
■ Some activities, such as consumer marketing, would remain outside the normal terms and conditions and be paid for through discretionary marketing development funds that were allocated base on the merit of the activity.
■ The final group of activities, the hygiene factors, were considered so fundamental to the role of the distributor that no remuneration would be offered or indeed needed.

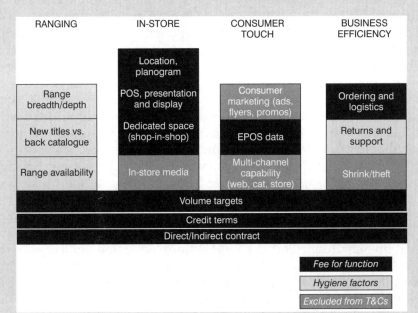

Figure 11.7 Illustrative compensation structure in a 'fee for function' model

The effect of this approach is to give the film and home entertainment distributor much more control over its channel, paying for what it wants the channel to do and pulling compensation away from partners that simply choose not to deliver. These hybrid types of compensation arrangements will become more common as the spotlight increasingly falls on ensuring that all distribution expense is making a positive contribution to business performance.

However, even this approach still positions the whole compensation negotiation between the supplier and the trade partner with the customer excluded. Why is this? Well, the answer lies mainly in the fact that the supplier needs the trade to 'complete' its offer. The trade is fulfilling all those needs we highlighted earlier, making the product available when customers want it, where they want it, configured they way they want, working the way they want in their business or home and supplied on a financial payment plan that matches their cash flow. These activities come at a cost and the supplier recognizes that it needs to compensate the channel for doing essential work in taking its products to market. Thus, we can expect the supplier to define that part of the compensation in some way. But, this is not the complete offering the trade channel provides to the customer. Each sale is a project and, as such, the customer should define the scope of specific services that it wants from the trade channel. 'Sophisticated' customers do this and negotiate their required package of services and related pricing to fit their needs exactly. But what if the customer has no idea what's entailed and what it should negotiate for? For example, would you know what should be done to service your car after one year's ownership? Ninety-five per cent of car owners probably have no idea as car technology is a fast-moving field and could not begin to negotiate the package of service required. Here the supplier (Ford, Nissan, etc) steps in and defines the one-year, 10,000-mile service that is required and encourages its dealers to offer a prescribed price. Customers can still indicate if they want the car picked up and dropped off, ask for the funny noise from under the dashboard to be investigated and request that baby-seat straps be fitted, all of which, if not covered under the warranty, will come at a price agreed between the trade player and the customer. So what we have is picture of compensation like Figure 11.8.

Partner role

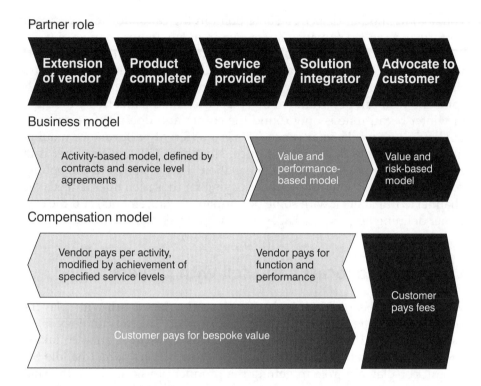

Figure 11.8 Business model and compensation model for different partner roles

At the top of the picture are our familiar partner roles. Below these, the business model shows the progression from supplier-related activities, defined by contracts between the supplier and its trade channel, to customer-defined activities where the customer is seeking to outsource work and risk in order to secure a certain level of performance (how good a job would you do of servicing your one-year-old car?). The price paid by the customer is directly related to the value and performance received or risk defrayed. Continuing our car example, you pay more at a franchised (or authorized) dealer than a workshop around the corner, but you know that the people working on your car are technically bang up to date on your model and should something go wrong after the service, you can take it back and expect them to sort it out, no questions asked. You are also sure that your three-year warranty is not invalidated. You might also get the car back from the service with a free valet or the use of a car while yours is with the dealer. You, the customer, are paying for all this and if you don't get it, you'll go to another dealer. At some point in the car's life, however, your performance and risk-management requirements might change. You are prepared to fix only the major problems, there is no warranty to protect and frankly, if the car was valeted it would only show the scratches and dings from your parking efforts in sharper relief. But what you do need is someone who can pop round and get it started on the first frosty morning of winter because he is only round the corner and doesn't expect you to book it in two weeks in advance. This is a different performance requirement and it comes at a different price. Note now that the customer is in control of the value/compensation equation. This is shown in the bottom part of Figure 11.8, with the supplier paying for those activities it needs the channel to fulfil (albeit with some performance requirements) and the customer defining bespoke packages of value and risk management.

Customer advocates and sell-with players

We have hinted earlier in this chapter about the role of 'sell-with' players, particularly in the role of advocate to customer. This terminology is, of course, that used by suppliers as it defines the role in relation to taking products to market. As the name implies, these players do not handle the product or play any role in getting the product physically from the supplier to the customer, work that is done by the sell-through players. However, these sell-with players can be crucial to the selling process in some sectors. This is usually the case where customers are ill-equipped or even incapable of defining what they want. You might think of it as a technical purchase and this applies in both the business and consumer markets. Architects and interior designers specify the products and often the brand of product to be installed in their designs. IT consultants specify the hardware and software architecture needed by businesses and are often asked to specify the products and brands required to build and implement it.

So, if the sell-with partner doesn't 'touch' the product, how does its business model work? In Figure 11.6, we indicate that the customer pays fees, which is the dominant compensation model as it is the customer who has initiated the purchasing process and gone to the player it believes best understands its needs and budget. This creates a challenge for the supplier who is now dependent on the customer advocate to recognize and specify or recommend its products over those of its competitors. The supplier's opening comes from the customer advocate's need to be sure it knows of the best-of-breed alternatives, new technologies and materials, etc, and to be sure it knows which problems each of the alternatives is best configured to solve. So the door is open to credible suppliers to inform and educate the customer advocate and suppliers should mange these relationships in much the same way as a key sell-through account. This means that the supplier should establish regular meetings, promote discussion of current projects and prospects, provide strong information flow in the form preferred by the customer advocate and generally do all it can to ensure that it is positioned in the customer advocate's thinking as top of mind, best of breed and a useful source of answers to technical problems.

All of this can be described as influencing sell-with partner behaviour, but can the supplier go further and reward the customer advocate, to create a commercial influence on recommendation? Care is needed to avoid compromising the customer advocate and placing it in a conflict of interest (see the case study on the financial services industry). Bearing in mind that reward can be both financial and non-financial, the answer is almost certainly yes. Familiar strategies are to provide resources that are valuable to the customer advocate, such as:

■ free technical help, demonstration and 'extra' products that enable the advocate to do its job at a lower cost;
■ training that goes beyond simple product knowledge, which displaces cost for the customer advocate;
■ broker introductions and leads sourced through the supplier's own networking, marketing and sales activities;
■ conferences and other events at attractive locations that serve as reward and motivation opportunities to the people of the customer advocate at no cost to its own business.

Financial services industry – who pays the trade?

The financial services industry is an interesting case, with many financial advisers (ie the trade channel) working for the customer but compensated through commissions paid by the suppliers (the pension funds and life assurance companies) on the products the advisers recommend and sell. This has long been recognized to be a situation open to abuse as there is clearly an inherent conflict of interest. Some advisers have rejected the conflict of interest and act only in return for fees paid by the customer. Others have tied themselves exclusively, and overtly, to the supplier they believe to offer best-of-breed products – their compensation comes in the form of commissions earned on the products they recommend. It tends to be the more sophisticated customers who prefer to pay the fees to an independent financial adviser, as they need sound advice and expect to source their products from a wide variety of suppliers. However, surely it is the unsophisticated customers who need even more advice? Quite possibly yes, but they are unwilling to pay for it when it is made an overt fee. They do pay for their advice, but because it is wrapped up in the overall price of the product, they believe it comes to them free of charge. As a result, many people are horrified when they try to exit from a policy part of the way through its term and find that most of the money paid into it for the first 18 months has gone on commission payments and the policy is worth much less than the monthly payments made to date. That's rather late to find out the price of the advisory service they have received.

In some sectors, suppliers have provided direct compensation for introductions or referrals that have led to sales. Here there are enormous challenges in measuring the degree of influence of the sell-with partner and even attributing a sale to a partner at all if the influencer is not in an existing relationship. An example of this is the impact that accounting firms have on the choice of accounting software chosen by small to medium-sized businesses. Microsoft, which is in the accounts package business through its Great Plains products, experimented with an approach that entailed asking the customer how it had chosen its package and who had influenced the sale. After trialling the approach for several months, the cost and administration burden was found to outweigh the leverage advantage gained. It was felt that the programme would need to be fairly pervasive across the accounting firms (which is a highly fragmented sector) to reach the tipping point at which Microsoft's compensation would positively influence sales. Too much manual work was required to identify the influencer, judge the impact of its influence and determine the appropriate level of compensation.

Sell-with players and strategic alliances

Not all sell-with players are customer advocates. There are many situations where two or more suppliers need to partner to offer a complete solution, yet neither is the customer advocate. One may be the solution integrator, or they may both be service providers. However, by forming a strategic alliance they may be able to generate higher sales volumes or better conversion rates or enter new markets than would be possible if they were to operate alone. If both parties are of equal market power, benefit equally from a sale and can collaborate effectively, the strategic alliance may need little more than shared sales planning and an equal commitment of resources to make it work. However, in most cases, one party is looking to leverage the market power of the other party and is seeking to find some way achieve that in a strategic partnership.

Figure 11.9 shows how the relationship can be promoted depending on the relative market power of the two parties and the time horizon to which they are working. If one party is relatively weak in market power, it helps if it can demonstrate that the stronger party will be able to generate significant revenue for its own offering as a result of the partnership. An excellent example of this is the way SAP software built its market share in markets outside its home market of Germany. SAP went to the big systems integrators such as Accenture and PWC Consulting with its ground-breaking but complex Enterprise Systems software and demonstrated that for every dollar SAP earned from software licence sales, the systems integrators would earn between 10 and 30 dollars of consultancy, installing and configuring the systems and the related change management work to adapt corporate customers' processes to get the best return on the investment. The systems integrators had to make some sizeable investments in skills and capabilities, and SAP made many of its courses available at negligible cost to lock in the alliance relationship. As a result, SAP had almost all the major systems integrators telling all their major clients to adopt the SAP applications, leading to a bonanza of work for them and market dominance in less than four years in many markets around the world, including the United States, for SAP. Had SAP offered a share of the margin on licence sales, the amounts involved would have been too small to interest the systems integrators and made a hole in SAP's profits. By focusing on the related revenue pull-through, SAP harnessed the marketing power of almost every solution integrator in the market.

Strategic partnerships (in this context) are built on shared expectations of long-term revenue generation. For them to be successful, it is essential that both parties invest time and money, and that there is a strong commitment

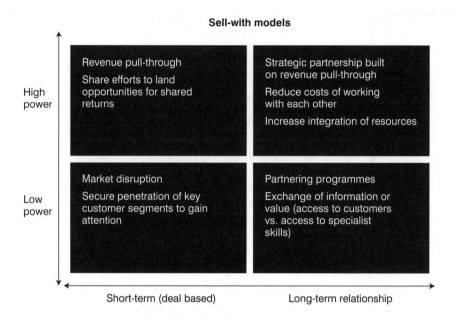

Figure 11.9 Matrix of possible 'sell with' models

from the top levels of both organizations. The best alliances are those focused on specific markets or opportunities and the relationship is built on predictability of outcome, on clarity of roles, and on communication and consistency. Above all, the relationship has to give each side a profit.

Applying this framework to your industry sector or channel

You may find the terms 'service provider' or 'solution integrator' hard to relate to the particular types of channel player with which you are familiar. And it can seem rather over the top to describe the classic trades of plumber or kitchen fitter, etc, in these terms. But don't be put off. Remember these are *role* descriptions, not *player* descriptions, and they are deliberately set in terms of the customer's context, not the supplier's. In our experience it is very helpful to think in terms of these roles as it can help suppliers clarify their channel strategies or go-to-market models. Indeed, Hewlett-Packard overhauled its entire European distribution model for its computer and printing products for business customers using this framework and improved its market position and distribution efficiency by so doing.

12

How the business model of the final-tier trade channel players works

Role defines business model

As we have seen in the previous chapter, the business model of a final-tier trade channel player comprises a mix of product resale and service provision. This mix can vary widely, from players where service provision makes up next to nothing as a proportion of sales in some instances to players where it can represent up to 100 per cent of the sales with no product resale at all.

Typically the proportion of services increases as you move from left to right of the partner types we have profiled (Figure 12.1). This reflects the higher value added and greater level of customization of the offering required to be competitive and effective in each role. We will examine the implications of this later on in the chapter.

Roles

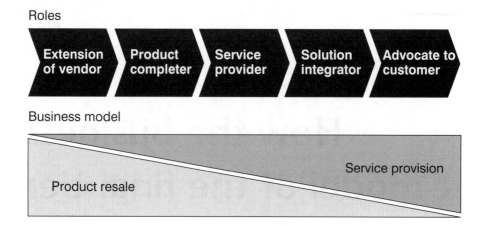

Figure 12.1 Typical product/service mix across spectrum of partner roles

The general trend across most industries as they mature is for the final-tier trade channel players to grow the proportion of their sales coming from services. There are a number of reasons for this:

■ As markets mature and growth rates slow down, final-tier players need to compete harder for their own growth. They find that service provision provides the basis for increased differentiation.
■ Better differentiation tends to drive higher margins from services.
■ Product resale wrapped up inside a service proposition can generate higher margins than just reselling a product without service.
■ Services tend not to be capital intensive, so making it easier to grow the business from a limited capital base

Although few of these players manage their businesses by splitting their 'product' and 'service' business models apart, it is helpful to focus exclusively on the service model for the next section of this part to understand its special challenges, which are quite different from those of the product model. We will reintegrate the two business models at the end of this part of the book.

Services come from people, either directly or indirectly (eg web-delivered)

Services are usually delivered by people, applying their time and skills, which has significant implications for the services business model. Consider the differences (Figure 12.2) between relying on products and people as the basis of the business model.

This analysis can be summarized in terms of the special challenges facing those managing service businesses and the response required:

- Volume sensitivity – need to manage the sales pipeline. High fixed costs need to be paid for each month.
- Fixed capacity – need to manage capacity utilization. Time of people cannot be inventoried to match demand, so demand must be managed to fit supply.
- Project/contract-based value delivery – need to manage recoverability. Unit of production is usually a project with a large number of variables, all of which can affect delivery time, cost and quality.
- People-based value delivery – need to manage people. People are tough to manage, and expect their managers to pay attention to their work/life balance, morale, career development, etc.

Managing a service business

We will look at how to manage each of these service-business special challenges in turn before putting together an overall model in the next chapter that shows the major value drivers and how they interact

Volume sensitivity – manage the pipeline

The margins of service businesses are highly sensitive to changes in the level of sales (or volumes). The profitability of the service is directly related to the volume of sales generated, because the cost of the people delivering the service is relatively fixed, either as salaried employees or contracted workers.

For example, Putney Plumbers Co has 50 qualified plumbers on its staff, each of whom costs $2,000 a month in payroll costs, and its overhead costs are $75,000 (this example could just as easily be a systems consultancy with 50 technical staff or systems analysts). This means that Putney Plumbers has to generate revenue of $175,000 a month in order to break even (50 plumbers @ $2,000, plus overheads of $75,000).

Now consider the following months' revenues and see how the gross margin and net margin perform (Figure 12.3). In a product business, we have seen that changes in gross margins of even a few basis points would

Activity	Product	People	Business model implication
Sourcing	Can usually be purchased within 24 hours	Can take months to recruit, train and integrate someone to be able to deliver a skilled service	Requires much longer lead-times to source people or skills Requires good visibility of sales growth to have the confidence to add to headcount Capacity is virtually fixed in the short term
Stocking (holding in inventory)	Can be held for some time	Time cannot be inventoried; it is like the seats on a plane, or rooms in a hotel. Once the plane has taken off, or the night has passed, no customer will pay for it!	Capacity must be sold for the period in which it is available; ie June time must be used in June and, more specifically, capacity on 23 June must be sold in advance and used on 23 June. Even more specifically, the time of each type of skilled employee must be used on 23 June
Matching demand	Product purchases and stocking levels can be varied to meet demand	People cannot be bought in and sold off, but expect to be employed for a period usually measured in years Subcontractors ease the issue, but with a negative cost and quality impact	This means that cost of sales is virtually **fixed** for the month, irrespective of sales volume Gross and net margins are volatile, linked directly to sales volume fluctuations
Purchasing on credit terms	Most product can be purchased on trade credit terms which vary from a few days up to several months	People prefer to be paid on weekly or monthly basis as employees. If hired as subcontractors, they usually expect payments each month	Timing of billing for services can be subject to customer acceptance or approval, creating a delay, while no matching credit is available on the supply side

Figure 12.2 Difference in business models based upon products or people

Month	Revenues	Cost of sales	Gross profit	Gross margin	Net profit	Net margin
January	$300,000	$100,000	$200,000	67%	$125,000	41.7%
February	$200,000	$100,000	$100,000	50%	$25,000	12.5%
March	$250,000	$100,000	$150,000	60%	$75,000	25.0%
April	$150,000	$100,000	$50,000	33%	–$25,000	–16.7%

Figure 12.3 Putney Plumbers Co revenues and margins by month

generate management's serious attention, but here, the margin in January is double that of April, simply because the revenue in January was double that of April. In a product business these two elements would be unrelated (other than if management decided to cut product prices to increase revenues in the slow month). The low gross margin in April reflects the cost of all the unused capacity, ie plumbers sitting around with nothing to do. In other words, Cost of sales has remained fixed across the four months even though Revenues has fluctuated widely.

Once a month has passed, there is nothing Putney Plumbers can do to with its unused capacity. This capacity is now also in the past and lost for ever. To minimize the damage of time not sold to customers, Putney Plumbers must plan to use this time as productively as possible – sending staff on training courses on the latest developments in U-bends, etc, or getting their holiday out of the way, if it can persuade its staff to take time off when things are quiet. In a plumbing business, it is possible to drum up extra business at fairly short notice, by ringing round past customers and offering winter check-ups, discounted boiler servicing and other offers to bring in any additional revenue it can. While this approach can help bring in marginal revenue, it has to be careful that it doesn't cannibalize its entire business income and train customers to wait for special offers. This need for the service provider to pre-sell a proportion of capacity is one reason why preventative maintenance and annual service contracts are seen as good value for customers. In these offers, the service provider is trading off margins for revenue certainty.

In the example above, the net margin's volatility is even more extreme, moving from super margins of over 40 per cent in January to a substantial negative margin of almost 17 per cent in April. This reflects the inherent risk in this type of business – almost all its costs are fixed in the form of salaries for around a year (depending on employment legislation) whereas its revenues are visible only a few days or weeks in advance. This gives some insight as to why emergency call-out costs are so high; it's the one time the plumber has to place a premium on its instant capacity.

In practice, no costs are truly fixed and even the payroll cost will be subject to accounting adjustments such as holiday accruals (which reduce the payroll cost to the company in the month that holiday is taken) and the constant effect of staff turnover. So the picture may look something like the chart shown in Figure 12.4.

This shows a somewhat seasonal pattern to the year with the levels of business in months 8 (August) and 12 (December) taking a hit as either customers or staff disappear on holiday, reducing revenue dramatically. In a well-established service business that has seen these patterns emerge over several years, this may not be a problem and the service provider will ensure that it has pulled in revenue to earn good margins in the other parts of the year to help ride out the loss-making or break-even months. The real challenge is to decide if a few months' worth of increased revenue represents genuine growth in the business or if it is just a 'bubble' or blip that will not last. If the levels of revenues rise for the next few months and Putney Plumbers is confident it is experiencing growth, perhaps from word-of-mouth referrals and its recent local radio advertising campaign, it may decide to increase its headcount to cope with the extra level of demand. However, if it has misread the situation, then it will have piled up some

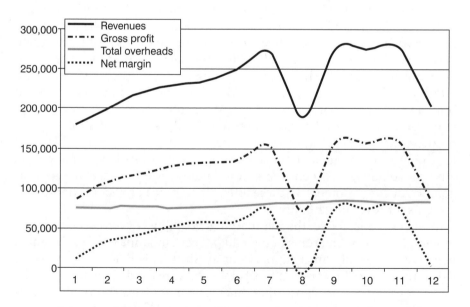

Figure 12.4 Illustrative service provider's business model profile by month

extremely tough months ahead as its new plumbers sit around underused and concerned for their future with the company.

What can the management of Putney Plumbers, or of any service business, do to ensure that it can manage this volume sensitivity aspect of its business? The best approach is to increase the visibility of its pipeline of future revenues and build up the future order book (sometimes called perversely order backlog). The further ahead it can book new business and schedule work for its plumbers, the higher the margins will be in each month and management can be more confident in its reading of the demand signals.

Each service provider will find that it has a natural 'horizon' for the visibility of its revenue pipeline. In the case of Putney Plumbers, that horizon may well be very short (one to three weeks) as plumbing work is more often corrective than preventative, with customers phoning up for help when things go wrong. Depending on the problem, customers may be prepared to wait for someone to come out and fix their problems, but beyond a certain period, they would rather go to another plumber. In service provider businesses where the service is planned and scheduled in advance, that horizon can be several months. For example, in information technology services or consulting work, the customer may be planning the work it needs up to 18 months ahead as it prepares the following year's budgets and allocates resources to projects. For these types of service provider, visibility of revenue could be 12 months or longer, but across a 'sales pipeline' of suspects, prospects, tenders or bids submitted and finally booked orders. Built into this pipeline is the sales cycle, which can often be three or more months as invitations to tender (or requests for quotation – RFQs) are received, qualified, and responded to through a process of multiple meetings culminating in a bid or tender document and then possibly several rounds of negotiations. Therefore the service provider's booked revenue will be around 3 months of the 12 months that it can see in the pipeline.

What most service providers will find is that the booked revenue will 'move', that is, it will be rescheduled from one week or month to another for a whole variety of reasons:

- business events at the customer forcing a delayed start;
- sign-offs and approvals taking longer than scheduled;
- quarterly budgets being frozen so projects are slipped back into the next quarter;
- sickness, change of roles, departures of key people on the customer side;

- earlier dependencies falling behind schedule if the work is part of a bigger project;
- non-delivery of some or all of the equipment or materials required for the project;
- non-availability of key customer personnel.

Note that none of these causes means that the revenue is cancelled, merely delayed. But to the service provider with its available capacity and fixed costs, the result is reduced revenue in a particular week or month with the big negative impact on gross and net margins that we have already seen illustrated above. The problems don't stop there though, as these slippages in scheduled work have a knock-on effect on available capacity in future weeks or months. If the service provider has, say, a small number of project managers that are critical to delivering pieces of work, these specialist resources will go from under-employed one month to overwhelmed in the next month as the delayed work gets added to the originally scheduled work. Easy options such as telling the customer that caused the problem that it will now have to wait are made more complicated by factors such as the desire to keep that customer happy as it is perhaps the provider's biggest customer or the delayed work may be the first phase of a long stream of work. Considerable judgement is required of the service provider's management team to allocate resources effectively to maximize short-term revenue and profitability as well as long-term customer relationships and future revenue.

With experience, service providers build up an air-traffic controller's picture of the different velocities of revenue moving through the pipeline and the likelihood of work slippage based on knowledge of individual customers, the types of work and even seasonality. They plan for the most likely slippages and take a seasoned view of how best to juggle the conflicting demands for resources. Best of all, they manage the future, as far ahead as they can, because they know that there's little they can do to manage the present and nothing they can do to preserve their stock-in-trade of time once it has passed.

Fixed capacity – manage capacity utilization

As well as the issue of demand management, the service provider has to manage the supply side, ie the service provider's own resources, with equal attention. The key to success is to have resources fully utilized for as much of the trading period as possible, maximizing the income generated from each person, without overdoing it and driving people too hard.

Generally, people like to be kept busy on productive work, and don't mind the occasional stint of late nights and weekends to deliver a contract by a deadline, especially if paid at premium rates. But there is a limit to the number of hours people can deliver month in and month out and sustained periods of overtime lead to quality issues, burnout and high staff turnover. People themselves are often a poor judge of their capacity to cope and will volunteer to take on more than they should, with the motivation of higher income, so it remains management's job to set guidelines and limits as to how much overtime can be scheduled in its job allocations. In setting these guidelines, management needs to plan how it uses overtime. If the demand is there, some reasonable level of overtime should be scheduled as demand-side slippage will tend to reduce the capacity actually required in a particular week or month. On the other hand, things do go wrong, requiring more work than planned, and customers will call up with emergency requirements. It is wise to keep some capacity free to cover these short time spikes in demand, and overtime is the easy way to absorb this.

Some people will 'hide', protecting their availability or that of the people in their teams or under their management by 'needing to be available for the big contract with ABC Co we are expecting any day now'. Management needs to retain control of these decisions or else utilization will very quickly fall below economic levels as pockets of resources go unused through this kind of protection. Experience helps judge when the bird in the hand should be serviced rather than keeping resources available for the bird in the bush.

Managing capacity utilization requires many trade-offs, not least between short- and long-term capacity, permanent and subcontracted staff, home-grown and bought-in skills, and aggressive and cautious recruitment plans.

In the short term there are constant challenges on the supply side. These challenges can include:

- sickness and absence of key staff;
- staff turnover with the loss of specialist skills as well as capacity;
- overruns on current projects requiring additional time of key staff;
- subcontractors failing to honour commitments;
- inexperienced or over-qualified staff being the only resources available, impacting either quality or cost of delivery.

Any or all of these factors can change the service providers' capacity and availability of key resources, and if they are not available, they cannot generate revenue. There is nothing more frustrating for a service provider than being supply-side constrained in a particular week or month – ie short-term capacity. Although the demand or booked work is available to be turned into revenue in the next period, the delay still hits the revenue in the current period, with the knock-on effect on gross and net margins. The trade-off here is between aiming for optimum efficiency (just the right number of the right mix of people) for high margins and delivering optimum quality (having backup of the right types of people) for long-term customer satisfaction and loyalty. Sod's law dictates that just as the scheduling of people against customer requirements is optimized, a call comes in from a key project manager or specialist saying that mother has died and he or she needs to take the next week off on compassionate leave. Solutions available include either carrying some level of additional resource to cover for this eventuality, with the additional cost, or developing a network of subcontractors with the relevant skills. Neither solution is ideal, and both have implications for costs, availability, and risk of lower quality.

Capacity and utilization planning requires a good understanding of the different technical skills and experience of each of the staff and teams as well as the requirements of each customer. This means that large service providers need to be able to classify and maintain a database of the skills of each of their people in such a way that as new projects or customer requirements come in, available resources can be identified and allocated. This can be tricky as skills do not easily conform to standard definitions. One customer manager at our example service provider, Putney Plumbers, may define the skills needed for a new customer contract as 'advanced heating systems and controls', whereas the plumbers with these skills may have defined them as 'CORGI qualification level 3', 'senior plumbing engineer' or even 'advanced *plumbing* systems and controls'. In a business with several hundred service people, these differences in how skills are defined may make the difference between poor and excellent scheduling of resources, with the attendant impact on revenues and margins.

Planning capacity for the longer term, ie for the next one to two years, to meet the business plan for revenue growth requires some strategic vision. Decisions need to be based on an informed view of which services, offerings, skills and resources will be needed as the market and customer requirements change in the future. The service provider needs to decide how to ensure it retains its differentiation and must understand which skills underpin this differentiation. Decisions need to be made whether to recruit from outside or develop people internally based on the degree of specialization of the service provider. Capacity planning needs to take into account recruitment and training lead-times given the availability of skills in the marketplace.

Service providers typically find it tempting to add to their headcount as soon as they see demand growing and the pipeline improving. The management teams of service providers are often dominated by people who are expert in the service the business is based on, but not necessarily experienced at making the business management decisions that ensure profit and growth. This means they tend to focus on the breadth and depth of their people and enjoy recruiting new skills and capabilities. However, they tend to underestimate the challenge of melding these people into productive teams that can be employed for a high proportion of their working time on profitable customer contracts. We'll deal with the complexities of managing people later in this chapter, but here the issue is one of when and how to expand the resource pool to match planned revenue and profitability goals. In making these decisions, the main considerations include:

■ How many people will need replacing through staff turnover?
■ Which specialty skills will experience growth in demand and which shrinkage?
■ What new services or offerings are we planning to introduce?
■ How many of each type of skill and depth of experience do we need?
■ How confident are we in our assumptions about growth and shifts in demand?
■ How seasonal or volatile is our demand pattern?
■ What is the right balance between generalist and specialist skills?
■ Which skills are critical to our differentiation and should be owned and protected?
■ Which skills should we subcontract out and which should we hire in?
■ How experienced are we at managing the types of skills we need?

People, or more specifically their hours, are the unit of production for a service business, so it is natural to want to grow the resource base because that underpins the ability to grow revenues. However, there is a real ratchet effect of adding to the headcount in that it may take three months to recruit and induct a new productive resource but, once added, there are legal (and simply human) barriers to removing that person if the demand does not materialize. Excess products can be sold off to realize cash (albeit at low or negative margins), but excess people may involve many months of excessive employment costs and the softer impacts of low morale, disaffected staff and the related impacts on quality and customer relations. Any decision to add to the capacity of a service provider is almost always a long-term decision and should not be made simply to resolve short-term staff shortages. It takes good judgement to know when to hire as well as which skills to hire, and robust management skills to decide when skills or resources are redundant and need to be moved outside the business. Some believe that only when managers have had to handle the process of making redundancies among their direct staff are they really equipped to make decisions to increase the headcount.

Project/contract-based value delivery – manage recoverability

For most service providers the unit of delivery is usually a project or contract which has to be fulfilled on time, within a fixed budget and to a defined standard of quality. (The exception to this is the simple offer of 'body shopping', that is, the hiring of people to a customer for a period of time – and the customer takes responsibility for the work to which they are assigned and its quality.) In all other cases, the service provider is delivering some form of experience or deliverable that is based on its ability to assemble the right team and resources, manage the sequence of work activities and deliver the scope of what has been agreed on time, to budget and to the required level of quality. In return for delivering the contract, the service provider wants to 'recover' as much of the value it has created as possible through price. From the service provider's perspective, it wants to be able to manage its recoverability in such a way that it makes a reasonable profit and retains a relationship with the customer that is good enough to encourage further business and referrals. It should be careful not to 'gouge' the customer or market by exploiting a particular unique situation or opportunity in the market that maximized short-term profitability, but at the expense of sustainable customer relationships. (See Peter Drucker's Five Deadly Business Sins, *The Wall Street Journal*, 21 October 1993, Section A, p 18.)

Perhaps the hardest part of the service provision process is agreeing what is to be done and the price to be charged for it. Each contract is unique, though many will be of a 'type', requiring the service provider to factor in many elements in making its pricing decision and to take account of risks and unknowns. The service provider must first understand what it is being asked to bid for... which can range from what seems fairly straightforward (such as 'plumber, replace my boiler') to extremely complicated ('outsourcer, take over and run my global accounting function, including all the underlying information systems'). An experienced service provider will know how to go about defining the scope, which questions to ask, which risks to anticipate, which options the customer might expect and where the real drivers of value might lie from the customer's perspective. It will know when to allow a contingency for risk or to define the contract for its work in such as way as to exclude the risk from its scope.

In terms of pricing the work, service providers at the more complex end of the spectrum will have established methodologies for delivering services and this will help them to break down the project or contract into phases, tasks and steps and then apply estimating guidelines to build up the number and value of the various resources required to deliver the scope defined. Even simpler services will comprise a number of components that can be broken out and priced up.

The result is a defined scope of work and a price that may be fixed or variable depending on convention (lawyers almost always work for variable prices, house painters for a fixed price) and the negotiating power of the buyer and service provider. In the case of services to be provided over a period, a service level agreement defines what is to be provided and some elements may be at a fixed price – such as running a help desk – and some elements variable – such as the number of users to be supported. The service provider will have built a target margin into the price, which will vary according to a number of factors, including but not limited to:

■ the market price for similar contracts, if it exists;
■ the market price for feasible alternatives (eg in-sourcing);
■ whether the customer is a must-win or retain account for the service provider;
■ whether the contract breaks new ground and offers a chance to establish a new service offering or master a new capability or technology;
■ whether the contract mops up available capacity that would otherwise be unutilized;
■ the cost to the service provider of the resources required;
■ the service provider's attitude to risk;
■ the service provider's proprietary technology or intellectual property;
■ the service provider's selling skills

It is the last item, selling skills, that can make or break the profitability of a service provider because these skills enable the service provider to build the expectation of value that the customer will derive from the contract or project. By selling skills we do not mean hard selling of the type associated with double glazing and time shares, but smart, insightful questioning techniques that uncover the value drivers in the customer's business and link the benefits of the project directly to them.

For example, Andersen Consulting, an information systems integrator and management consultancy (now known as Accenture), was able to grow at rates of 50 to 60 per cent in Europe during the late 80s and early 90s while charging a premium of 30 per cent compared to its direct competitors. How did it do this? It invested heavily in understanding the industry sectors it was targeting and built a clear picture of the way systems applications could address the fundamental challenges worrying chief executive officers. It took care to ensure that it also addressed the concerns of the chief technology officer and chief information officer, who were the targets of its competitors, but focused its pitch on the issues that drove shareholder value, the stock price and the compensation schemes of the boards. It talked in terms of reducing inventory levels, accelerating time to market of new products, increasing customer yields and returns on assets, etc. By talking the language of the board, Andersen Consulting made its projects more valuable to the board, and the additional few million dollars on the price really didn't seem to be important in that context. Andersen differentiated its own offering by promising differentiation for its customers, and this showed up in its margins. One important point to note is that Andersen invested thousands of hours and millions of dollars in enabling its partners and managers to apply its hard-won selling advantage systematically by training them in its 'Winning New Business' methodology and putting them through three-day-long proposal writing courses.

So far we have talked about the front end of project/contract-based value delivery – effectively how the service provider defines the bespoke value proposition of each individual assignment for each customer. The back end is equally important – value delivery. Having made its promise, the service provider must now fulfil it. This requires project management skills, risk management skills, people management skills (see Section 12.3.4 below) and quite frankly, a fair hand from lady luck. The best-managed projects can sometimes be derailed by adverse events completely outside the service provider's control, ranging from the sudden incapacitation of someone whose skills are critical to the loss-in-transit of some key component of the solution (through theft or disaster) or the incompetence of other players involved in a multi-provider project assembled by the customer. One could argue that effective risk management would anticipate these risks and put in place contingency plans, but there is a probability–cost trade-off that rules out covering every eventuality.

Bad luck aside, the service provider should be equipped to handle the many dimensions of bringing in the project on time, within budget and to the specified quality. The methodology that underpinned its ability to estimate the price correctly should also enable the service provider to manage and control delivery. Steps, tasks and phases of the project/contract should be performed in the right order, with the relevant dependencies identified.

Some tasks will take longer than estimated and consume more resources, but the good project manager will have contingency built in and accumulated from the tasks that take less time and resource than expected. In all projects there are variables that are under the project team's control, some that are under their influence and some that are outside their control or influence. Experienced project managers can exercise their influencing skills to keep things on track and will have protected themselves from the things they cannot.

For example, in many projects or contracts, work gets held up or extended because the starting point is not as expected – legacy IT systems are not as described by the customer, the plaster under the wallpaper is rotten, the pipework connected to the boiler does not meet building regulations, etc – so the service provider is required to do extra work. To ensure margins are not damaged, this work needs to be paid for, and a tight contract and firm project management will ensure that it is down to the customer to pay for it. This concept of getting paid for all the work performed by a service provider is called **recoverability**, ie recovering the full price for the value actually delivered. One way to think of this is that full recovery is when the service provider receives 100 per cent of its target revenue for the contract. Sometimes a service provider will concede some recoverability, usually for 'marketing' reasons such as:

- Constant demands for minor bits of additional work would annoy the customer.
- Forgoing some recovery is seen as a price worth paying to improve the prospects of winning a subsequent phase of work or another project from the customer.
- The service provider should have anticipated the problem and bears the cost to maintain its image or reputation with the customer.

The other cause of poor recoverability is the service provider's own problems in delivering the project. These usually result in some form of overrun in terms of resources consumed and it is simply not down to the customer to pay for the service provider's problems. Examples of these problems include:

- poor-quality work that needs to be redone or enhanced;
- learning curve on the part of the service provider or individuals on the project team, resulting in the work taking longer and consuming more resource;

- staff scheduling inefficiencies meaning that staff employed on the project were over- or under-qualified for the work required (but were the only resources available at the time);
- using subcontractors to substitute for the service provider's own resources that have left the service provider or been deployed onto other, more critical projects;
- using additional resources to supplement the team in order to hit deadlines;
- estimates proving over-optimistic;
- delays or substandard performance by suppliers chosen by the service provider.

Most service providers can cite a number of projects in their history which have become legends for the number of disasters that accumulated and resulted in a low or even negative recoverability. There have been a number of IT projects for the public sector in the UK that became so bad that the service provider was terminated or made to pay penalty payments for missing deadlines or delivering systems that provided only a fraction of the functionality promised in the original contract specification.

Where service providers often lose out on recoverability is on the grey areas where the customer has changed the specification along the way, often for good business reasons, but the cost of which has not been flagged by the service provider. An example is when the contract period is stretched out, through non-availability of the customer's own resources. This means that the service provider is on the contract for longer and almost always has to commit more resources, even if they are stretched out and scaled down over the longer time period. The increased amount of 'put down and pick up' work incurs resources. However, it is often difficult to tie this type of issue down in contracts and usually the service provider takes a hit on recoverability as a result. This is often down to the relative power in the relationship between the customer and the service provider. Many large corporate and public sector customers have learnt to hold the promise of future work or threat of loss of future work as a double-edged sword to the throat of the service provider. This erodes the service provider's ability to fully price the cost of 'change orders' or scope increases, and thus their recoverability.

People-based value delivery – manage people

Managing people is not a simple numbers game. People are tough to manage, and expect their managers to pay attention to the variety and mix of their work experience, work/life balance, morale, training and development and offer them career progression, etc. In many ways the demands of the people responsible for delivering the services are at odds with the demands of the customer and even that of the service provider itself (Figure 12.5).

Each time the service provider generates an opportunity to win a new customer, bid for new business or start a new project, it has to balance these potentially conflicting demands in the way it allocates its people to contracts and customers. Each individual decision will come out in favour of one of the three stakeholders and to the possible detriment of the other two, but over time it must maintain a fair balance. It is too easy for weak management to succumb to the 'squeaky wheels' and concede to the most demanding customer, most strident contract manager or most disaffected member of staff. Strong management requires the ability to assess the business dimensions of long-term customer value, development of service team capabilities and managing the career development of individual members of staff. Management also needs to be able to explain the basis of its decisions and persuade everyone involved of their merits. This requires interpersonal skills on the part of its managers, strong team management skills across the company and excellent communications and selling skills to make the case for resourcing and scheduling decisions.

Larger service providers invest heavily in the people management infrastructure to ensure that all members of staff experience best-in-class training, personal development, feedback, evaluations, and pay and benefits so that they want to stay and build their careers with the service provider. In return the service provider secures a loyal, motivated, appropriately skilled team, seasoned in customer service and the service provider's offerings and differentiation, that can be called on to go the extra mile when needed. The best service providers have the mechanisms in place to track performance, identify the good, poor and non-performers and address problems early if necessary. Good talent management systems will give transparency to the availability of staff, the depth and relevance of their experience and the staff's own expressed preference for future work experience.

The more 'high end' the services being offered by the service provider, the more critical the ability to retain and develop the specialist people that deliver them. The departure of a single person, or worse, a team of seasoned specialists, could be catastrophic for the service provider as this often goes hand-in-hand with client defections and further staff departures,

Dimension of work	People expectations	Customer expectations	Service provider expectations
Match of experience to requirements	Variety of work that offers fresh challenges and personal development to increase 'personal capital'. Do not want to be doing the same type of work all the time	Highly experienced and expert people that have done this type of work many times before and can deliver faultlessly every time	People expert enough to deliver the work on time, on budget and to the required quality, without being over-qualified and thus too expensive, or too inexperienced and thus requiring intensive supervision and allowance for learning curve
Scheduling	Steady work without too much pressure involved in meeting the deadlines. Time off for vacations when convenient for family commitments, etc	As quickly as possible, with plenty of time allowed for client sign-offs. Resources available to meet demanding deadlines without interruption	Steady full-time work scheduled over a fixed period with no downtime or breaks
Continuity of staff	A reasonable period spent working on one customer followed by the opportunity to move on to bigger, more prestigious customers. Opportunities to be involved in putting together bids for new work at new clients	Same staff all the time, so no requirement to orient the service team and minimal distraction for own staff. Can be expected to understand client expectations without these needing to be spelt out. No distractions or absences	Flexibility to rotate and assign staff to where there is the best fit. Need to move best performers to highest-risk or most valuable customers. Able to assign best staff to bidding for new work and new clients

Figure 12.5 Conflicting expectations of the service provider's stakeholders

possibly to a direct competitor. It may take months, if it is even possible, to go out into the market and recruit replacements, and once on board it may take up to a year for the new people to reach full productivity as they master the unique approach of the service provider. A service provider can spend thousands of dollars on expensive training and skills upgrading for its people and it should regard this as an investment that needs protecting to secure the expected return.

Equally, service providers offering basic services will feel the impact of high staff turnover, as it will impact customer service, team continuity and general experience levels that enable service teams to handle the hundred and one issues that arise in service delivery.

Service-based business model

Using the same value creation (VC) tree framework model as explained in Chapter 8, we can take the major elements of the typical service provider income statement and balance sheet and present them as a map of the business model. This model shows how all the different dynamics interact. Every decision taken within the business affects how the business performs and the VC tree shows how these effects cascade up the tree to change the value created or destroyed. (As a reminder, value created is the level of profit made in excess of the cost of the capital deployed to generate those profits.)

As we have seen, the service-based business model is all about leveraging human capital, rather than working capital as in the case of the product business. Therefore, with a relatively small amount of capital deployed, the service provider's value creation is heavily dependent on its operating profit. Mapping the key management levers we have reviewed in this chapter to the value tree framework shows how the emphasis works through the left-hand side, the income statement dimension of the business model (Figure 12.6).

On the right-hand (balance sheet) side, working capital is still important, because service providers usually do not have substantial capital financing and thus need to husband their limited cash resources.

In the following chapters we work through each of the key elements of the framework, highlighting the key measures that matter and the implications for service provider management.

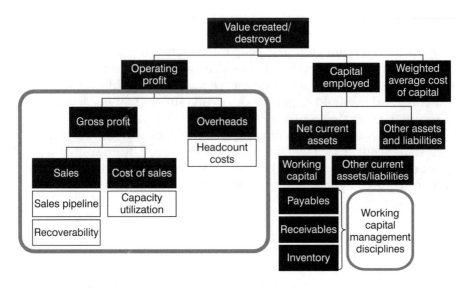

Figure 12.6 Value creation tree for a service provider

Overview of service business model measures

To show how the service business model measures work, we will use an example, XYZ Co, a service provider with a value creation tree as shown in Figure 12.7. The elements in the light shaded boxes are the standard financial measures that apply to any business, and show the financial statements set out as a logic tree (see Chapter 8 for full explanation of this framework). The elements in the darkened boxes represent the measures specific to a service provider and are never shown in any external reports. They are, however, critical dimensions of the service provider's business model and will be at, or close to, the top of the internal management reports. Because there are so many variations in types of service provider and the business models they operate, there is more variety in terms of types of measure and less formality about how measures are calculated.

The following chapters will define the measures that matter, discuss the variations based on what we have seen in the real world and set out what we recommend as best practice. We will explain why we have selected a particular measure or definition, so that you can make up your own mind if that measure or definition is right for your business. You will not find many of these measures in financial textbooks, but some of them are referred to in specialist books on managing professional service firms (such

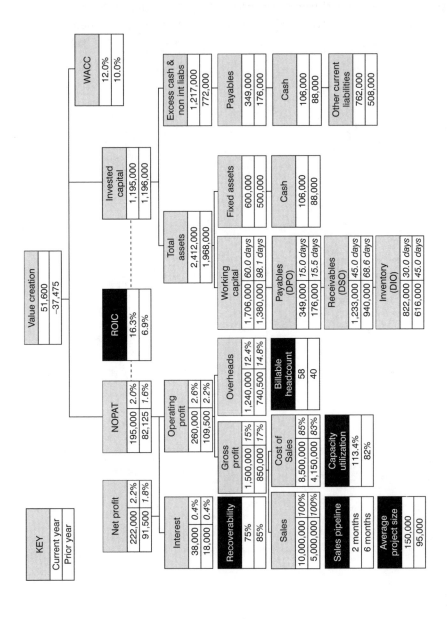

Figure 12.7 XYZ Co (a service provider) value creation tree

as David Maister's *Managing the Professional Service Firm* (New York: The Free Press, 1997)). Because there are no formal accounting standards or generally accepted definitions for calculating these specialist measures, it is essential that you ask how each company has calculated the measures you see.

13

Sales and utilization

Sales

As we have seen in Chapter 12, the level of revenue in any week or month has a critical impact on the overall profitability of a service provider. However, the matter of what constitutes revenue or, rather, when to recognize it is much more complicated than for a product business.

Revenue recognition

Recording sales or revenue recognition in a service business is surprisingly one of the most subjective areas in a service provider's financial statements and is quite open to abuse or manipulation. In theory, you should look at the accounting policy of the service provider to see what approach it takes, but even if you can decipher the accounting jargon, it is often written in a code that would pass the non-accountant by. Why is this area so complicated? Let's look at XYZ Co and ask some questions.

XYZ Co has three types of service income streams:

■ large contracts with multiple phases spread over periods of up to 15 months;
■ small contracts that typically take around 3 months to complete;
■ fixed-term service, support and maintenance contracts.

Now, in the case of the **large contracts**, when might you consider a sale is made? Is it:

A. When the customer calls to commit to the contract?
B. When the customer signs the contract?
C. When the first consultant arrives on the customer's site?
D. When the first month's work is completed?
E. When the first month's work is signed off by the customer?
F. When the first month's work is paid for by the customer?
G. When all the work is completed?
H. When all the work is signed off by the customer?
I. When all the work has been paid for by the customer?

These options have been laid out in an order that accountants would recognize as having the most 'aggressive' at the top and most 'cautious' at the bottom. Few people would be comfortable recognizing all or even some of the income on a contract at point A and equally few would think the company should wait until point I before recognizing any income. Fifteen months is what accountants call a 'long-term' contract and under international accounting standards, revenue and the related profit should be recognized as the work is carried out, *provided the outcome can be assessed with reasonable certainty*. In simple terms this means that options D and E are the most widely accepted revenue recognition points depending on XYZ Co's practices. Note the words in italics, which mean that as the revenue is recognized and the associated profit is booked, XYZ Co must look at the way the contract is going and be sure that it will not make a loss a the end. If a lower than planned profit or even a loss is looking likely, then it must reduce the profit it books accordingly. (We'll look at the profit dimension and how XYZ Co will deal with recording the attributable profits in Chapter 14.)

Revenue recognition practices will depend somewhat on the rigour with which XYZ Co controls its projects and the way it records the activity of its billable staff (ie the ones that work for customers to earn income). At the high end and increasingly towards the low end of the service spectrum, time sheets are kept to allocate hours to specific customer contracts. Extending these time sheets by the billing rates for each grade of staff will give a 'gross revenue' that can be recognized. Taking note of the words in italics means that the progress of the project should be assessed against the time charged in. If the project manager assesses that the work in a phase is 35 per cent complete, but the hours recorded extended by their billing rates equates to 45 per cent of the total phase contract price, a judgement is required. If the nature of the work is such that more expensive resources are required early on, it may be decided that the project is on track to be completed for no more than the contracted price and all the revenue may be booked. If, on the other hand, the resources are more or less a consistent mix over the delivery of the phase, then XYZ Co should book only 35 per cent of the contracted revenue and 'write off' the additional 10 per cent of effort spent getting to that point. If it did not do this, XYZ would run the risk of recording revenue in, say, the first three months of the work but still having to spend time working to deliver the phase in month 4. But with no 'billable capacity' left in month 4, there would be no income to recognize. This would mean that XYZ Co would have recognized income too early, something that cautious accountants would prefer to avoid. Note that there is a judgement call involved and facts that show the judgement to have been wrong may come to light later on in the phase. This does not mean that XYZ Co should go back and restate its income for earlier months, but simply shows the need to be careful and err on the side of caution when making the judgement around the time of finalizing the revenue for a given month.

The same principles apply to **small contracts**, though here there is less scope for error and it may be acceptable to divide the revenue over the number of months of the contract to keep things simple. Given XYZ Co has a mix of long and short contracts, and already operates a time-recording system, it is likely to apply exactly the same approach to revenue recognition to both types of contract. It may spend less time on the judgement calls as both the margin of error and the size of contracts are smaller.

One point to watch is when XYZ Co moves into a new line of service or writes its contracts in a different way (changing the risk it bears); it will be less experienced in making these judgement calls and even small contracts could deliver high risk. Over time, most service providers learn how to recognize revenue sensibly and it is best if the judgement calls are made by the project managers who are one step removed from any pressures management may be under to hit a particular total revenue target. Once management teams catch the disease of 'revenue smoothing' by influencing their view of when the revenue on contracts should be recognized, it is hard to shake off. These marginal practices usually come to light when there is a dip in revenues yet everyone is still working away furiously delivering contracts on which there is no income in the month. More serious troubles and cash flow problems are often just around the corner in these situations, so service providers need to guard against fooling themselves with their own revenue 'management' practices – the cash balance brooks no such manipulation.

The third type of income is from **fixed-term service, support and maintenance contracts**. These can be in the form of fixed- or variable-price contracts or a blend of the two with a fixed and a variable element. The fixed-price contract is effectively like an insurance policy for the customer, where the contract price is the insurance premium and XYZ Co takes the risk on the number of 'claims' or call-outs it will have to service. A low number of call-outs will result in a healthy profit and a high number of call-outs can generate a loss for XYZ Co. Typically, service providers simply divide the contract price by the number of months covered and take the same amount to income each month. The costs then fall in the month incurred. Over a large number of contracts and months, this evens itself out and results in a fair revenue treatment. Only if the service provider knows something different should it adjust this approach, for example it may know that it will receive a higher proportion of call-outs in the last three months of a contract. If it has the data and track record to demonstrate this to be the case, it may allocate a higher proportion of the fixed-price contract revenue to the last three months. The variable-price contract will usually follow the basis of variation. For example, if the number of call-outs determines the price, then the number of call-outs in any one month will determine the revenue for that month, using either an actual call-out price (if it varies) or standard price.

Measuring the pipeline

Given the nature of services, almost all service providers make their sales in advance of the time they book the revenue. As we saw in Chapter 12, lengthy sales cycles require service providers to make their sales as far ahead of actually booking the revenue as possible. This visibility of revenue, the sales pipeline, is a critical success factor and the service provider must be able to measure it effectively and consistently. The most effective tool available to the service provider to measure its pipeline is a schedule of the revenue booked and visible, by time period, either weekly or monthly. Different names are applied to this management tool, including Sales Schedule or Forward Order Book or Sales Pipeline, and many other names. An example of one such 'sales schedule' is shown in Figure 13.1.

Note that the date of the schedule is shown as mid-July, so the sales schedule shows actual sales (in $000s) for the first six months of the year and an up-to-date projection of sales in each of the months for the second half of the year. It is vital that the schedule is updated on an event-driven basis, ie every time there is news of a sales win or an expected slippage.

In the example shown, sales have been running ahead of the business plan for the first six months (which is why the 'to convert' numbers are

Sales Schedule – Category 1

Sector	Client	Description	Job No.	Current year												Total
				Jan	Feb	Mar	Apr	May	Jun	Jul	Aug	Sep	Oct	Nov	Dec	
Auto	ABC Co	Technical project	ABC342	11	10	10	10	10	10							61
Manf	DEF Co	Strategy project	DEF001	22	22	10	16									70
Ret	GHI Co	Investigation project	GHI233		25	17	17	15	5							79
Ret	GHI Co	Second phase	GHI234					5	15	15	15	15	15	15	15	110
Auto	JKL Inc	Technical project	JKL040					30	20	25	25	30	35	30	5	200
Manf	MNO Co	Technical project	MNO002	10	15	15	15	15	15	15	15	15				130
Airl	PQR Co	Strategy project	PQR027			15	15	15	15	15	15	15				105
Com	STU Co	Investigation project	STU004	25	25	20	10	5								85
Com	WXY Co	Technical project	WXY112													0

| Total CAT 1 | | | | 68 | 97 | 87 | 83 | 95 | 80 | 70 | 70 | 75 | 50 | 45 | 20 | 840 |

| Business plan | | | | 65 | 75 | 75 | 75 | 75 | 75 | 75 | 80 | 80 | 80 | 80 | 80 | 915 |
| To convert | | | | -3 | -22 | -12 | -8 | -20 | -5 | 5 | 10 | 5 | 30 | 35 | 60 | 75 |

Figure 13.1 Example of an order book shown in a sales schedule

shown darkened and negative). However, in mid-July, there is still some work to be done to win business for July ($5,000 short) and an increasing amount to be sold for the other five months of the year. This is very typical of a service provider with, say, a one-month sales cycle, but of course would be rather worrying if the sales cycle was, say, three months... unless of course there's lots of business about to be closed. The schedule above is called Category 1, which in this particular service provider means actual confirmed sales (which can still slip even after confirmation), and it defines Category 2 as work which has been bid for or a price quoted and a bidding document or quotation submitted to the prospective customer or client. Category 3 is used to denote opportunities that the sales team have identified and are hoping to be the subject of either a bid or quotation. To qualify for Category 3, the service provider has decided it must be able to quantify the likely value of the work and estimate the likely schedule for the work.

Figure 13.2 shows how the rest of the sales pipeline might look in Categories 2 and 3. Note that there is a column for the probability of winning the work, which is used to drive the line 'weighted Cat 2' as a crude way of estimating likely revenues from the pipeline. It is also much more likely that the work scheduled for each month in Categories 2 and 3 will slip, as there are many more steps before the work is confirmed. Like Category 1, this schedule should be updated on an events basis and monitored with a high degree of frequency by the management team.

Calculating the pipeline from these numbers is usually done using some variation of this formula (Figure 13.3).

It is up to the service provider to decide how stringently it applies the test of probability. Looking at the actual numbers in the sales schedule, the pipeline can be summarized as shown in Figure 13.4.

Comparing this to the average targeted sales by month of $80,000, as shown in the business plan (for the period August to December), produces a pipeline of 4.6 months (ie $369,000/$80,000).

Is this good or bad? The first factor to take into account in assessing this pipeline is the typical sales cycle. If this company takes only a month to convert leads into sales, then a pipeline of almost five months is excellent. On the other hand, if the sales cycle is typically six months, then things are not looking nearly so good. As we can see from Category 1, there is still $75,000 of sales to make in the next five months to hit business plan for the year as a whole. Looking at Category 2, the weighted probability of future bids is only $109,000, so there is a high chance that the company will miss its business plan, unless its probability assumptions are extremely accurate. While the overall pipeline number (4.6 months) is helpful, care must be taken in its use, as it grossly oversimplifies the situation. Of more relevance

Sales Schedule – Category 2

Organization	Description	Date of first contact					Jan	Feb	Mar	Apr	May	Jun	Jul	Aug	Sep	Oct	Nov	Dec	Prob total	Grand total
																			Current year	
ABC Co	Technical project	09-Feb												15	25	25	25	25	12	115
ABC Co	Technical project	09-Feb															25	25	5	50
QWE Co	Strategy project	30-May											15	5	15	15			37	50
RTY Co	Investigation	10-May													3	3	7	3	8	16
GHI Co	Investigation	01-Feb													5	10	5		10	20
FDE Co	Technical project	27-Jun											5	5					7	10
EEW Co	Strategy project	15-Nov	20-Dec	Green	50%	Call on 30/7									15	15	15	15	30	60
SUBTOTAL							0	0	0	0	0	0	20	25	63	68	77	68	109	321
Weighted Cat 2							0	0	0	0	0	0	15	9	25	28	19	14	109	109
Category 3																				
ASD Co	Technical project	08-May		White	10%	Submit bid									25	25	25	25	10	100
JKL Co	Strategy project	01-May		Black	10%	Agree scope									15	15	15		5	45
SADF Co	Investigation			Grey	10%	Meet board											25	25	5	50
WER Co	Technical project	19-Apr		Robinson	50%	Meet tech dir											50	50	50	100

Figure 13.2 Examples of a sales pipeline shown in a sales schedule

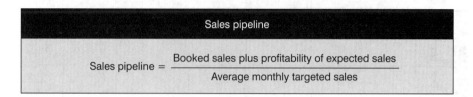

Figure 13.3 Sales pipeline

August Cat 1	$70,000	
September Cat 1	$75,000	
October Cat 1	$50,000	
November Cat 1	$45,000	
December Cat 1	$20,000	
Total Cat 1		$260,000
Weighted Cat 2 (Prob total)		$109,000
Cat 3 (ignored as too uncertain)		$0
Total booked sales plus probability of expected sales		$369,000

Figure 13.4 Illustrated summary of sales pipeline

is probably how the pipeline is changing over time. If it is increasing, that is definitely good, but this increase may not be driven by near-term sales, so immediate revenues could still take a dip. And if the pipeline is decreasing, then urgent attention is needed to ensure that opportunities to win more contracts are being generated. If the pipeline is shortening, this is a real problem. If management is doing its job it will be reviewing the full profile of the sales schedule every week or even more frequently, so the sales pipeline number is just an overall measure for the record.

In our example VC tree for XYZ Co (Figure 12.7), the sales in the current year have doubled over the prior year, which looks like a terrific result. But, and this is a very big 'but', its sales pipeline has fallen from six months in the prior year to two months in the current year, a real collapse. How could this have happened – it can't be very realistic, can it? Well, unfortunately, this example is an all too real illustration of one of the biggest issues facing service providers – 'feast and famine'. When (particularly smaller) service providers land some big projects, they become totally focused on delivery and take their eye off the sales pipeline. This issue is often exacerbated by the fact that the process of bidding for new business requires the time of the more senior billable people to scope the work, prepare the technical sections of the tender documentation and estimate the work effort. When the demand for their time is consumed in delivering current work, these resources are not spending time helping to win new work. In larger service providers with dedicated sales teams this challenge can be more easily overcome, but in smaller service providers, the sales effort is often headed up by one or more of the founders/key executives who lead on the technical front and thus are heavily involved in both sales and delivery. For these service providers, when one or two major contracts are won, the pipeline can suddenly shoot up to six or even nine months. This causes the company to heave a collective sigh of relief that sales are taken care of for a while and the focus switches to delivering these big new projects. However, it's not easy to switch selling activity on and off, and once 'put down' the sales task is a hard one to pick up again. As we shall see from the other measures, XYZ Co is wrestling with so many challenges caused by the doubling of business volume that management can easily have become distracted from focusing on the pipeline.

Utilization

Utilization is the key measure of productivity used in service providers. It is a powerful measure as it can be applied to the entire service part of the business, individual divisions or teams and even each individual billable member of staff. High utilization means that a high proportion of the time of billable staff is going into productive, revenue-generating work.

Calculating utilization

Different service providers will have adopted different ways to calculate utilization but in most cases it will be along the lines of the formula shown in Figure 13.5. Billable time is the time spent working on agreed customer contracts or projects, usually tracked by being recorded on time sheets by billable staff against specific customer projects. Standard time is the number of hours or days that a billable person should be available to work in the relevant period.

For example, a full-time person will work 52 weeks less, say, 4 weeks of vacation less, say, 2 weeks of statutory holidays = 46 weeks, or 230 days or 1,840 hours on an 8-hour day. Some companies may factor in a standard allowance for sick days or training days, so reducing the standard time further. Most companies will *not* factor any overtime into the standard time as this creates the wrong impression culturally – most employees need to

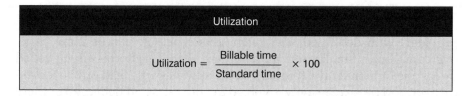

Figure 13.5 Utilization

understand how utilization is calculated and applied and they will not be happy to see overtime built into the measure.

Utilization is a sensitive number as it is often used in assessing individual or team performance and to judge personal productivity levels. Therefore, when calculating the measure on a month-by-month basis, the standard deductions of personal vacation and statutory holidays should be removed from the denominator. This is a calculation that needs to be done each month using the 'actual month', as shown in the example in Figure 13.6.

Thus, even though this individual took two weeks off in July, his or her utilization will show as 100 per cent for the period he or she was available to work. Note that in February and September, this person's utilization was in excess of 100 per cent, which simply means that hours worked on customer contracts was in excess of standard hours, something that indicates a high level of productivity, which is good for the service provider's profitability. In some higher-end services, the service provider will pay its more senior staff a fixed salary without overtime (which is effectively built into the worker's compensation level). In these companies, high utilization translates into super-profits because the hours represented in an excess of 100 per cent utilization are revenues with a zero cost of sales.

Month	Billable hours	Statutory hols and vacation taken hours	Standard hours	Adjusted standard hours	Utilization
	A	B	C	D = (C − B)	E = A ÷ D
January	160	0	160	160	100%
February	160	8	152	146	110%
July	80	80	160	80	100%
August	80	0	160	160	50%
September	172	24	168	144	120%

Figure 13.6 Example of utilization calculation

The calculation works for groups of people, teams, divisions, etc, as well as it does for the individual. Simply aggregate the total hours of each billable person and calculate using the aggregated numbers.

Managing utilization

In our example service provider VC tree (Figure 12.7), XYZ Co is showing utilization as 82 per cent for prior year and 113 per cent for current year. What do we make of these figures? Is the increase in productivity always a good thing? Could this measure be increased further?

Given we are dealing with people here, there is a natural limit to the amount of utilization that can be sustained over time without suffering a fall-off in quality, burnout and increased staff turnover. We have all experienced short bursts of working intensively and put in the hours to get a job completed by a deadline, and some of us thrive on this kind of pressure. However, most of us need a bit of time off to decompress and recharge our batteries after such a gruelling period of work and many companies in the service business operate a time off in lieu (TOIL) scheme, which effectively gives back to employees some of the hours spent in excessive overtime. This helps them to reduce the total overtime bill and enhances employee satisfaction. In this way, any peaks in utilization driven by deadlines will be matched by troughs as official or unofficial TOIL kicks in.

Over several months, the pattern of an individual's billability may look as shown in Figure 13.7. Note that the employee does not have the same number of hours/days each month. December and January suffer from the seasonal holidays and February is known in the trade as a 'short month'. Generally as a very crude rule of thumb, utilization levels need to be kept in the range 85 to 115 per cent. Less than 85 per cent means low revenues per billable person, with the knock-on effect in terms of profitability. Sustained levels much above 115 per cent tend to lead to problems over time of quality through tiredness burnout on intellectually or physically demanding work and ultimately people will leave, increasing rates of staff turnover. This rule of thumb works at group, team or divisional level as well, though care is needed to review the individual statistics to ensure the average is not made up of several workers doing excessive overtime and a few shirkers or people with the wrong kind of skills dragging the average down.

As they grow, service providers generally need to create groups or teams of people to help foster the different specializations that may be needed. Often multidisciplinary teams are needed to deliver solutions to customers, but if specialists don't work alongside their fellows from time to time,

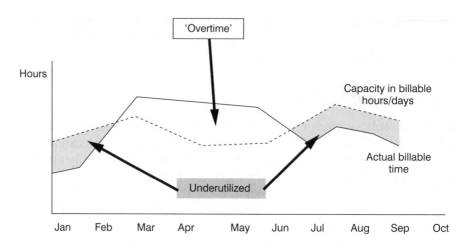

Figure 13.7 Example of an individual's utilization pattern for a year

they will fail to learn and pass on best practices or be able to stay on top of current developments in their field. By giving people a sense of identity and focus associated with their core discipline, these aspects of their development can be managed by the group or team manager. It's not unlike houses and classes at school, where pastoral care is exercised through the house (equivalent to the discipline-based team) and the daily coursework is managed through classes (equivalent to the project team). While there are many excellent development aspects to the management of people through groups or teams, there is a downside for utilization. Typically the group or team leaders are involved in the scheduling decisions affecting their resources and these leaders tend to have a point of view as to which projects/contracts will be best for their people (focusing on their team members' personal development). However, this point of view often runs counter to maximizing utilization and a firm hand is required to ensure that people are assigned to current projects/contracts and not kept back for some potential project that would 'be better development' for the individuals concerned.

Like all measures, a simple number does not give the whole story. One of the keys to success in a service business is finding ways to put people to work for large chunks of time without distraction. That way, every hour of every week of every month for several months is billable. And all the things that people find to fill their days when they are not busy, such as personal admin, keeping up to date on technological or industry developments, etc, somehow get squashed down and absorbed into the hours billed to customers.

Average project/contract size

The single most effective way to achieve the service provider nirvana of deploying lots of people full-time on single customer projects is to sell big projects or contracts. Not only that, but each project tends to have a certain 'overhead' in terms of selling and negotiating effort, project set-up and button-up, project management and so on, which has to be repeated for every single project. Selling fewer, bigger projects reduces this overhead in proportion to the revenues, increasing productivity and margins as shown in Figure 13.8.

In scenario A (dotted line), our worker is employed full-time on one big project through to the end of June, takes some vacation in July and then ramps up on another big project from August onwards. In scenario B (solid line), a different worker is deployed across a number of smaller projects of one month or less, some of them quite intense and others that do not require much time at all. The smaller projects rarely dovetail neatly, which means that there are gaps between projects of zero utilization, which kill the overall average. In this example the worker in scenario A is 22 per cent more productive (higher utilization) than the worker in scenario B, even

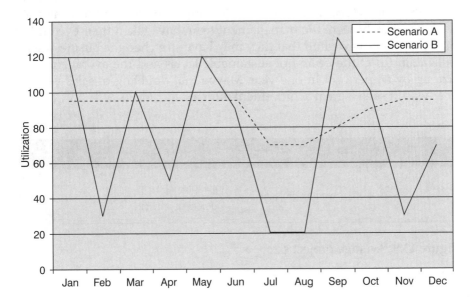

Figure 13.8 Comparison of utilization under two project size scenarios

though not an hour of overtime was worked, compared to well over 100 hours of overtime for the poor worker in scenario B.

Smart service providers have learnt the lesson that bigger projects drive productivity and margins and use it to increase their chances of winning such projects. As a very rough rule of thumb, any project that requires more than six months' full-time work for a billable resource can be discounted up to 30 per cent from normal prices and still deliver higher margins than projects lasting a month or so. This rule of thumb is somewhat governed by the margins being made on the services concerned, so should be tested within each company to find the level of discount that can be sustained.

Average project/contract size gives a good indicator as to how well the service provider is doing in improving this 'effectiveness' measure over time (Figure 13.9). In the case of XYZ Co, it has substantially increased its average project size from $95,000 in the prior year to $150,000 in the current year. It would be interesting to investigate whether this is the result of most of its projects increasing or if it is the effect of one enormous contract distorting the overall picture. The former would be good for the business model of XYZ Co, whereas the latter might not just distort the picture, but distort the business as well, making XYZ Co unhealthily dependent on one contract or customer. When this happens, the major project often sucks up all the best resources, consumes senior management's exclusive attention and other projects and customers suffer, impacting longer-term sales. As we have already seen, the management team have taken their eye off the pipeline and now we find that they may have stretched the business, with utilization up at the ceiling of sustainable levels and the average project size up by 60 per cent in one year. Maybe that doubling of sales year on year wasn't such a great achievement after all…

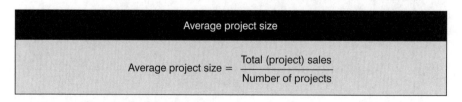

Figure 13.9 Average project size

14

Gross margins and recoverability

Gross margin

One of the primary drivers of the increase in services provided by the final-tier trade channels has been the potential of earning higher margins than is possible simply by reselling product. However, the potential to mismanage margins is also higher, underpinned by a lack of understanding of how margins are measured in service businesses. In Chapter 12, we showed how cost of sales is virtually fixed in a business where service is provided by in-house employees who are on fixed salaries (ie not subcontractors). This means that as sales fluctuate, so gross and net margins fluctuate, or in economists' terms marginal revenue becomes marginal profit, dollar for dollar. In other words, once a business moves above break-even, the next $100,000 of sales goes straight to the bottom line as $100,000 of gross and net profit. Although this is somewhat of a simplification, it is an accurate representation of the dynamics of margins in a fixed cost of sale business. This means that if the management takes care of the sales, it is also taking care of the margins and overall profitability of the business.

So how can we talk about the higher margins in services, if they are entirely driven by sales? The fundamental economics we have described above and in Chapter 12 are helpful in understanding the dynamics of the overall business model, but not in managing the business on a day-to-day basis. Imagine you are the sales person who brought in that last $100,000 of sales as a single contract to take the company up and away from break-even. What was the margin on it? Surely we have just said it was 100 per cent? Bonus please! Well, if you did claim your bonus on this basis, you would not be too popular with the other members of the sales team who have also sold some sizeable contracts in order to reach break-even for the period. Did they all make negative gross margins on their sales? Of course not. The answer lies in what accountants call taking a full costing rather than a marginal costing approach. In full costing, the resources consumed by a contract are charged against its revenues, just like product cost of sales is matched to the product sales revenue. In this way, every contract sold shows a positive gross margin (assuming it was priced above the sum of the resources required) and margins of different projects can be compared on a like-for-like basis.

Note that under this accounting approach, a service provider could sell four projects in a period, all at substantial gross margins, and still make a loss. Look at the example shown in Figure 14.1 for a service provider with a total payroll cost for its billable people of $600,000.

Contract	Sales	Cost of sales	Gross profit	Gross margin
A	$100,000	$50,000	$50,000	50%
B	$150,000	$90,000	$60,000	40%
C	$50,000	$20,000	$30,000	60%
D	$200,000	$120,000	$80,000	40%
Unused resources		$280,000	–$280,000	
Total	$500,000	$600,000	–$100,000	–20%

Figure 14.1 Example of project/contract and overall profitability

The key line is clearly the 'Unused resources', sometimes call unallocated resources. This is the payroll cost of the time of people for whom there were no projects on which to work in the period. It is vital in managing a service provider to understand the impact of unutilized resources on the overall profitability as well as to know how to maximize the profitability of the projects that are sold.

It is not easy to tell what is happening in the business model of a service provider, if you are reviewing the external accounts, because of the alternative ways of accounting for the unused resources. There are three alternatives:

▪ Treat the cost of all billable staff as cost of sales, regardless of utilization.
▪ Do not charge any people costs into cost of sales and show it all as overheads.
▪ Treat the 'used' time of billable staff as cost of sales and leave the unused resources in overheads.

Compare the accounts of the three companies shown in Figure 14.2. All have achieved the same level of sales and net profitability. Company A has adopted the first of the three accounting options, treating the full cost of billable resources as cost of sales, giving it a low gross margin. Company B has adopted the second accounting option, treating all its people costs as overheads, giving it very healthy-looking margins indeed. Company C has taken the third option, charged in the cost of the time required to earn the sales to cost of sales, leaving the balance of unused resources in overheads. None of these is wrong, though accountants would prefer the third option, as it adheres to one of their core principles of matching costs and revenues as closely as possible.

What are the typical gross margins that can be earned for service? As a very crude approximation, low-end services look to multiply the fully loaded payroll cost (ie including social taxes, insurances, etc) by a factor of

	Co A	Co B	Co C
Sales	1000	1000	1000
Cost of sales	300	300	300
People cost of sales	400	0	250
Gross profit	**300**	**700**	**450**
Gross margin	30%	70%	45%
Overheads	200	200	200
Salaries	0	400	150
Operating profit	**100**	**100**	**100**
Operating margin	10%	10%	10%

Figure 14.2 Alternative accounting treatments of people costs

3 and high-end services by a factor of 5. This means margins (excluding the cost of unused resources) of 33 per cent for low-end services and 80 per cent for high-end services, a very wide range but one which reflects the potential to deliver value for customers as well as the degree of competition for the particular services on offer. Note that these factors are used for setting 'prices' or rates used to price up contracts, and that the local market situation, length of pipeline, seasonality and the level of unused resources will all play a part in the final rates actually achieved in practice.

The more differentiated the service, the higher the potential margin that can be earned. Domestic trade services such as plumbers, electricians, decorators, etc, have recently seen their margins improve as their time-poor, cash-rich customers become more willing to pay for trustworthy, reliable workers, who clean up after themselves and can do the increasingly technical work required. Plumbers who specialize in installing luxury bathrooms complete with wet areas, power showers, self-demisting mirrors, etc, can demand very high rates, once they have established their reputation and can provide top-drawer references. Equally, the plumber who is prepared to come out at all hours of the day and night to unblock sewage pipes can also command high call-out rates, but only for the 'distress purchase'. It will not be able to command such high rates for regular plumbing maintenance and installation work unless it is operating in an area where there are few plumbers to meet everyday demand.

Similar examples can be found in all other service sectors, whether they be for consumer or commercial customers. Applying the framework of types of service providers helps to fix a pattern to the types of margins earned, based on role in the value chain and the level of value delivered (Figure 14.3).

This should be taken as a very rough guide to target margins for service business models, but should help you to evaluate if the intended role for a service provider is being borne out by its margins. In our experience, most service providers perceive themselves to be at least one role to the right of this model than they really are, and the actual margins earned expose the self-deceit. While moving to the right appears to be the best move possible, there are real challenges in achieving this, as discussed in Chapter 11. In terms of the business model, these high margins come with the increased risks of the specialization being eroded over time, fewer customers and opportunities that demand the specialist skills and more time needed on the part of the service provider to remain current and to communicate its high-end capabilities through thought-leadership activities. On the other hand, the low-margin end of the spectrum has to maintain extremely high levels of utilization in order to cover its costs and make a net profit.

Roles

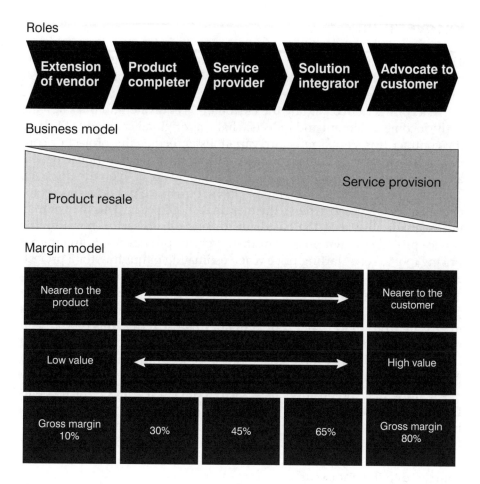

Figure 14.3 Typical service provider gross profit margins by role

In the case of XYZ Co, margins are quite low, in the mid-teens, but this service provider has put all its billable team's payroll costs into cost of sales because its utilization is above 100 per cent – in other words, it has no unused resources. So if its billable capacity is fully utilized, why are its margins so low? We don't know anything about where it is on the service provider spectrum, but the average project size suggests it is doing more than basic low-value work, so the decline in gross margin from 17 to 15 per cent should be quite a concern for the management team. There are some clues in the numbers as to why this might be the case, and the first of these clues lies in the next measure...

Recoverability

The final factor affecting profitability is recoverability. This is essentially the proportion of the fully priced resources consumed by a contract or project that the customer actually agrees to pay for (Figure 14.4).

'Final contract price paid by the customer' is equivalent to the sales line in the income statement and reflects what was originally agreed at the time the contract was signed plus any variations agreed as the project or contract has progressed. 'Total resources used' are the time of in-house people and any external people or services bought in to deliver the contract. 'Standard prices' refers to the target prices the service provider has set for each of its resources to achieve the margin it should earn. This may or may not be made visible to the customer depending on sector, norm or the service provider's own policy. For many service providers it is an internal pricing tool to set a starting price when estimating or quoting for a project, and from which the service provider may choose to discount.

In the case of XYZ Co, recoverability has slipped from 85 per cent in the prior year to 75 per cent in the current year. This is a little like discounts increasing from 15 to 25 per cent and, put in those terms, this is clearly an alarming shift in the business model and one that needs investigating immediately. Which of the possible causes of low or falling recoverability reviewed in Chapter 12 could be at work here?

We know that the business has exactly doubled its sales (which equals the final contract price paid by the customer on all its projects) year on year, but because the recoverability rate has fallen, XYZ Co has actually had to increase its resources used to deliver those projects, ie 200% × 85/75 = 226%. This is the amount of additional work deployed in the current year compared to the prior year.

Let's look at how it has attempted to cope with this on the supply side:

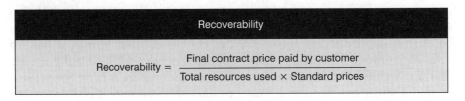

Figure 14.4 Recoverability

- Billable headcount is up from 40 to 58, an increase of 45%, but this would have been spread over the year, so on average this would represent an increase to capacity of 22.5%.
- Utilization is up from 82 to 113%, an increase of 37%.
- Combining the two gives an overall increase in in-house capacity deployed of 168% (ie 122.5% × 137%).

How has XYZ Co managed to deliver 226 per cent extra work with an increase in deployed capacity of 168 per cent, a gap of 58 per cent? The most likely answer is that it has used subcontractors, and while this has plugged the gap in capacity, it has given rise to other issues. Subcontractors will almost always cost more per hour or day than in-house people, and this additional cost shows up in higher cost of sales, which has reduced the gross margin. Even the best and hardest-working subcontractors will take time to climb the learning curve of the service provider's internal methodologies and in-house ways of doing things, requiring more time and resource than an experienced employee. However, the risk with subcontractors is that they will not bring the same level of commitment to the project as an in-house person whose future career prospects are bound up with the service provider's success. They may not be of the quality expected or promised and could even disappear part-way through the project. However, over time a service provider may build up a network of proven and reliable subcontractors whose skill sets are known and who in turn know how to work alongside the service provider's in-house teams. This offers the best of both worlds: high-quality, predictable resources and lower fixed costs, enabling capacity to be flexed to match demand. The one downside remains a higher cost per hour, though this may be offset by higher productivity, especially if self-employed.

So it seems that XYZ Co has pursued the goal of growth taking on bigger projects, but paid a high penalty in terms of increasing its fixed cost base, damaging recoverability, reducing its gross margin and taking its eye off the ball in terms of maintaining a healthy pipeline. It could be heading for disaster as it now has to meet the payroll costs of 58 people but has just two months' of sales on its books. You can bet that the management team will not be sleeping well, assuming they can read the business model as well as you now can.

15

Working capital management

The cash-to-cash cycle

Let's now turn to the balance sheet and see how well XYZ Co is managing its cash-to-cash cycle and if it might be able to weather the storm until more contracts can be booked into the sales schedule (for more explanation of the key ratios used in this section, see Chapter 6).

In most service businesses there are very few assets and liabilities in the balance sheet that are not part of the cash-to-cash cycle, or working capital of the business. You may come across the occasional exception – a long-standing highly profitable service business may choose to invest some of its accumulated capital in a property that houses its working premises, which we would argue is dipping into another business model altogether and nothing to do with running a service business. Indeed, one could argue that this is a risky move as the business may outgrow its premises. A call-centre-based business may invest in the IT systems that power its out-bound calls and control its telesales scripts, but generally these are small items on the balance sheet. The real investment required to underpin the long-term sustainability of a service business is sufficient working capital to enable the service provider to pay its staff and subcontractors (and the 'overheads' suppliers) on time, bill its customers and wait for them to pay. In a well-run service provider, the level of working capital is relatively small compared to that of an equivalent-sized product business. In a poorly managed service provider, it can balloon alarmingly to levels that could be compared to a product business.

Let's look at the elements of the working capital cycle for a service business: supplier credit, inventory/work-in-progress and customer credit. These are directly comparable to the product-business working capital cycle covered in Chapter 6, but with some very significant differences that reflect the nature of a service business. The cycle starts with the sale of a contract in which key business arrangements, including the phasing of the work, a billing schedule and credit terms, are defined. Many service providers operate a project accounting system in which each contract is assigned a project account with a unique number or identifier to aid in accumulating charges and credits. Once this account is opened, the time cost and other costs of work done on the project are charged in. The largest item will be the time cost of in-house workers (using time sheets) and sub-contractors (using either invoices or time sheets). Most workers and sub-contractors expect to be paid monthly, taking cash out of the service provider's bank account. Effectively each hour charged into the project is accounted for as both sales revenue and cost of sales in the income statement and unbilled work-in-progress on the balance sheet. Depending on the system being used for the project accounting, the time is captured at both payroll cost and billing rates (ie the price the customer pays). Many service providers use long-term contract accounting rules to recognize an element of attributable profit as the project progresses, so the unbilled work-in-progress *will be recorded at billing rates – or sales prices*. Note how this is very different from a product business which records its physical inventory *at cost prices*. This is one of the few times that accountants will allow the principle of 'accruals' (ie putting transactions into the right time period) to override the principle of 'prudence'. Not all service providers do this, and some will accumulate work-in-progress at cost prices and only recognize the profit element when the work is billed out. Given that the difference between these two approaches is so significant, it pays to ask how each service provider records its work-in-progress. At agreed points in the project, the service provider invoices the customer for the work completed to date, or for a predefined amount like 33 per cent of the contract, and this effectively removes that amount from the unbilled work-in-progress and puts it into customer receivables. At the end of the credit period agreed in the contract or whenever the customer decides to pay, the bill is paid and the service provider receives the cash back into its bank account. This cash-to-cash cycle looks as shown in Figure 15.1 for XYZ Co in the current year.

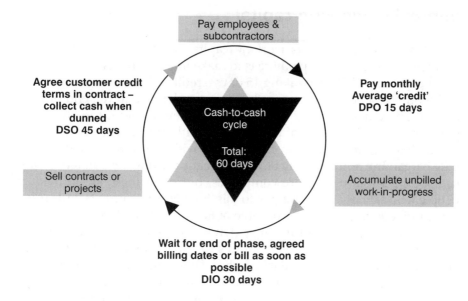

Figure 15.1 The cash-to-cash cycle for XYZ Co in the current year

Is this good or bad? Has XYZ Co improved its grip on working capital? Overall, the working capital cycle is now 60 days, or two months, which is often regarded as an average benchmark for service providers – effectively 'one month to bill and one month to collect' is the rule of thumb often heard. This compares to 98.1 days in the prior year, which is over a month longer and would generally be regarded as fairly appalling. To put it into context, if XYZ Co had not improved its working capital cycle at all, it would have needed another $1 million dollars of cash in the business by now (the extra 38.1 days × $10 million sales). Given it has total capital employed of $1.45m, this might have been difficult to find! No bank would grant a loan or overdraft for this sort of amount, especially as it already has other current liabilities, made up of the overdraft and a few sundry liabilities, of $762,000. The only realistic source of the additional funds required would have been shareholders… on the promise that the business was growing fast. But this sort of radical refinancing takes time, so it is just as well that XYZ Co has grasped the nettle and improved its working capital cycle in the way it has.

Improving working capital

Could XYZ Co improve its working capital further? Let's look at each element and see what scope there is to make improvements.

On **payables**, XYZ Co is taking 15 days' credit, as it is paying its workers and all those subcontractors hired in to meet demand at the end of each month. There may be some overheads suppliers where it can stretch its payment terms, but many of these will be with utilities and services providers that it cannot afford to alienate and with which it is likely to have little bargaining power. It may be able to negotiate longer credit terms with its subcontractors if they are companies, but often these are individual people who cannot afford to agree to this. So there appears to be little room for improvement on the days payable outstanding (DPO) measure.

XYZ Co has 30 **days in inventory** (DIO), which means that on average each contract is clocking up one month's worth of activity before it is billed out to customers. Can this be improved? There are two ways to improve this measure, depending on the management and negotiation skills of the company and how the contracts have been defined. If XYZ Co has managed to agree that work on contracts can be billed at the end of each month, its first action is to set up the month-end processes so that as soon as the last working day of the month is completed, time sheets are sent in by everyone involved in working on projects (employees and subcontractors alike). These can be reviewed and the related costs are added to the project's work-in-progress balance. Invoices are immediately drawn up and sent out to the customer, removing the balance from inventory/work-in-progress and posting it into accounts receivable before the accounts are closed off for the month. In this way, there will be virtually no inventory at month end, apart from the usual odds and ends that clutter up any portfolio of contracts. If XYZ Co cannot manage to negotiate monthly billing, it may try to secure stage payments or agree a billing schedule.

Its second strategy is to secure an up-front payment 'to secure the resources to be committed to the project' or similar words. This is the equivalent of taking of a deposit to secure a hotel room or a holiday booking and is quite reasonable if XYZ Co is effectively committing its scarce resources to a project. These advance payments can be for whatever XYZ Co can negotiate; 50 per cent of the contract price would be excellent, 33 per cent good and 20 per cent not too bad. The real advantage of these up-front payments is that they create 'negative inventory', because the bill has taken costs out of inventory that haven't yet been incurred by working on the project. In practice, accountants keep these negative balances separate on the balance sheet, call them 'income in advance' and put them in with accounts payable, but the effect is still to reduce the working capital cycle by the equivalent number of days' worth of advance payments received. Taking this principle further, XYZ Co can negotiate its billing schedule so that effectively each payment is an advance payment, with only a small proportion of the contract price to be paid after all the work is signed off on completion. Depending on the work schedule, some of these payments may be partially in advance and partially in arrears, but in every case where the billing is going out of inventory ahead of or in the same month as the work, the month-end balance will be close to zero or even negative. The best way to think of the effect of this is that the service provider has accelerated its cash flow by a month or more. Figure 15.2 is an example to show how the difference in terms negotiated will affect the end of month balances.

Note how by negotiating the billing schedule shown in the lower half of the table, the business has managed to avoid any month-end inventory balance at all and even starts off with $50 of income in advance. This is a substantially better working capital outcome than results from accepting terms that state that invoices can only be submitted monthly in arrears. Using this approach, XYZ Co has plenty of potential to reduce its days in inventory balance further and should aim to reduce it to, say, 20 days initially and then see if it can go further. It will take time to implement this new strategy as it will only be able to negotiate better trading terms on new contracts and projects. XYZ Co may have to concede some margin in its pricing to secure these trading terms, and the merit of doing this will

Month	Beginning inventory balance	Work done on project	Invoices raised	Ending inventory balance
Contract terms agreed: Invoice monthly in arrears				
Jan	$0	$50	$0	$50
Feb	$50	$150	$50	$150
Mar	$150	$100	$150	$100
Apr	$100	$0	$100	$0
Contract terms agreed: 33% up front, 33% one month, 33% on completion				
Jan	$0	$50	$100	–$50
Feb	–$50	$150	$100	$0
Mar	$0	$100	$100	$0
Apr	$0	$0	$0	$0

Figure 15.2 Example of how differences in contract terms affects end of month inventory balances

depend on how closely it is likely to bump up against its overdraft limits. There will often be customers who won't accept such terms, so XYZ Co will have to decide if it is willing to work with them or possibly to charge a (hidden) premium in its pricing to these customers to cover for the adverse impact on its cash flow.

Once the invoices are invoiced to the customer they become **receivables** and XYZ Co has to get them paid as close to its credit terms as possible. Again these will have been the subject of negotiation when the contract was set up, and powerful customers may be able to impose their 45-day or longer payment terms over XYZ Co's stated 30-day terms. Currently XYZ Co's days sales outstanding (DSO) are running at 45 days, down from 68 days in the prior year, which is a substantial improvement. Generally, the higher-end services tend to go through more approval processes with higher levels of management on the customer side which can slow down payments, whereas the lower-end services get paid more quickly for the opposite reasons. Can XYZ Co improve on 45 days DSO? Possibly, depending on its customer base. If it is serving the public sector or very large corporate customers, the chances of improvement are pretty slim. One strategy that we have seen work well on large contracts is for the service providers to negotiate that 80 per cent of each invoice is paid straight away on 15-day or 20-day terms and the remainder is paid when the invoice has been fully checked out and signed off. This type of arrangement usually requires a reasonable track record of working together to have been established and the customer to have built up a high regard for the accuracy and reliability of the service provider's contract delivery as well as its billing systems.

When the income stream is from fixed-term service, support and maintenance contracts, it is not unreasonable for the service provider to insist that these are paid for on a monthly standing order or direct debit, with the first three months paid up front to reflect the costs of setting up the contract initially. It may be a tough negotiation to secure that three-month up-front payment and it is easy to concede it in the interests of landing the contract and customer relationship. But added together, these up-front payments can represent a substantial cash float, which helps to compensate for the typically lower margins earned from this type of income. Indeed, taking a portfolio approach to its income streams is a powerful strategic option for management, optimizing cash flow from service and support contracts, optimizing utilization from larger contracts and optimizing margin from smaller but more strategic contracts. However, management should always ensure that it is securing the best possible trading terms from each type of income stream, and not feel its job is done when the contracts are won.

From this analysis, we can see that there are some areas in which XYZ Co can improve its working capital management and accelerate its cash-to-cash cycle (which is the sum of DSO and DIO less DPO), from the current 60 days down to something approaching 30 to 45 days. Shaving 15 days off the cycle at the current level of business would free up $410,000 of cash (sales of $10m × 15/365), which would help enable it to meet its monthly payroll until the pipeline of new contracts is built up. However, all the improvements we have discussed are more easily done when negotiating new contracts and not at all easy to introduce to the existing contracts or customers.

16

Value creation and growth

Value creation and improving the numbers

Now we have looked at the two sides of the value creation tree (VC tree) separately, we can look at the way they come together and assess whether XYZ Co has done a good job overall of running its business in the last two years (notwithstanding potential troubles ahead!). In Chapter 8 we set out the principles behind value creation, ie that the operating profit generated should exceed the cost of the capital invested in the business to generate that profit. As we have seen, a service business should not need much capital beyond its working capital, so it should be able to create value with a reasonable level of profitability. Figure 16.1 gives a reminder of the VC tree for XYZ Co.

In the current year XYZ Co has created value of $51,600, which is a tiny outcome for $10 million of business, but it is an improvement over the value destroyed in the prior year of $37,475. How has it managed to turn the situation around? If you look at the invested capital for both years, you will see that they are almost identical, but in the current year the larger scale of business has pulled the net operating profit after tax (NOPAT) up above the cost of that invested capital. Even so, the margin of error is very small and the real culprit here is the low gross margin, which barely covers

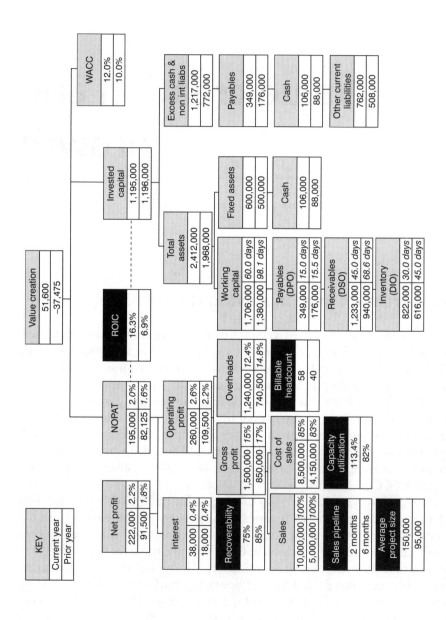

Figure 16.1 XYZ Co (a service provider) value creation tree

overheads and leaves a very small operating margin of 2.6 per cent on sales (up from 2.2 per cent in the prior year).

You may have noticed that the cost of capital has increased from prior year to the current year – up from 10 to 12 per cent. Remember that this is XYZ Co's cost of capital, not the general cost of money in the marketplace, and as such is a risk-adjusted cost of capital. This means that the providers of capital (shareholders, banks and other financing sources tapped by XYZ Co) have decided that the distinctly uncertain outlook for next year has increased the risk in the business and as such have increased the return they want from their particular capital provision to the company. Thus XYZ Co had to earn a higher NOPAT in order to create value to compensate for the extra risk it has built into the business. But it needs to do better, much better, if it is to have a long-term future.

We have looked at various options for improving the business performance as we have reviewed each of the key measures in turn, but we need a strategic framework for sorting out XYZ's business model. Putting the issue of tight working capital control to one side (dealt with in Chapter 15), what are the options available to XYZ Co for improving its profitability?

The framework shown in Figure 16.2 focuses on the two key measures of profitability, gross and net margin, and is based on measuring gross margins after deducting the cost of time used on customer projects. Clearly, if the service provider is achieving high gross and net margins (ie it registers in the top right-hand quadrant), it should maintain whatever it is doing, as long as a review of the future prospects in the sales pipeline indicates that this situation will continue. Equally clearly, if the business is suffering low gross and net margins (ie it registers in the bottom left-hand quadrant) and the separate strategies set out in the other quadrants don't arrest the decline, it should review its whole proposition and consider refocusing or restructuring the entire business model.

The more interesting and challenging situations are if the business registers in the other two quadrants. In the top left quadrant, where net margins are adequate but gross margins are low, this combination suggests that there is no problem with utilization, but perhaps with commanding sufficiently high prices for the value delivered. Service providers may find that they are simply not charging enough for the service they provide and management should experiment by **increasing prices** systematically to find at what point they start losing competitive bids. It may be that *some* prices for *some* services should be increased, for example any emergency call-outs or other crisis-response-type services. Perhaps seasonal pricing may apply, with discounts for low season and premium (or normal, but higher) pricing for high season. Accounting firms regularly

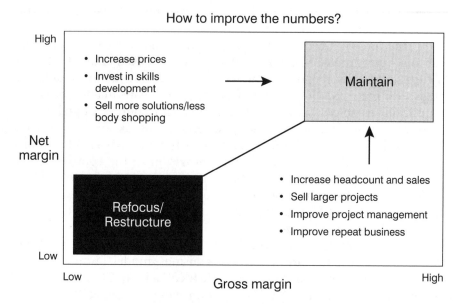

Figure 16.2 Options available to service providers for improving profitability

offer services at lower rates when out of the busy end-of-year reporting season (their busy season is the three months following 31 December and to a lesser extent the period following 31 March) and charge their partners and staff out at higher rates on more 'risky' work such as business valuation work or litigation support work.

The second factor to investigate is the skill set of the billable team; is it up to date and fit for market? Could a greater investment in **skills development** command higher prices and does the team have the skills to sell the value it is really delivering to customers? Is the mix of skills aligned with market trends? What are likely to be the next services opportunities and how well do the current skills position the service provider to respond? It is better to implement a rolling plan of continuous technical and personal skills training if possible, but it may be appropriate from time to time to make a strategic investment in a major new area or technical development. The alternative to organic skills development is skills acquisition, in the form of either recruitment or acquisition of a company or business. This is a big, strategic, decision and should be based on a solid strategic assessment of the company's own situation, long-term goals and feasible options.

The third option is to change the mix of business and **sell more higher-end 'solutions'** that deliver greater value. This will reduce the proportion of the business that comes from services that are more akin to 'body shopping', such as outsourced technical support, etc. Many service providers make the strategic decision to 'go up-market', offering higher-end services in the expectation of richer margins, only to fail. Each case is different, but often the cause can be linked to the fact that the culture and management style appropriate for the people that deliver lower-end services simply does not work for the people capable of delivering higher-end services. In the IT sector many corporate resellers found their margins under pressure simply installing hardware and networks with related support services and sought to move up-market into the area dominated by professional services firms, installing applications and integrated information systems. But simply importing people, or in some cases, whole teams with the skills to do this proved unworkable. The salaries, career development expectations, calibre of management and quality of customers were totally different to those the world corporate resellers were used to and they failed even to understand why their new recruits became disaffected so quickly and left. Computacentre, one of Europe's leading corporate resellers, attempted to move into the SAP software installation business and invested heavily in recruiting and building up the team for it, before finding it simply could not make the business model work. A combination of internal challenges with the team and difficulty in establishing credibility in this market space finally took its toll and Computacentre finally pulled the plug on the business after about three years. It has since refocused on IT infrastructure services. Perhaps the stand-out exception to this general trend was the purchase of Price Waterhouse Consulting by IBM, but here the entire operation and management team were acquired and initially left intact as IBM worked out how best to slowly integrate the two operations and cultures. In many ways IBM's services team were merged into PWC, rather than the other way around.

Let's examine the options in the other quadrant, high gross margins but low net margins. This suggests that there isn't enough volume to cover the unused capacity and overheads. Either the **level of sales needs to be increased**, absorbing the unbilled capacity, or, if utilization is already high and the business is capacity-constrained, possibly the billable **headcount should be increased** (healthy margins suggest a strong demand for the service provider's offering). We will address some of the issues associated with managing growth in the last part of this chapter.

Closely related to increasing sales is the strategy of **selling larger projects**. Larger projects increase business productivity all round, with higher sales per sales effort and, once sold, higher utilization levels over sustained periods. It may be smart to trade off some of the strong gross margins through aggressive pricing to win bigger projects and increase net margins as a result of eliminating the fallow periods in the 'feast and famine' cycle typical of shorter-term projects. Larger projects may mean changing the target customer or adding new capabilities to expand the range of service offerings, neither of which should be attempted without careful weighing of the considerations. Often, winning larger projects means targeting larger customers or the public sector. Is the service provider equipped for the longer, more demanding sales cycle? Can it meet the minimum requirements in terms of certifications, insurance, bonds or whatever other hoops it will have to jump through? Will it have credibility and an acceptable track record? Can it carry the larger risks associated with larger, often more complex, projects? This may mean a step up in **project management** skills and disciplines in order to control these risks and to ensure that the extra revenue generated actually improves the bottom line. Failure to invest in the right project management skills and experience could mean that all the larger projects deliver is larger problems and bigger risks, so that the extra revenues become absorbed in project overruns and fixes.

The final strategy, which all service providers should embrace at all times, is to increase the level of repeat business. There are many reasons why a service provider should do this:

■ Repeat business is often not put out to competitive tender so there is a much lower sales effort required to negotiate the scope and terms of the work.

■ Repeat business often follows on directly, enabling the team to remain in place with no downtime and no learning curve, induction time, etc. Even if the work does not follow on directly, the 'pick-up' time is greatly reduced, benefiting both service provider and customer.

■ An invitation to repeat working for a customer is often accompanied by a greater level of trust placed in the service provider by the customer, widening the potential scope of services that can be provided and opening the door to higher-end services.

■ Working within a familiar customer environment reduces the risk of unknowns, scoping errors, wrong assumptions, etc, improving the potential for both higher margins for the service provider and keener scoping and pricing for the customer.

■ New service offerings can be piloted with customers inside a strong working relationship where both parties can invest in the risk and return – the customer gets a potentially valuable service at a greatly reduced price and may gain a competitive advantage, though with more disruption over a longer period than is ideal; the service provider proves the service offering and irons out the teething issues but possibly at a loss on the project.

Repeat business will be a key strategy for XYZ Co, with its dangerously short sales pipeline and overstretched resources. Existing customers are more likely to yield quicker sales cycles with less sales effort required. The projects are likely to be less risky as client environments will be familiar and client expectations more likely to be matched to XYZ Co's standards and performance.

As we have seen, the service provider business model is just as challenging to get right as the product-based business model, with perhaps more of the 'softer' elements in terms of the people and team management dynamics. Applying this strategic framework should help most service providers to select the right strategy or combination of strategies to improve their business performance, while keeping a tight reign on working capital management, enabling the delivery of substantial value creation.

Managing growth – the integrated product and service business model

As we showed at the start of this chapter, most final-tier trade channel players operate a blended business model with some element of both product resale and service provision. In some cases, these two elements are inextricably linked, with customers expecting the products to be supplied as a seamless part of the solution they are buying. In others, customers expect some degree of service and support as part of the package when buying products, but will then specify specific services to be delivered on a discrete basis. In both cases, the business models have to be synchronized in terms of the customer experience. But this does not have to be the case in terms of managing and controlling the business model and we strongly recommend that the integrated business be managed separately in terms of product and service business units and in terms of the customers/contracts as represented in Figure 16.3.

Management needs to be able to identify and manage the product and service business models separately, given the very different margins, working capital and specialist measures that apply to each model. In addition, it should be able to take an integrated view of each contract/project

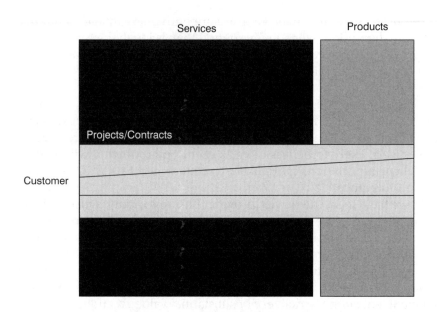

Figure 16.3 Two-dimensional business management: business model and customer orientations

and each customer relationship. Using modern accounting systems, this two-dimensional view of the business should be possible for any size of final-tier trade channel player of any complexity. The rationale for this approach is further reinforced when contemplating managing growth, given the way the constraints work in the two models: in the product model, working capital is the key constraint on growth, whereas in the service model, productive headcount and billable capacity will usually constrict growth before working capital (assuming the demand is there for both models). The two models also tend to have different cycle speeds with different reaction times needed – product businesses need faster responses in terms of changing the product lines listed and stocked, whereas the service business needs to be sure it is responding to an upturn in demand, not a 'blip', as increasing billable headcount is not easy to undo. As we have seen with XYZ Co, the risks of taking on too much new business too quickly can overwhelm the business and the management team, leaving the business vulnerable to disaster. It is much more difficult to extricate XYZ Co from the situation at the end of the current year than it would be to turn around a product business facing similar consequences from over-expansion. The lead-times with adding and removing or even changing people is measured in terms of months and quarters, rather than days or weeks with products. These different 'rhythms', constraints and risks of the two business models are the fundamental reason why product and service business models should be kept separate and managed differently.

Managing growth is very dependent on being able to 'read' the sales pipeline and getting close enough to customers to be able to sense the level of demand ahead. It requires an ability to segment the market so as to be able to define offerings that meet the different needs of each segment and to gauge which offerings are going to experience the higher levels of demand. This places an onus on the management team to adopt a disciplined approach to business planning and to project the possible dynamics of the business models under their control. Sensitivity analysis (essentially modelling a variety of realistic alternative scenarios) should help identify which are the more and less risky options to pursue and how well the business can respond. We have seen several service businesses get caught up in the excitement of landing some new customers or major contracts and gearing up the business in terms of both headcount and debt to finance the extra working capital, without considering the possibilities once the contracts are completed. The consequences were universally dire and involved the founders and principals of these businesses losing control of their business, or suffering a severe setback that took a year or more from which to recover. On the other hand, we have seen small players become very large players through careful assessment of the opportunities they have generated, positioning their offerings to be in the high-growth segments of the market and adapting their internal culture as they have grown. These are the businesses that have been able to finance growth through good net margins, a firm grip on working capital management and maybe just a little luck.

17

How to sell to final-tier trade channel players

What we mean by selling to final-tier trade channel players

Just as selling 'to' a distributor is really about selling the business case for a commercial relationship or making the business case for a particular product or category, so selling 'to' a final-tier trade channel player is about demonstrating how you can deliver business benefits from working together. The final tier is not the end customer, but a route to market to the end customer, and as such represents a critical element of your distribution model. You may be a vendor looking to go to market through the final tier either directly (in which case it is your only tier in the channel) or through distribution, or you may be a distributor looking to increase your market reach and coverage to strengthen your own value proposition to vendors. In both cases, you have to demonstrate that your value proposition is more compelling than the competition in order to win and retain share of the final tier's business. To get the optimum channel value proposition, you need to apply your insight into how their business models work to construct a stream of commercial benefits that both meet their needs *and* exploit your unique advantages to the full.

For example, as a leading brand you can offer a final-tier trade channel player the benefits of strong customer demand (sustained by a roadmap of new products or technologies and backed by substantial end-customer marketing spend), low cost of selling and a robust support infrastructure.

Or as a niche brand, you can offer exclusive dealership status with high margins and a high degree of account management (we shall explore both these positions later on in this chapter).

In the approach we proposed for selling 'to' distributors in Chapter 10, we advocated starting with an analysis of the distributor's strategy. However, in the case of the final tier, this is usually not feasible simply because of the numbers of players involved and, additionally, the numbers of *types* of players involved. You need to research the business models and objectives of the channel player types you want to engage in order to define your channel strategy. This research will enable you to size and prioritize the business potential of each channel type and to determine the key elements of your channel propositions.

Keeping your channel value proposition in tune with the market

Smart suppliers run partner advisory boards that engage a cross-section of relevant partners in regular dialogue (say every six months) and use these boards to test their channel value propositions or planned changes. Partners are generally quick to say what they don't like about planned changes, though are not so good at making proposals that suit the channel as a whole, restricting their suggestions to ones that will benefit them uniquely! Partners will sometimes volunteer what the competition is or will be doing with their channel value propositions, though often with some embellishment in an attempt to lever some improvements from the supplier running the advisory board. Experienced suppliers know they have to navigate this continuous 'negotiation' and keep the dialogue at a strategic level, parking the tactical stuff for partner account managers to deal with in one-to-one meetings.

Segmenting the final-tier trade channel

Your final-tier channel value propositions should be the commercial expression of your channel strategy. It should set out a segmented approach to working with your different channels, showing how to plan to reach and serve each customer segment. It should spell out:

- what role you want the channel to play in terms of market access, demand generation and fulfilment;
- on which customer segments each channel player should be focused (for example, large global customers are addressed by the direct sales force, large national and mid-sized customers are served by Gold dealers and small-sized customers by Silver and Bronze dealers handled through distribution);
- what functions you, as their supplier partner, want to pay the channel for fulfilling, through margin or functional discounts or marketing funding;
- the standards of accreditation and resources you expect them to dedicate to your brand and the level of support and other benefits on which they should base their activities;
- what you expect them to deliver in terms of volumes of business and at what cost to you.

In return you can set out your channel value proposition, based on the economic needs of each type of partner. Segmentation enables you to allocate resources according to your business priorities, for example allocating greater margin rebate incentives to the dealers who recruit more mid-sized customers to your brand, or you can reward your Gold dealers for capturing new large-sized accounts from specific competitors or perhaps for achieving up-sell or cross-sell objectives.

By segmenting your final-tier trade channel, you improve your chances of understanding your channel economics in terms of cost per lead, cost per sale and cost to serve for each customer segment. For example, suppliers using the retail channel will find their national retail partners demanding margins of between 30 and 50 per cent for placement on their shelves and expecting to see their products turning 20 to 25 times a year serviced by professional distribution, in return for national coverage and substantial volumes. However, this may still prove to be more economic than attempting to reach the same consumers through other types of retailer that have less buying power (perhaps buying through the 'cash and carry') and needing extensive advertising support but providing less effective market access and lower volumes.

For the rest of this chapter, we will assume that you have a clearly defined channel strategy that meets your business objectives and provides a framework for building compelling channel value propositions. (There are plenty of books on how to define your channel strategy, including the excellent *Marketing Channels* by Stern, El-Ansary, Coughlan and Anderson, 2006). So from here on, we will focus on what the channel players are looking for from you.

What the final tier looks for in a vendor

The single most significant dimension of your channel value proposition for any channel player of any type is predictability. In dealing with any vendor, all channel players look for a predictable source of commercial profit, so they can invest in the relationship with confidence of the return it will generate. This predictability is surprisingly difficult to deliver and many vendors have created a reputation over the years of 'dipping in and out of the channel', meaning that at one time they have established a 'pro-channel' strategy, working with indirect channels to drive their go-to-market strategy for a year or so, then they have switched emphasis to their in-house direct sales force, pulling (usually the largest) accounts and deals away from the channel. Partners that have invested in winning the account over time suddenly find the relationship ripped away from them by the vendor with little or no compensation. Why would vendors do this? Perhaps they are concerned about account control (fearing the channel could switch-sell to another vendor brand), or are responding to the customer's expressed desire to be managed directly by the vendor. Whatever the short-term reasons, the effect is to send a clear signal to the channel that the vendor is not serious about its commitment to working with channel partners over the long haul. Even vendors that claim to have seen the error of their ways and now commit to a long-term pro-channel strategy will find that the channel has long memories and will be slow to embrace the new channel proposition.

Final-tier trade channel players understand that vendors usually don't want to hand over the entire market to them. Most of their vendors will have a segmented approach and have allocated only part of the market to them. The channel players don't have a problem with this so long as they can see that their vendors have a clear channel strategy and well-defined rules of engagement that they can work from. The channel's perspective is 'tell us where we can make money and stick to it'. Even rules that say 'the top 200 named accounts will be served by our direct sales force' are acceptable so long as the channel understands the criteria that defines 'top 200' and the process and frequency for moving accounts in and out of the list.

Long-term partnering with the channel is essential where the channel is required to invest in the relationship – either by the vendor or by the market – to fulfil its role. For more technical products, this investment can mean adopting a long-term positioning alongside the vendor's brand, dedicating significant numbers of marketing, sales and technical people to being trained up in the vendor's products, dedicating part of the infrastructure such as technical support, spare parts inventories, bench and diagnostic equipment and attending vendor conferences and events. Examples of final-tier trade channels that have done this include information systems installers such as Accenture or PriceWaterhouseSystems that have specialized in SAP's software; trade installers of specialist equipment such as stairlifts, conservatories, kitchens; dealers in earthmoving equipment such as JCBs or Bobcats; and petrol stations that take a franchised shop or coffee station.

Once the groundwork of a consistent set of rules of engagement, backed by a sustainable channel strategy, is in place, the vendor's challenge is to sell the commercial relationship so that it can recruit and retain the right channel players as go-to-market partners. The vendor's channel value proposition needs to be cued into the specific pressure points on the business model normally experienced by the channel players it is selling to. Proper research by independent consultants will help uncover the real opportunities to differentiate your proposition and thus which elements of your channel value proposition to emphasize. Channel players are more likely to share the detail of their business model and be more objective in describing the features of different vendors' channel value propositions that work best, and why, to an independent third party than they would to the vendor's own account managers, with whom they are going to have to negotiate annual and quarterly targets. They are also more likely to engage with someone who seems to understand their model in depth, perhaps with a financial background, something few account managers tend to have.

At the end of this sub-section we set out a table showing the suggested areas on which to focus by channel player type. First, however, we shall cover the key dimensions of an effective channel value proposition, to provide you with a checklist for building your channel value proposition. These dimensions are growth, profit and productivity.

Growth – Most if not all of the partners that you want to engage with your channel value propositions will have growth ambitions. Check the following for relevance and, wherever possible, quantify the value of the benefit stream:

- Brand
  - Do you have a commanding market share or can you demonstrate growth in market share (overall or within key categories or key segments)?
  - What investment in marketing are you making to sustain or improve your market share?
  - What impact is this investment having on customer awareness and preference ratings?

- Positioning
  - Are you positioned for growth in terms of the new technologies, key market categories or segments?
  - Does your brand offer credibility that the channel can 'borrow' or leverage to strengthen its sales and marketing proposition?

- New markets
  - Do your offerings open up new markets for the channel, perhaps through a new price point or new functionality?
  - What market research can you share that shows the future direction of the market and where partners need to be positioned?

- New customers
  - Will your brand or offerings bring the channel new customers?
  - Where is your marketing activity focused?
  - Is your marketing spending increasing?
  - Do you have a lead-sharing capability backed up by lead-generation activity?
  - Will you send sales people to co-sell along side the channel's own sales force?
  - Do you have an end-customer sales force that will pass leads on to the channel?

- Address new/unmet needs
  - Will your offerings help your partners increase their penetration and relevance to their existing customers?
  - What research and insights can you share about unmet needs or emerging needs to demonstrate the relevance of your offerings?

- Stream of new technologies and products
  - Can you demonstrate that you will be able to respond to future demand through a roadmap of new technologies and products?

- Revenue pull-through
  - Will your channel partners be able to generate additional revenues from installing, servicing and supporting your products (sometimes revenue pull-through can be many times the revenues from reselling the actual products)?

- Joint business planning
  - Can you jointly pursue new opportunities through focusing your combined sales and marketing resources?

Profit – Although many partners will focus on gross margins and gross profitability, it will usually be in your interests to widen the whole business case to include all the elements of the income statement that come into net margin and net profitability. As a vendor many of your marketing funds will be taken as a reduction in the channel player's marketing costs, so will only show up in contribution or net margins. Check the following for relevance and, wherever possible, quantify the value of the benefit stream:

- Contract definition
  - Do you offer any aspect of a protected market space for a particular channel partner that will improve its ability to earn higher margins? This protection can be in the form of explicit exclusivity, such as a franchised territory, or implicit through restricted access through accreditation (by product range, size, resource commitment, certification, etc).

- Margins
  - What level of front-end discounts, back-end discounts, functional discounts, rebates, bonuses, volume rebates, etc, do you offer?
  - How does the timing of when margin is earned vary?
  - What targets and standards must the channel partner achieve to earn the different levels of margin?
  - What margin protection do you offer, such as price protection (against price changes), inventory protection (against loss in value of inventory) or returnable inventory, etc?
  - What margin protection do you offer to those who have invested in the pre-sales process and capabilities (accreditation, authorization to sell technical products, etc)?

- Margin mix
  - Does your brand offer a richer margin than the competition because it offers higher-end solutions, more opportunities for cross-sale and up-sale?
  - What level of marketing support and positioning for the channel do you offer to reinforce the higher end sales?
  - Does your brand require a greater level of service and support from the channel player, or command a premium for its skills? (Anyone who has seen the difference in servicing labour rates for an Aston Martin compared to a Ford will understand this point.)

- Soft funds and marketing funds
  - What funding do you provide?
  - How restrictive are the activities which qualify for your marketing funding?
  - What agency support and resources do you provide for the application of these funds?
  - How quickly do you approve and pay claims for marketing funds?

- Overheads
  - What infrastructure do you provide that reduces the overhead costs of your partners?

- Standardized systems and processes (perhaps made available over the web through partner portals)

- Technical backup, knowledge bases, online documentation

- Training (not just in your products, but in generic skills such as core technology, diagnostic processes, project management, integration, sales or interpersonal skills)

- Professional sales and marketing resources (ranging from artwork and templates to sales support and marketing services such as PR).

Productivity – this is perhaps the least well-exploited aspect of many vendors' channel value propositions and can best be thought of as the dimensions of doing business that the partner could not deliver itself (or not economically). For example, a regional dealer simply could not build a globally recognized brand that has customers walking in demanding named products. Nor could it afford to design and develop the rigorous training that its technical sales and support people will need to keep at the leading edge of technical developments. (On the other hand, neither could the vendor acquire local market knowledge and customer insight to the degree its channel partners have built up over many years.) Check the following for relevance and, wherever possible, quantify the value of the benefit stream:

- Lead generation
  - Do you distribute leads to your partners?
  - Do you actively generate leads (either continuously or in promotions)?
  - Do you manage lead distribution, to your better-qualified or more responsive partners?
  - Do you facilitate partner lead broking, so that partners can team up to pursue a lead?
  - Do you provide lead registration, so that partners can pursue a lead on your behalf exclusively, or with your assistance exclusively?

- Co-branding
  - Do you provide access to other leading brands through co-branding or co-marketing brands?
  - Do you develop segment-specific marketing initiatives? (eg Hewlett-Packard, Vodafone and Microsoft all teamed up to put together bundled deals aimed at the small/medium-sized business market.)

- Marketing
  - Do you provide (or provide access to) marketing services, PR, marketing services agencies, etc?

- Resource alignment
  - Do you provide resources or undertake activities that multiply the productivity of the partners' own resources such as sales training, business management courses, etc?
  - Do you integrate your technical support and sales support capabilities (so that you don't compete with each other)?
  - Do you provide some form of relationship management (eg partner account managers) who can help ensure the partner's strategy is aligned with the vendor and manage the vendor's processes and resources to the partner's benefit?

- Have you lined up other strategic alliance vendors to provide preferred status for your partners (eg banking, insurance, legal, accounting, etc)?
- Do you use your bulk-buying power to access resources and services that would not be available to the individual channel player (eg courses at world-class business schools) or to secure lower prices for the channel?

■ Asset deployment
  - Do you provide consignment inventory (ie the channel only pays for the inventory when it sells it)?
  - Do you provide floor-plan financing (ie effectively cheap loans for inventory)?
  - Do you offer your own or a third party's trade receivable discounting service (ie so the channel can receive most of the cash from its trade receivables immediately and the balance when its customers actually pay)?
  - Do you offer schemes to help your channel partners set themselves up or to acquire the specialized equipment they need to run their operations?

(All of these options are effectively using the strength of the vendor's balance sheet or its cash resources to create advantage for its partners.)

You will need to tailor this list as you develop and refine your channel value propositions, but an excellent approach is to challenge each of your internal business functions to set out all the ways they support (and could support) your partners. Not only will this bring forward opportunities to offer your channel partners some unique advantages from their relationship with you, it will encourage 'channel thinking' in the parts of your business that perhaps do not typically engage with the channel partners.

Set out in Figure 17.1 is a table showing which elements of a vendor's channel value proposition are more likely to appeal to the different final-tier trade channel types (using the different channel roles set out in Chapter 11).

It is essential that, once you have determined your channel value propositions for each of your channel segments, your account managers who manage the relationship with your channels are properly briefed and updated regularly. Few vendors invest enough in this and run the risk that each account manager is underselling (or worse, miss-selling) the value proposition relevant to his or her set of channel partners. Vendors that make the investment in explaining not only their channel value propositions but

Value proposition	Extension of vendor	Product completer	Service provider	Solution integrator
Growth				
Brand	✓	✓	✓	
Positioning	✓	✓	✓	
New markets	✓	✓	✓	
New customers	✓	✓	✓	✓
Address unmet needs	(✓)	✓	✓	✓
New technologies/product	(✓)	✓	✓	✓
Revenue pull-through			✓	✓
Joint business planning			✓	✓
Profit				
Contract definition	✓	✓	✓	
Margins	✓	✓	✓	
Margin mix	✓	✓	✓	✓
Soft funds/marketing funds	(✓)	✓	✓	✓
Overheads	(✓)	✓	✓	✓
Productivity				
Lead generation		✓	✓	
Co-branding			✓	
Marketing		✓	✓	
Resource alignment		✓	✓	✓
Asset deployment	✓	✓	✓	✓

Figure 17.1 Relevance of a vendor's channel value proposition to different channel roles

also the logic and data behind them usually secure a stronger position in their channels and can ride the storms of channel feedback from the occasional wrong turn or mismanagement with greater resilience. In many cases, account managers need training in understanding their partners' business models and the core economics that drive them to be able to sell their channel value propositions effectively. Commercial and financial skills are not usually a strong point among account managers, whose background is often in sales or product marketing, and for whom 'finance for non-financial managers' courses do not make enough of a connection to their day-to-day dealings with partners to be of use.

It is often just as critical HOW a vendor deploys its channel value proposition as WHAT it comprises. For example, if the only person from a vendor that a channel partner sees is an account manager every few months (in the run-up to quarter-ends), who is a different person every other time, it is going to interpret that as a lack of genuine partnership intent. On the other hand, if the vendor is given an account manager who takes the time and trouble to understand its business, and is exposed to the vendor's senior management who explain its strategy, and apparent breaches of channel strategy are pursued and resolved promptly, the channel will conclude that the vendor is serious about its channel relationships. Clearly, vendors will make more effort and investment in the deployment of their channel value proposition with their strategic partners – the 20 per cent of their partners who deliver 80 per cent of their revenue – than their other partners, but they need to remember that channel sentiment as a whole will respond to the vendor's overall posture to the channel.

The best vendors regularly survey their channel partners to ensure they are tracking the competitiveness of their channel value proposition and the effectiveness of its deployment. Shown in Figure 17.2 is an example of how well one vendor is meeting the expectations of its low-end value added resellers (VARS) in the form of a map.

In this example, the vendor has broken out its channel value proposition by Business, Relationship, Marketing and Support. The black area charts

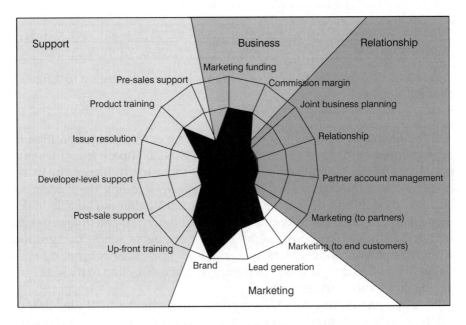

Figure 17.2 Example vendor profile against low end VAR channel value proposition

how well it is doing on the individual dimensions of these elements. It can also be very effective to ask your channel partners to rate your strongest competitor as well as yourself in these surveys in order to assess the gap between you. There is nothing better for fostering effective channel relationships than to constantly seek feedback as to how well you are doing **and then to act on it**. Business results are a lagging indicator of the competitiveness of your channel value propositions – by the time sales and share of account start to slip, the rot is well established and it will take time to reverse. Channel surveys are leading indicators, if well executed, and when done regularly can pick up issues or opportunities that can be dealt with before business performance is damaged.

What the final tier looks for in a distributor

Distributors compete with other distributors for their share of the different segments of the final-tier channels. Unlike vendors, they do not have their own end-customer brand pulling power to attract new channel players. But they do have other weapons, primarily their product range, which is of course multi-vendor based. The leading broadline distributors will have long-standing relationships with all the major brands and many lesser brands, making one-stop shop a core element of their proposition. On top of range they need to get the basics of availability, price, responsiveness and credit right. They may also offer services that leverage their scale, for example specialized logistics such as drop shipment (shipping direct to the end customer on behalf of the final-tier player), consolidation (assembling a complete assortment of products from multiple vendors for a single shipment to an end-customer) or special packaging (such as for retailers, who require bubble packs to prevent theft). Depending on the sector, they may also offer other services such as outsourced marketing services, project management and financing.

In most markets you will find a handful of leading broadliners competing for 'first call status' of the final tier – ie the distributor that the final tier will call first for 80 per cent of its requirements. Below these will be an array of distributors who can't secure a distributorship with all the leading brands, so will compete on some other basis, such as a brand or category specialization, better service levels (in some dimensions at least) or a commercial dimension such as offering credit lines to accounts that struggle to get sufficient credit from the broadliners. Most of these 'other' distributors will need to select one or more segments of the channel on which to focus in order to offer a finer-tuned proposition than the broadliners can hope to achieve. In addition to the basics of product availability, competitive prices and credit, these distributors will place greater emphasis on the added value services that are aligned with the needs of their chosen customers in the final tier.

For both the broadliners and specialized distributors, the same channel value proposition framework of final-tier needs applies and forms the basis for the checklist: growth, profit and productivity. Check the following for relevance and, wherever possible, quantify the value of the benefit stream:

Growth

■ Brand
  - Do you offer all the brands necessary to meet the needs of your chosen channel segments?
  - How many brands do you distribute on an exclusive or semi-exclusive basis?
  - Are you increasing your share of distribution for any key brands?

■ Positioning
  - What preferred distributor status do you have with vendors that will enable you to offer superior marketing or technical support to your customers?
  - Are you positioned for growth in terms of having distributorships with the emerging brands, technologies, product categories?
  - Do you publish a catalogue or product listing that serves as a reference guide for the end customer market?
  - Do you manage segments of channel partners on behalf of your vendors?

■ New markets
  - Do your offerings open up new markets for the final tier, perhaps through securing new distributorships or being an early distributor for new technologies, categories or franchises?
  - Do you offer (better) training in the new technologies and products that will help your channel customer catch the next wave of opportunity?
  - Do you offer a higher level of technical support (pre- and post-sale) than your competition?

- New customers
  - Do you run marketing programmes and offer marketing services that will help the final tier recruit new customers?
  - Where is your marketing activity focused?
  - Is your marketing spending increasing?
  - Do you administer co-marketing funds on behalf of your vendors?

- Joint business planning
  - Do you help your final-tier players with their business planning?

Profit

- Margins
  - How many brands do you distribute on an exclusive or semi-exclusive basis?
  - What level of front-end discounts, back-end discounts, functional discounts, rebates, bonuses, volume rebates, etc, do you offer?
  - How does the timing of when margin is earned vary?
  - Do you charge for delivery in ways that improves the final-tier margins?
    - Free delivery for orders above a minimum order size?
    - Free delivery for back-orders?
    - Lower charges for multiple ship-to points than your competition?
    - Reward smart ordering behaviour on the part of your customers?

- Margin mix
  - Do you offer a range that includes brands and categories that offer a richer margin than the competition because it offers higher-end solutions, more opportunities for cross-sale and up-sale?

- Overheads
  - What specialized logistics services do you offer that minimize the costs for the final tier?
    - Drop shipments (to end-customer locations)?
    - Labelling, packaging and invoicing services (to the end-customer on behalf of the final tier)?
    - Multiple ship-to points (for final-tier customers who have multiple locations such as retailers)?
    - Delivery to desk (as opposed to back door)?
    - Consolidation (of multiple products to enable a single shipment of say all the elements of a project to an end-customer)?

- What marketing services do you offer that can save the final tier from needing to invest in its own marketing resources and can provide expertise that it could never afford?
- What technical support and back-up do your offer your final-tier customers, pre- and post-sale, that saves them from needing to invest in these resources?
- What infrastructure do you provide that reduces the overhead costs of your partners?
  - Standardized systems and processes (perhaps made available over the web through partner portals)?
  - Technical back up, knowledge bases, on-line documentation?
  - Training (not just in your products, but in generic skills such as core technology, diagnostic processes, project management, integration, sales or interpersonal skills)?
  - Professional sales and marketing resources (ranging from artwork and templates to sales support and marketing services such as PR)?

Productivity

- One-stop shop
  - What proportion of each final-tier segment's product needs do you distribute?

- Resource alignment
  - Do you provide resources or undertake activities that multiply the productivity of the partners' own resources such as technical training, sales training, etc?
  - Do you provide some form of relationship management (eg partner account managers) that can help ensure your final-tier customer's strategy is aligned with that of the vendors that you distribute?
  - Do you use your bulk-buying power to provide resources and services that would not be available to the individual final-tier customers?

- Asset deployment
  - Do you provide advantageous credit facilities or credit terms compared to your competitors (perhaps for specific segments of the channel)?
  - Do you provide consignment inventory (ie the final tier only pays for the inventory when it sells it)?

- Do you provide floor-plan financing (ie effectively cheap loans for inventory)?

You will need to tailor this list depending on what type of distributor you are and on which segments of the final tier you focus. Larger distributors will try to leverage their balance sheet strength by taking the big deal discounts and leading with price and/or credit facilities, whereas smaller distributors will try to leverage their specialization with customized support and service.

Many distributors experience some level of churn in their customer base as final-tier players seek to avoid becoming over-dependent on one distributor or to increase the credit lines available to them (three distributors giving a credit limit to a single player will usually be greater than the credit limit any one distributor will be willing to provide). In competitive markets, the battle can focus entirely on price and availability, as the distributors sign up to volume discount deals from the vendors and then seek to offload the higher volumes to their customers. However, this is a short-term game and ultimately does the market a disservice, as the final tier has to ring around all the distributors to find the best price for every product it sells and the distributors gain no advantage or loyalty from the other dimensions of their value proposition. Mature markets are characterized by fewer price-led propositions and stronger business-focused propositions, which actually do more for the final tier's efficiency and productivity.

Managing the account relationship

Whether you are a vendor or distributor, you will need to decide what level of account management is cost-effective for your array of partners. Key partners (typically the 20 per cent of your partners that deliver 80 per cent of your revenues or profits) should be managed on a strategic basis, sharing long-term plans and leveraging each others' strengths. There are two critical success factors: a strategic account management process; and a properly skilled strategic account manager.

The *strategic account management process* should engage the top-level management of both the vendor/distributor and the final-tier partner and ensure that there is sufficient alignment and focus in both businesses on helping each other achieve its business goals. Set out in Figure 17.3 is an outline of the process that should be driven jointly by the relationship managers of both parties.

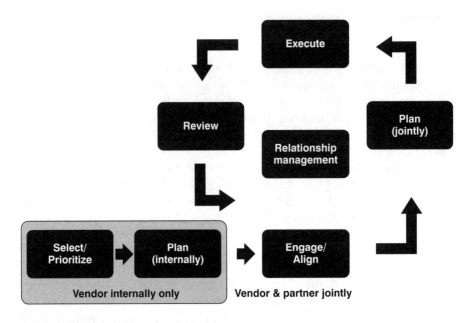

Figure 17.3 Strategic account management process

Strategic account managers (SAMs) have one of the most demanding roles in business, sometimes termed a 'boundary role'. SAMs need to be able to establish themselves as trusted business advisers to their final-tier partners by virtue of their status in their own company (ie ability to command resources and influence priorities), commercial business skills, strategic insight and strong focus on shared business goals. Often drawn from a sales background initially, their role is actually very little to do with selling (in fact a selling mindset would be counter-productive), and all to do with general management of the teams and resources of two companies. It is essential that they understand the channel economics of their partners as well as how their partners impact the economics of going-to-market inside their own company.

In our experience, many vendors set up excellent account management processes, appoint their top managers to the SAM role with their key partners and then fail to recognize the damage inflicted by their internal compensation and incentive structures. They set annual and quarterly targets which force the SAM to bring the conversation down to the level of securing orders to hit volume targets and potentially distort the run-rate business. This often fatally wounds the ability of the SAM to re-engage the partner in establishing strategic programmes to capture key segments, build joint assets that would command competitive advantage or create offerings that leverage the unique combination of their capabilities. Very few vendors tie meaningful compensation to the achievement of unique milestones developed in the joint strategic account plan. Instead they impose a series of standardized growth volume, margin and logistics targets which can often run counter to the spirit of the strategic partnership they are seeking to build. These vendors will cite the need to hit quarterly targets to maintain their own share price and influence stock market sentiment, which is quite understandable. But these short-term goals need not be entirely at odds with building long-term competitive advantage and it is merely intellectual laziness to set targets and base compensation only on the short-term dimensions of the commercial relationship for which the SAM is responsible.

The real purpose of account management is to 'grow the pie' of business opportunity for both the vendor and its partners, rather than fight over the share of the pie – sometimes termed a zero-sum game. To do this effectively requires joint business planning on an annual basis and some regular reviews during the year. Vendors can often bring market research and market-wide insight to the process to complement the more focused insight from the partner. By sharing their strategic goals, common objectives can be defined. The joint plan, leveraging the special advantages of their combined resources, should be signed off at high enough levels to ensure both organizations are committed to fulfilling the plan. Targets and incentives can be agreed for the personnel in both the vendor and its partner based on the plan. Wherever we have seen this approach implemented effectively it has always led to substantial gains in market share, profitability and competitive advantage.

Some rules of thumb for making compelling business cases

There are some generic strategies that vendors (or distributors) should employ to maximize the competitiveness of their channel value propositions. These strategies are usually differentiated based on market share position as this fundamentally changes the economic viability of different strategies and creates different dynamics in the business models.

If you are a market share leader

If you are a **market share leader**, you usually have the strongest brand and you will be able to spread the cost of your end-customer and trade channel marketing activities over a higher number of unit sales. As the (or a) leading brand, you should be leveraging the benefits of demand pull in your channel value proposition. The advantages of money margin, productivity and volumes should be highlighted to overcome the usual disadvantage of low margin:

■ Money margin – or the gross margin in dollars will make a substantial contribution to fixed costs as most of the vendor's trade channel partners will see sales of the vendor's brand at something close to or above market share. These volumes would be hard to replace and even at low gross margin percentages will represent substantial gross profit.
■ Productivity – usually a leading brand has done all the marketing needed to create demand for its products, so the trade channel's effort in selling these products is greatly reduced. In addition, the burden of technical support is often reduced through greater market familiarity and higher customer knowledge. The greater level of business between a leading brand vendor and its partners can (and should) support more intensive account management, joint business planning and customized investments and activities, all of which should drive greater productivity and increased partner profitability
■ Volumes – depending on the category, carrying the leading brands denotes a status and credibility on part of the trade channel partners that converts into higher volumes of business for them. This often brings 'carry-along' business from end-customers as well as the opportunities to cross-sell and up-sell off a bigger revenue base. These benefits are multiplied for the senior tiers in a multi-tier partner programme.
■ Gross margin percentage – the downside is that leading brands are by definition the most widely distributed, creating downward pressure on the gross margin percentage that can be earned on them by the final-tier trade channels. In many cases, the final tier will use benchmark products from key brands to articulate the competitiveness of its price proposition, dragging margins even lower. And vendors can exacerbate the problem by offering volume deals on their highest-volume products, forcing the final tier to pass these discounts on to the end-customer ('passing it to the street') to make sure it in turn can offload its increased inventories.

If you are a small vendor or new entrant in a category

For **vendors who do not command strong market shares** or offer an end-customer brand with high awareness, the channel value proposition will be based on very different economics. Vendors in this position will be asking the final tier to actively sell their brand against the more established leading brands. The final tier will only do this if it can see an attractive economic return for its efforts, which will typically include high gross margins. Given the brand is not widely distributed, the final-tier players that do take it to market will not be competing with each other on price. It is likely that margins will be better than for the leading brands, providing the offering is competitive in terms of its end-customer functionality. Indeed it may well be that it is complementary to the leading brands and as such offers the final tier a high margin component of a solution that falls 'under the radar' from the end-customer's perspective.

An example of this is that retailers will often make a higher margin on the accessories than on the core product that is sold at the same time (sometimes even more money margin). It's not unusual for a customer to have done their internet searching and found the cheapest source of the core product (because as a leading brand it is highly benchmarked), and then accept the retailer's suggested accessories without even pausing to fish out their credit card. The result is that that unknown accessory vendor has delivered a very attractive channel value proposition by enhancing the overall basket (total paid by a customer), enriched the margin in both percentage and dollar terms and done so with a lower investment in inventory, shelf space commitment and with no marketing cost whatsoever. These principles will apply in any situation where there are complementary or peripheral products to highly distributed 'core' products and these vendors should have no trouble building attractive channel value propositions for their final-tier partners.

As a market share minnow, you are offering your partners an open market landscape, but equally virtually no brand awareness or visibility. The key factor that your proposition must include is credibility for your offerings. Typically this will be built around some high-profile reference sites or sales that borrow the credibility of the customer. In a business-to-business context this could be some early direct sales made to Fortune 500 corporations or a government department or agency. In the small to medium business context, you may need to seek approvals or certifications from relevant trade associations to demonstrate validity. In the consumer market, high-profile sports or entertainment endorsement is valuable, though it must be relevant to your target market. Alternatively, well-placed

PR or editorial endorsement can be the difference between success and failure in convincing the final tier to take your products to market. Finally, securing one high-profile final-tier player as your partner may be the key to convincing others to take you seriously. In the consumer market in the UK, Harrods is often given very attractive deals by its smaller vendor suppliers in return for the enormous kudos of being able to say 'on sale in Harrods'.

Different channel types will have different concerns that the small vendor must anticipate and pre-empt:

■ Retailers will be interested to know how fast production can be ramped up if the trial quantities of the product sell well. Going to a national chain of grocers may not be the best first-channel partner if it will expect you to be able to meet orders for several hundred thousand when the first order of ten thousand sells out quickly. You may need to start with regional grocers to give your capacity the chance to ramp up.

■ Trade dealers will want to know what level of technical support and backup they can count on if the product requires specialist installation or fitting. Being told 'we can get back to you in 10 days' just won't wash with the channel if it has customers expecting the work to be finished on time.

■ Integrators will want to know just how well you have tested your products across the array of permutations and combinations that they could be working with, for similar reasons.

If you can overcome these issues and offer a high margin on a credible offering, your channel value proposition's final ingredient should be the high degree of influence your partners will have with you as a vendor. They will be a big fish in a small pond and, depending upon your ability to be responsive, you can enable them to offer their customers something closer to a tailored or customized solution than they could with a leading brand. This may not seem material, but many of your partners will value this, especially if they see you as a future winner, and their ability to position themselves with their customers will be enhanced.

Selling 'with' the final tier in an advocacy role

So far in this chapter we have dealt with the channel as 'sell-through' partners, ie they take your product to market on your behalf. However, there are many players in the final tier who do not 'touch' your product but can make or break your chances of building sales to end-customers. We termed these players 'sell-with' partners in Chapter 11 and highlighted how critical it can be to include them in your channel strategy. Equally, it is important to define a channel value proposition for them to ensure that they are 'on-side' and will endorse your brand and products. Key to this is to help them do their job as customer advocates – they need to be experts in all new technologies, developments, market trends, etc. Their role, credibility and of course income is entirely dependent on really being experts with some degree of objectivity. You will enhance their capability and not compromise their objectivity by maintaining a dialogue with them through seminars, bulletins, briefings, conferences, relationship managers, etc. They will anticipate and filter your claims of market-leading innovations and product breakthroughs, but equally will listen intently to your technical updates, especially if you align your briefing teams with theirs. This means that if you have your technical people talk to their technical people, you will gain far more credibility than if you unleash your sales and marketing forces. Companies like IBM and Microsoft have hosted technical and consultant briefings for years. They have learnt to balance a few attractions (venues are often Venice, Monaco, Las Vegas) with the hard-edged technical symposiums and throw in a few nice dinners. The technical community in most categories receives fewer boondoggles than the sales and marketing communities and appreciate being paid attention. In the healthcare and pharmaceutical industries, there are now strict guidelines on what the drug companies can legitimately do to educate and brief their principal advocates – the prescribing doctors (after years of abuse where doctors were flown out to exotic locations for their 'education'), but in most industries common sense sets the boundaries of what works before it becomes counter-productive.

Those vendors that deliver genuine technical briefings and updates build up a reputation over time that stands them in good stead with the advocate channel. Vendors do not always have to be the host and in many sectors independent advocates are the host and they seek to impress their clients with the quality and seniority of the vendor people they can get along to their customer conferences. In the IT sector, leading advocates like Forrester and Gartner will mount many conferences aimed at different communities and use the chief executives, chief technology officers, etc, of some of the top brands to ensure they pull in a good audience. These provide the vendors with a double benefit: they get to put across their view of the world (with their products and technologies at the centre) to the end customer or sell-through partners and to influence the thinking and trendspotting of the leading advocates in the industry. Smaller and emerging vendors will have to set their sights a little lower, focusing on more niche advocates and lower-key events and forums.

Conclusion

The channel will only take relevant and competitive products and services to market so it is essential to pay attention to the basic offering from an end-customer's perspective. However, while necessary, a better mousetrap will not be sufficient to persuade the channel to take it to market. For that you need a compelling channel value proposition, which speaks in economic terms to your potential partners' business objectives. Segmenting your channel enables you to segment your channel value proposition, so that it is relevant to the business model of each type of partner. For your more strategic partners you need to go even further and investigate their particular objectives and the pressures on their business model in designing a proposition that enables you to take best advantage of the unique combination of resources in your two organizations.

Part 4

Retailers

18

The role of retailers

Retailers and retailing

What distinguishes retailers from all other types of final-tier players? The generally accepted definition of retailing is that it consists of selling products and services to the **ultimate consumer** for private consumption. And by and large that's whom retailers sell to, though not exclusively as small business will also often use retailers for convenience (and sometimes for price). You will have noticed that the definition makes no mention of shops or stores. Many retailers today go to market through many selling motions, including stores, catalogues, mail-order, online and tele-sales. In this section we are going to focus on the store-based retail selling motion, ie selling through physical retail premises, located in places that are convenient for the target customer. We will touch on the business models of the other selling motions later on. The core proposition of the store-based retail channel is convenience, product choice and comparison, touch and feel, trial, advice, confidence through physical presence in backup or ability to return and the intangible dimensions of 'experience' such as image, entertainment, indulgence, etc (why else would so many garments purchased on a Saturday afternoon in a glitzy store never make it out of the bag once they have been taken home?).

In the store-based selling motion, the goal of the retailer is to select the best location, attract its customers to come to the store, get them to 'shop' the store, get them to buy the 'best mix' (ie most profitable lines) in the store and finally to get them to come back again. As the store is built or fitted out, the retailer needs to communicate its presence and forthcoming opening so that it can hit the ground running. Once open, it must build up its customer base through aggressive advertising and promotion, refining its messaging and targeting as it learns more about the catchment area of the store. Depending on the store, the category and its competition, customers may be prepared to travel up to 100 miles to visit a store or be unwilling to go further than a 15-minute drive. Once at the store, the retailer needs to draw the customer in through attractive window displays or good visibility of its most attractive products (which is why grocers always put fresh fruit and vegetables at the entrance of their stores). And once the customer has been enticed inside the store, the retailer needs to draw them further in and around the store by smart layout and merchandising. Increasingly retailers are grouping items together in 'solutions' rather than simply by categories. So clothing stores group polo shirts, chinos and pullovers in matching colours, with accessories like belts and shoes. Grocers group rices, sauces, naan breads, curries, samosas, etc, together with other dips and accoutrements of an Indian meal, with similar displays for other cuisines such as Chinese, Italian, Mexican, etc. Software stores merchandise the same product in multiple locations to catch the different types of shoppers in their stores: those who know what they want, the browsers who could be tempted, the novices who need help and the shopper who always wants what's in the 'top ten' list. The goal is to encourage the customer to buy a bigger 'basket', spending more than they intended, and ideally to have traded up from the value range to the premium range or from 'good' to 'better' to 'best', increasing both money margin and gross margin percentage.

The store-based retail channel is a fairly high-risk channel as errors made in site selection may take more than a year to identify and even longer to correct. Customers can move (traffic often moves from one end of a town to another if a big mall is opened or a major supermarket relocates), and competition can open up nearby, raising the bar for store fit-out and product range and lowering it for prices. Once built and staffed, the core costs of the retail operation are relatively fixed, putting pressure on the retailer to drive sufficient volumes and secure high enough margins to cover these costs. To respond to these challenges, retailing has increasingly become a science, with software tools to support decision making right through the process from site selection to **ranging** (how many models and sizes to offer in each category and in what depth) to **planograming** (how to lay out the merchandise to maximize sales). Even the colours, lighting, background music and special odours pumped through the air conditioning are now chosen based on research into customer responses.

Given the pressures on retailers, it is not surprising that they have developed a reputation for dealing with their suppliers somewhat brutally, demanding outrageously high margins, the right to return products that don't sell (or don't sell fast enough) and asking to be paid for just about every aspect of their operation – listing fees to include a product in their store, special payments for putting products in prominent positions and high traffic areas in the store, marketing fees for including products in their promotions and marketing and even fines for deliveries that turn up late or errors in quantities or invoices. Many retailers have become massive brands in their own right with the power to make or break a supplier's access to consumers through their presence in the market and share of a particular category. For example, at one time, Dixons electrical stores were in just about every high street in the UK and their share of the electricals market was approaching 70 per cent. If you were a vendor in the electricals sector, you had to secure a presence in Dixons to have any hope of making sales and you had to pay the price through very high discounts, fees and marketing funds as well as committing to run major communications programmes aimed at drawing your customers into Dixons stores. In return you could count on high volumes and brand visibility, although in many categories Dixons was competing with your products using its own-brand products at a lower street price.

Retailers do not all fit one mould, however, and there are significant differences in approach that reflect their scale (national retailers, regional retailers, independents), core proposition (mass merchants, category killers, specialists) and price positioning (price leaders, service leaders), as shown in Figure 18.1.

There will usually be a wide variety of approaches even among competitors in the same arena, with, for example, one mass merchant going for a price leader strategy and another mass merchant for the full service approach. Every retailer must ensure that the core proposition is conveyed consistently across the customer experience. Customers visiting the discount club Costco accept that the concrete floor, industrial shelving and bulk packs are integral to the retailer's ability to offer the lowest prices. In department stores, customers expect to pay top prices for the fashion lines presented in glitzy surroundings and handed over beautifully wrapped and packed in snazzy carrier bags. Where retailers lose out is if a key part of the proposition is missing or below standard, for example the temporary 'Saturday boy' in the photography shop who knows even less about the two cameras you are considering than you do and picks up the box to read the specification to you.

Type of retailer	Get customer to the store	Get customer to shop the store	Get customer to buy best mix	Get customer to return to store
National retailers eg Tesco	Advertising in national media, sponsorships, stores everywhere	Standardized store layout and merchandising	Promotions, use of high spot locations in store	Loyalty programmes
Regional retailers	Advertising in regional media, store density in region	Standardized store layout and merchandising	Promotions, use of high spot locations in store	Store density in region
Independents ie local stores	Community-based marketing	Range and choice	Advice	Service and support
Mass merchants eg Tesco, Carrefour, Wal-Mart	Comprehensiveness of range	Store layout and merchandising	Promotions, use of high spot locations in store	Convenience of store location and coverage of weekly needs
Category killers eg Toys 'R' Us, Carphone Warehouse	Category-led communications, usually price led	Choice and assortment	Promotions, use of high spot locations in store	Loyalty programmes, comprehensiveness of range in category
Specialists eg Barnes and Noble	Targeted communications	Advice, choice and assortment	Advice	Quality of service
Price leader eg Costco	Price-led communications	Store layout and merchandising	Drive volume through 2-for-1 type deals	Everyday low prices
Service leader eg El Corte Ingles	Service-led communications	Advice, choice and assortment	Advice, choice and assortment	Quality of service

Figure 18.1 Types of retailer customer value propositions

Customers tend to go to the retailers with which they are familiar and in whom they feel a certain level of comfort. This is a direct response to the in-store experience which, if well executed, will resonate with customers and encourage them into the store and keep them in the store for longer. Large retail groups will operate multiple store formats to attract subtly different customer segments, especially in the fashion clothes sector. Mass merchants will carry several different propositions and place them in separate areas to appeal to multiple different segments. In Tesco, the value lines are always on the lower shelves within a category, while its premium brands are typically grouped in solution clusters on the end caps and in special areas in the store, with warmer lighting and less buzz, encouraging a browsing rather than a shopping-list-ticking-off approach.

To vendors or suppliers, the retailer's primary role as a channel is to deliver customer traffic to their products. More importantly, it is to deliver a well-defined set of customer segments with a predisposition to buy their products. In choosing to go to market through retail, suppliers are engaging with a high-cost channel and need to ensure that they are geared up for the demands of servicing this channel, in terms of both the customer volumes demanded and meeting the demands of the retailers, financially, logistically, and in terms of marketing support and account management. It is not a channel you dabble in. Retailers have long memories for suppliers that couldn't meet their side of the deal and will be reluctant to re-engage with a supplier who has let them down in the past. Understanding the retailer's business model, as set out in the next chapter, is key to negotiating your products onto the retailer's (best) shelves and staying there, and it is essential that you know what you want out of the channel before you go anywhere near it.

Catalogue and online retailing

Many of the constraints on the retailer's business model have traditionally been overcome through the adoption of the catalogue and, more recently, the online selling motions. In fact, these two motions are often combined as ordering has migrated from mail (ie mail order), through call centres to online, though many retailers continue to operate call centres in tandem with their websites. These selling motions enable retailers to:

■ offer an almost unlimited range of products in breadth and depth that no physical store could match in terms of capacity;

- in the case of catalogues, increase convenience, allowing shoppers to browse and buy 'in the convenience of their own home' as expressed by so many retailers;
- in the case of online, increase opening hours to 24/7, making themselves available whenever the customer wants to buy, without the attendant cost in store and payroll costs;
- increase reach in terms of being accessible to any customer in the world with a phone or online computer, without needing to establish anything more substantial than a local language website;
- offer customization of the product before it is delivered, such as finishing, engraving, configuring, etc.

Relatively few retailers have embraced the catalogue selling motion, however, as it suffers from significant barriers to entry, including the enormous up-front cost of catalogue production and distribution, as well as requiring stable prices for the life of the catalogue. Recent print production processes have helped overcome some of these disadvantages and catalogues have experienced a resurgence as online ordering has multiplied the convenience dimensions of this selling motion.

The volumes purchased through the online selling motion have accelerated from the time of its arrival, though not as fast as some of the early predictions which implied that the only traffic visiting stores by now would be tumbleweed. The factors underpinning this growth are that it offers all the advantages of catalogues but without the need to fix prices for any time and, although the artwork and layout costs remain, there is a one-off cost to establish a website that can be maintained and updated at a fraction of the cost of repeated catalogue production costs, with the ability to responding rapidly to consumer demand.

However, as many early online retail operations discovered, there are some severe disadvantages too:

- the challenges of drawing the customer to your online store, especially if you do not already have an established retailing brand and the costs of maintaining top-of-mind awareness, when the competition is only a click away;
- making the online shopping experience as easy and intuitive as possible for the different consumer segments targeted;
- the challenge of up-selling and cross-selling customers to buy more than the specific product they have come online to buy;
- the inability to answer immediate questions or handle objections;

- establishing trust in the mind of the customer in the absence of a physical presence and any tangible reputation;
- competing with the 'manufacturer direct' competition and other online competition, making for intense price pressure;
- overcoming delivery logistics challenges, with many domestic customers requiring out-of-hours delivery slots;
- overcoming payment logistics challenges with increasing risk and fear of internet fraud;
- the need to provide for 'reverse logistics' in the event the product delivered is faulty, not as ordered or simply not wanted by the customer.

Many of the online-only retailing propositions that sprang up in the early days of the internet sought to dislodge the 'expensive and cumbersome' store-based retailers through the double play of price-led and convenience-led advantage. However, with the notable exception of Amazon, virtually none of those players survived to the era of Web 2.0 and it is instructive to consider why this is so. The primary reason these online-only retailers failed is that they did not create sufficient awareness of their offer. Second, they were unable to engender sufficient trust in the mind of customers to persuade them to overcome the usual barriers of innovation in adopting new buying and paying habits. These retailers served only to shovel vast amounts of venture capital into the hands of the advertising agencies hired to create new brands and draw the traffic, but they usually ran out of cash before the volumes of online traffic reached break-even levels. This was an expensive education in the value of the physical store as a communications vehicle and its role in the select and buy process experienced by a customer. What we see now is the reverse situation, with the so-called dinosaurs of retail establishing slick and effective online experiences that leverage fully their trusted positioning with the customer. Effectively it was easier for the store-based retailers to move online that it was for the customers to shift to the web-based retailers.

As the online retailing selling motion has matured, the major retailers have increasingly blended their channel proposition, allowing customers to browse in one channel, order in another and select either in-store collection or home delivery from any channel. This has led to some interesting pricing strategies, with the online and in-store prices becoming more aligned and the emergence of smart ranging strategies as the fast-moving lines are carried in store and the slower-moving (but often more profitable) lines made available online or through a catalogue, sometimes even through an in-store booth.

There is no doubt that online retailing is going to continue to grow, but the early predictions that it will be at the expense of the store-based selling motion are wide of the mark. Increasingly consumers will demand the ability to drift across multiple selling motions and expect seamless transfer and a consistent experience as they do so, requiring that retailers be present in each selling motion to avoid losing business to those that are. The retailers' challenge will be to harness the internet-based technologies to control their costs, build stronger consumer insight and deliver relevant service to each of their customer segments.

19

How the retail business model works

Role defines business model

The retailer's business is all about volumes. The more products it can sell out of its stores, the more times it will earn a margin and the more productive will be its space and its employees. And with high volumes it will be able to turn to its suppliers and demand higher margins (ie discounts) and bigger marketing payments for bringing large numbers of customers to their products. Retailers (and analysts) headline their performance in terms of volume productivity, such as sales per store, sales per square foot, sales per employee, etc.

To grow, retailers add stores and aim to increase their sales per store and will trumpet their success if they can do both at the same time. Adding stores is a relatively straightforward, predictable process that bolts on volumes, adds to market coverage, increases customer reach (increasing customer convenience) and increases buying power, which can be turned into higher margins and lower prices. Increasing sales per store requires fine-tuning of category mix, selection of product lines, ranging, merchandising, more effective marketing and tight management. In other words, increasing sales per store is the real test of a retailer's strategy and management team and this is the litmus test for analysts rating a retailer's performance.

Let's take a look at an example retailer's accounts and see how their role shapes the economic profile of their business. Throughout this part of the book we will use MNO Co Retailer as our model (Figure 19.1).

There are some key characteristics to retail financial statements:

- *High operating cost* (10.8% – $413m on sales of almost $4bn) – while operating costs vary by type of retailer, they all incur significant marketing costs in order to draw traffic to the stores and, unsurprisingly, significant costs of store operations.
- *Minimal receivables* ($48m on a business with sales of almost $4bn) – retail is often referred to as a cash business. This means that a retailer does not usually give credit to its customers, so its takings are banked each day as cash (customer credit-card payments are paid to the retailer by the credit card company within 24 hours, making them almost as good as cash or cheques). Even the retailers that do offer some form of customer credit do not usually hold the credit on their own books, using either a third-party finance company to provide the finance or an in-house

MNO Co Retailer financials

	$m			$m
Sales	3,829	**Fixed assets**		139
Cost of sales	3,311	**Current assets**		
Gross profit	**518**	Inventory	399	
Overheads	413	Accounts receivable	48	
Operating profit	**105**	Cash	323	
Interest	5	**Total current assets**		770
Profit before taxation	**100**	**Current liabilities**		
Taxation	40	Accounts payables	378	
Profit after taxation	**60**	Other	87	
		Total current liabilities		464
		Net current assets		306
		Long-term liabilities		119
		Net assets		326
		Shareholders funds		326
Income statement		**Balance sheet**		

Figure 19.1 MNO Co retailer financials

finance company, which will hold the credit balances on their books, paying the retail company immediately.

■ *Relatively fast-turning inventory* (8.3 times) – the balance sheet amount includes all types of inventory, including the products passing through distribution centres, the stockroom at the back of the store as well as the products on display on the shop floor. It is also an average across the entire range of products stocked. Clearly our example is not a grocery store as some grocery stores achieve inventory runs of 25 times per year or better. However, our example retailer, MNO, carries a large stock of spare parts and accessories for its main products so its inventory turns are dragged down by this. We'll see in Chapter 20 how the management team can improve this rather poor performance.

■ *Big payables* ($378m against inventory of $399m) – given MNO's inventory isn't turning that fast for a retailer, it is still only financing a tiny fraction of its investment in inventory. Many large retailers exploit their dominant position relative to their suppliers and extract payment terms of 90 or even 120 days. To the degree to which their payables exceeds their inventory (note there are no receivables to finance), these retailers are generating a 'cash float' which they can bank and on which they can accumulate interest. The more powerful the retailer, the more it is able to demand lengthy payment periods from suppliers, even the major brands. Global grocery retailers such as Tesco, Carrefour and Metro/ Makro generate significant interest income from this aspect of their business model, enriching their net margins.

■ *Assets are approximately equal to long-term liabilities* ($139m against $119m) – this is because most retailers lease their stores in order to maintain flexibility in their property portfolio. This is a key retail success factor, enabling them to move up to bigger premises or to move to newer malls in more vibrant parts of the town or even relocate to higher-traffic parts of the same mall. The retailer's own investment is usually limited to shop fit-out, which typically lasts less than five years. Depending on the retailer's positioning and sector, fit-out costs can be extremely expensive, but necessary to create the right environment to attract its target customers and encourage them to spend more time in the store. Retailers may own their 'back office' assets such as distribution centres, IT systems and maybe corporate offices, but generally all free cash flow is channelled into inventory.

Note that there is nothing that would distinguish the retailer's gross or net margins as these will vary significantly by retailer (as do inventory turns in practice).

It becomes easier to see how the retailer's business model works if we rearrange the components of its financials into the same logic tree structure we have used for the other types of channel business model. Figure 19.2 shows the highlights, focusing on the elements that are specific to the retailer.

For full definitions of all the measures see Chapter 20, but to understand the core of the retailer's business model we need to review how different types of retailer perform on the key performance areas shown at the bottom of the figure.

The first of these is *productivity of space* (Figure 19.3). Note: Not all retailers report using the same basis for store square footage. The majority of retailers report sales per foot on a gross basis – this includes all square feet, including in-store storage and office space. However, many retailers report data based on selling (retail) space, which is typically between 60 and 90 per cent of gross store space.

Note how there is an obvious correlation between average store size and sales per store, with the stand-out exception of jewellery stores, where Tiffany's extraordinarily strong performance and exceptional average ticket size distort the picture for this type of retailer. The domi-

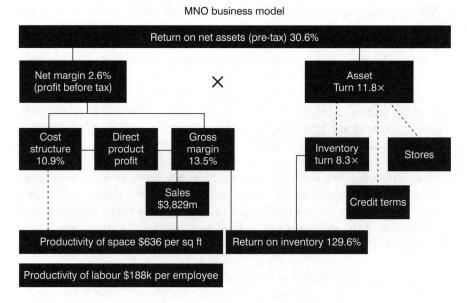

Figure 19.2 MNO business model

Type of retailer	Sales per sq ft	Basis	Average sq ft per store	Sales per store
Jewellery stores	$1,280	Gross	4,211	$7,152,256
Grocery and pharmacy stores	$623	Selling	22,607	$11,528,783
General merchandisers – large format	$467	Gross	132,743	$61,675,931
Clothing and accessory stores	$314	Gross	30,062	$8,396,376
General merchandisers – mixed format	$240	Selling	99,403	$23,984,611
Home furnishings	$240	Gross	24,284	$5,261,032
Book retailers	$230	Gross	19,473	$4,373,423
Sporting goods	$180	Gross	49,923	$9,284,224
Electronic stores	$174	Gross	28,213	$22,454,050

Source: www.Bizstats.com

Figure 19.3 Productivity of space measures for different types of retailer

nance of grocery stores in terms of the average household spend and their sophistication in terms of merchandising and marketing shows in their ability to drive almost double the productivity of most other types of retailer in terms of sales per square foot. The other strong type of player in this regard is electronics stores, which benefit from large-ticket items that do not require much space (such as cameras, MP3 players, computers, etc).

The second performance area is the *productivity of labour (or employees)*, which is more to do with the retailer's basic proposition than the quality of its employees (though well-trained, knowledgeable staff do make a difference, as we show below). Retailers choose whether they are a high- or low-service store and balance this with their ability to sell and trade up customers through the range, choice and depth of products on display and through merchandising displays. Typically we think of supermarkets in the grocery sector as low service, where the shopper browses and chooses products based on what's on the shelf. The role of staff is limited to restocking shelves and pointing customers in the direction of a particular product. In comparison, department stores tend to be high service, with staff selected to match the customer demographic ('people like us') and well trained in advising customers to select products that meet their needs. Clearly the department store format will need more staff, and possibly more expensive staff, on the shop floor than the grocery supermarket.

Figure 19.4 shows the comparisons for the different types of retailer. Note how the highest sales per employee measures relate to types of retailer that require high investments in the store format yet suffer from very low margins – gasoline or petrol stations and motor vehicle dealers. To overcome these barriers, successful petrol stations are open for long hours and experience very high volumes of traffic and motor vehicle dealers have the benefit of big-ticket sales, ie each sale is many thousands of dollars. At the other end of the scale, hardware, miscellaneous, book and clothing stores secure high margins (between 30 and 50 per cent) to compensate for their low sales per employee measures.

The third performance area is *return on inventory*, of which the most common measure is gross margin return on inventory (investment), shortened to either GMROII or GMROI. We looked at this in detail in the part on distributors where it is also a key measure, for much the same reasons that retailers use it – it can be broken down into its two key drivers, 'earn and turn' (Figure 19.5).

For retailers a healthy GRMOII means that they are earning decent margins and turning their inventory relatively quickly. Any categories or products that are not performing well can be quickly analysed to see which aspect of performance is the cause.

Type of retailer	Sales per employee
Motor vehicle and parts dealers	$375,440
Petrol stations	$214,916
Electronic and appliance stores	$198,704
Nursery and garden centres	$198,428
Home centres	$181,883
Furniture and home furnishing stores	$148,476
Supermarkets and other grocery (expect convenience stores)	$141,141
General merchandise stores	$131,780
Health and personal care stores	$130,244
Sports goods, hobby and musical instrument stores	$114,100
Convenience stores	$109,481
Clothing and clothing accessories stores	$106,548
Book, periodical and music stores	$104,089
Miscellaneous store retailers	$103,733
Hardware stores	$98,710

Source: www.Bizstats.com

Figure 19.4 Sales per employee for different types of retailer

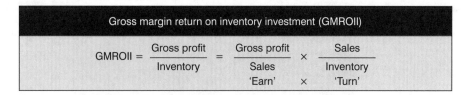

Figure 19.5 Gross margin return on inventory investment (GMROII)

Earn and turn

Retailers often describe their entire business model in terms of 'earn and turn', referring to the need to maximize the margin (earn) and the number of times they can earn that margin or velocity of inventory turn. At a very simplistic level, one can classify all retailers as tending towards one of these two models: **high earn and low turn**; or **low earn and high turn**.

Of course, there are retailers that fall into the other possible models, but relatively few because market forces either erode their advantage, if they are high-earn and high-turn players, or drive them out of business if they are low performers on both counts. Set out in Figure 19.6 is a mapping of types of retailer in terms of their typical earn and turn characteristics.

As highlighted before, the general merchandise stores (which include grocery) have managed to engineer high earn and turn models, through their buying power and professional management disciplines. In any sector, there will be retailers that have found ways to operate with either a higher earn or a higher turn than usual, but the whole sector can undergo a shake-out if a major player finds a way to outperform its competitors on both fronts. Amazon used its online proposition to improve its earn and leveraged the inventory of its publishers to minimize its investment in inventory, giving it high turns as well. Amazon's success sent shock waves rolling throughout book retailing and forced its competitors to respond through enhancing their in-store propositions, adding 'clicks' to their 'bricks' or sadly in many cases caused smaller independent retailers to go out of business. In the clothing category, Benetton developed a supply chain that enabled it to communicate the demand signal back to its factories in terms of colours and fashions and adjust its inventory several times a season, helping it to keep in stock only those lines that were selling well. This helped Benetton avoid the need to run end-of-season sales at punishing discounts, which enabled it to maintain excellent margins and sustain a high rate of sale, through avoiding stock-outs when there was a run on a particular colour or line.

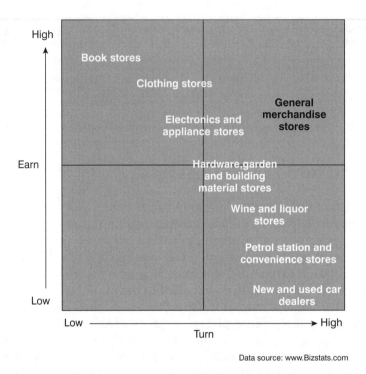

Data source: www.Bizstats.com

Figure 19.6 Mapping of types of retailer in terms of their typical 'earn' and 'turn' characteristics

Most retailers operate to a natural 'rhythm' of inventory turn, which is governed by their store size and format, ordering and inventory management processes and systems and physical stocking and handling procedures. For larger store formats, this rhythm will vary by major category (such as furniture, fashion, and electricals categories in a department store). This rhythm or natural rate of turn will shape the economic profile of the products a retailer wants to stock and sell. Grocery stores will not be interested in products that turn at half the rate of the rest of their lines, even if they offer a superior margin. For many years, this mindset tended to keep the higher-end, luxury foods out of supermarket-format grocery stores. Even a margin of up to 80 per cent on foie gras, stilton or expensive wines would not compensate for a turn that could be low single digit (when the average is mid-twenties and climbing). Plus with perishable items, the risks of spoilage and complete write-offs are much higher. More recently, rising disposable incomes, shifting consumer demographics, home eating trends and better packaging have started to make these types of products turn much more quickly and so even unusual fruits and vegetables have entered the store.

Layout and planogramming

Retailers think of products as needing to earn their place on the shelves in their stores. Their stores are bound by concrete walls and there is a finite amount of shelving in the store on which products can sit. And not all shelves are equal, so those products that sit on the most visible shelves (just below eye level) in the most highly trafficked parts of the store (front third, biased towards the right-hand side) need to justify their location or else the retailer will be shifting these products to the second-division locations. The map of where categories are sited in the store and where each product sits on the shelf is called a planogram. For large retailers with hundreds of stores, they may have a single generic planogram (fresh produce is always by the door, bread at the back of the store, etc) or planograms for different types and sizes of store and to allow for different local demographics. The level of top-down control and direction will vary with some retailers, allowing a reasonable degree of local autonomy to suit the local demographic, and others controlling everything centrally, even to the point of sending photographs of the displays along with the planograms.

Retailers have to balance category range and depth with economic performance. For example, in grocery stores, toilet rolls are poor contributors with their bulky space-occupying packages, yet no retailer would consider dropping the line! In fact Costco, one of the most economically fine-tuned business models in retail, regards toilet rolls as a major traffic builder, with an enormous proportion of its household customers timing their visits to Costco based on when they are about to run out – just take a look at the proportion of trolleys going through the checkout loaded with a mega pack of toilet rolls next time you are in one of their stores. The key is to make the product work for the retailer in other ways, so the toilet rolls are almost always stacked towards the back of the store at the end of higher-margin lines, pulling customers through the store and past these potential margin earners twice.

In any store there are several areas that can generate especially high rates of sale because of their visibility and the proportion of the in-store traffic that passes them. These are typically the areas around the check-out or cash point and queuing lines, 'end caps' or the ends of aisles, and 'dump bins', which are the bins or simply spaces for pallets in open areas towards

the front of the store and near the entrances and exits. These special locations can be used in different ways, to put the spotlight on:

■ products currently under promotion or supported by a current advertising campaign;
■ fast-moving products, which can be in both their normal/category location and in these high-attention zones to ensure there is sufficient
product on display;
■ high-margin accessories or impulse-purchase items that can benefit
from catching the customer's eye;
■ end-of-line items that are discounted to clear ('manager's specials') and
can be taken off the category space to make room for new lines;
■ special purchases or deals offered by suppliers under volume discounts
that need to flow through the stores quickly;
■ solutions or combinations of products that go together logically to make
a set, supported by display panels that explain the logic (to trade the
customer up from buying a stand-alone product).

These high-spot locations tend to stand alone and often bear no relation
to the categories around them. This is in contrast to the care that goes into
how a category is laid out to align with the customer's 'decision tree' and
to influence their selection of product. The customer's decision tree is the
retailer's key to understanding how to set the display. For example, in the
category of hair products, should the retailer group the products by
brand, by type of hair, by type of product, by size, or by price point?
Before we give the answer, compare the two decision trees shown in
Figure 19.7, which are the result of detailed research and observation.

Note how they differ – hair care starts with type of product, but in the
soft drinks category, many retailers and brands have found that customers are more loyal to the form (eg cans) than the brand. Customers would
rather switch brand than take out bottles if they went into the store to
buy cans.

In the hair care category, customers are looking for a layout that helps
them identify the type of product first, then to match their hair type, then
to suit their budget and finally to select the size they want. The smart
retailer will set the layout to support these browsing and purchasing behaviours, setting the category vertically (supported by signage and shelf labels)
and using their eye-level shelves to influence choices of brand and the
right-hand side of the shelf for the larger sizes to encourage the customer
to trade up a brand or size. These are decisions that can be influenced,
whereas no customer will be persuaded to buy shampoo when they want

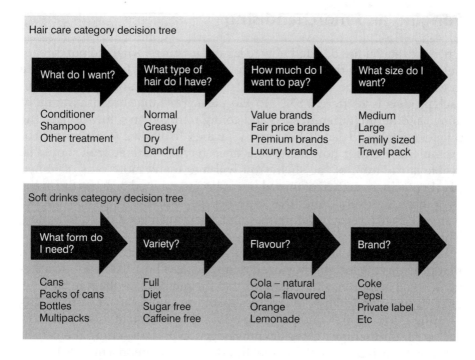

Figure 19.7 Customer decision trees for the hair care and soft drink categories

conditioner, or products for dry hair when they have normal hair. Bundles (shampoo and conditioner) and promotions (eg two for one) can be adjacent to the relevant product or size.

In the soft drinks category, retailers need to set the category by form first (ie standard-sized bottles, super-sized bottles, cans, multi-packs) and then, within each form type, start to subdivide by sugar/caffeine content, then flavour and finally brand. They may provide dumps or end caps dedicated to a particular brand (if sufficiently compensated), which may be near the category or elsewhere in the store, perhaps near the barbecue section in the summer. Some elements in the category may be repeated in multiple locations, so the cans and small screw-top bottles will also be in the lunch/snack zone, and in a mixer zone in with the alcoholic drinks category. Kodak used to aim to have its old-style film products on sale in 24 different locations in a department store.

Ranging and merchandising

Once the retailer has decided how to lay out its stores, where to put categories and how to set them out, it has to decide how much space to allocate to each category and how many SKUs (stock-keeping units – each size of each product is a different SKU) to allocate across range breadth (different items) and depth (different sizes and configurations). In some formats, the retailer even has to decide how many 'facings' to allocate to each item. For example, in a grocer, how many cans of each type of tinned fruit should be visible at the front of the shelf? You will find many more cans of tinned peaches facing you than of tinned pears, because tinned peaches fly off the shelf at a rate several times that of tinned pears and the retailer does not want the shelf to empty before the shelf-stacker can get around to replenishing it.

Large retailers and major brands can afford to do the consumer research that provides the insight they need to understand how to lay out the category. Some brands become so expert that the retailer asks them to be 'category captain' and hands over to them the responsibility for organizing ('setting') the entire category, including their competitors' products. Kellogg's, for example, is the acknowledged expert on setting the cereals category, which can contain several hundred SKUs (spend a minute browsing the sheer variety of cereals, flavours, sizes of packet, etc, next time you are in a big grocer). Kellogg's has built years of research and experience into its allocation algorithms for space and location and can set the cereals category for any type of retailer in any location of any size. The retailer doesn't just hand over its shelves to a major brand, of course, but sets demanding objectives in terms of required improvements in sales and margin per square foot, inventory turns, proportion of sales made from products on promotion, even the average basket size related to key brands. And it expects to see a number of special programmes and promotions that are unique to its retail brand.

The retailer needs to synchronize its category merchandising and stocking levels with the key seasons and the major brands' advertising and promotion campaigns, so that demand is met with supply in store. To do this many retailers plan their promotional calendars up to nine months ahead, wanting to know what their suppliers will be introducing in terms of new products, promotional campaigns and how much they will be investing in marketing dollars and merchandising funds. Some categories are highly seasonal (garden products), others are tied to range updates (clothes) and technology breakthroughs (electricals, computers, cameras) and yet others are event or even weather driven. For many years, Coca-Cola dominated the sales of soft drinks for grocers because it could guarantee to restock the category several times a day if summer temperatures soared, with its local bottler-based logistics. Different store formats lend themselves to different point-of-sales material. Specialist shops can adopt a comprehensive 'dressing' to align with advertising and marketing campaigns and harness the increased awareness and preference generated. Stores that do not have the space for extensive posters and display materials may employ leaflets and mail drops in the local community, backed up by greeters or in-store demonstrations and trials. Generally all of these are either provided or paid for by the suppliers whose products are under promotion, plus a payment to the retailer for the privilege.

In merchandising the store, there is a considerable difference between retailers which are visited by their customers on a regular basis, such as grocery or department stores, and those which are visited only occasionally by any one customer, such as speciality stores. The challenge for high-frequency stores is the need to stimulate interest and demand, drawing attention to the current promotions and programmes essential to increasing the average basket and enriching margins. Customers resent major resets that cause them to have to relearn the layout of the store, so regular recycling of the end caps and dumps becomes critical. However, more recently, the use of generic mailers and adverts containing basic 'calls to action', such as 'Bar B Q ingredients and sauces are on special offer for this weekend only', have been replaced by coupons printed on till receipts and direct mail sent to loyalty-card-carrying customers. Point-of-sale (POS) data capture is becoming increasing sophisticated, allowing retailers to target their offers at customers who are most likely to respond. Thus, offers for gluten-free cakes and biscuits can be targeted only at customers who have bought gluten-free bread, and incentives for bulk packs of pet food can be targeted at pet owners. These marketing techniques help the retailers address their greatest challenge – getting the customer to come back. In fact retailers want the customer to come back sooner and more often and smart marketing strategies based on tracking customer behaviour can be very powerful. These techniques are not restricted just to the fast-moving consumer goods in mass merchant stores, but can be just as effective when applied to other types of retailer, including speciality stores. For example, a digital camera will potentially trigger the need for a whole host of additional purchases such as memory cards, cables, a tripod, extra lenses, followed by a photo printer which in turn will require ink, paper, paper trays and then an external hard drive to store all the photos taken and so on. By timing its offers and incentives carefully, ie in relation to the customer's original purchase, the retailer can accelerate these purchases and ensure they are made in the same store (the consumer may not even have thought of their digital camera store as somewhere to consider purchasing a hard drive).

Increasingly, as customer-based data becomes available, retailers are recognizing that customers are not all equal. Analysis of many retailers' customer profitability has shown that typically the top 20 per cent of customers deliver 50 per cent of the retailer's profit (and the bottom 20 per cent actually cost the retailer money to do business with). Until recently there was very little the retailer could do about this as it puts out its wares and invites customers in to shop. However, with targeted communications and offers, loyalty cards and further technologies, retailers will effectively be able to offer differentiated service levels, pricing and unique offers to those customers who deliver the greatest value to them. And in the process, if they happen to drive away their least profitable or loss-making customers, retailers won't be too disappointed. More likely they will be able to engage these customers in such a way as to change their buying behaviours to become profitable for the retailer. Customers can be quick learners, as evidenced by their learning to buy from carpet shops only during sales, as these seem to come around ever more frequently with ever-bigger discounts.

Retailers need to learn to adapt their business models fast too or else those that 'pile them high and sell them cheap' are going to find themselves outplayed in the very competitive environment of modern retailing.

20

The measures that matter and how to manage with them

Sales (or takings or revenues)

In retail, everyone pays attention to sales. Chief executives expect to see yesterday's takings on their desks by 10.00am or earlier each day, probably broken down by geography, type of store, perhaps time store has been open or since it was last refitted and with comparisons to the same day last year. And everyone else in the management chain will be scrutinizing the sales for their part of the business. The reports may also include sales for the week to date, month to date or year to date, again with comparisons with the same point last year.

Let's look at two retailers, Mums' Stores and Dads' Stores, and see what sort of year they have had (Figure 20.1).

The headline in simple sales terms is that Dads' Stores has outperformed Mums' Stores by increasing its sales by 20 per cent compared to 12 per cent. But this hides some interesting differences between the strategies of the two retailers:

■ *Average store size* – Mums' Stores clearly operates a big store format, with its average store size in terms of sales space well over 35,000 square feet compared to Dads' Stores with approximately 11,000 square feet, but

Mums' Stores' newer stores are smaller than average so that by the end of the current year its store size has fallen to 96% of the previous year. Dads' Stores on the other hand is opening bigger stores increasing its average store size by 3% (Figure 20.2).

■ *Store openings* – Mums' Stores is slowing its rate of store openings from 10% in the prior year to 9% in the current, whereas Dads' Stores is on a steady 12% increase in its store portfolio.

	Mums' Stores	Change over prior year	Dads' Stores	Change over prior year
Sales prior year $m	$4,095,879		$1,007,314	
Sales current year $m	$4,575,682	112%	$1,205,128	120%
Prior year sales of stores that have been open one year or more	$3,891,085		$926,729	
Current year sales of stores that have been open one year or more	$4,209,627	108%	$1,084,616	117%
Stores open at start of prior year	250		300	
Stores open at start of current year	275	110%	335	112%
Stores open at end of current year	300	109%	375	112%
Sales per store prior year (average)	**$15,603,348**		**$3,172,643**	
Sales per store current year (average)	**$15,915,415**	102%	**$3,394,728**	107%
Sales space (000 square feet) at start of prior year	9,950		3,200	
Sales space (000 square feet) at start of current year	10,250	103%	3,750	117%
Sales space (000 square feet) at end of current year	11,000	107%	4,250	113%
Sales per square foot prior year (average)	**$406**		**$290**	
Sales per square foot current year (average)	**$431**	106%	**$301**	104%
Prior year average store size	38,476		10,945	
Current year average store size	36,957	96%	11,268	103%

Figure 20.1 Summary of performance measures for Mums' Stores and Dads' Stores

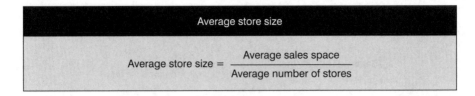

Figure 20.2 Average store size

■ *Sales per store (or store productivity)* – here Dads' Stores has clearly done well, growing at the rate of 7%, which exceeds the gain in average store size of 3% (Figure 20.3). Mums' Stores has actually done even better because although it has only improved store productivity by 2%, it has done this with a *reduction* in average store size of 4%. This is reflected in the fact that it has grown its sales space by only 7% compared with store increases of 9%. Dads' Stores by contrast has added 13% of sales space, more or less in line with its store count gain of 12%.

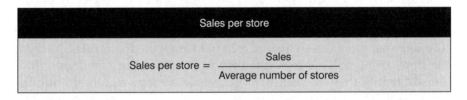

Figure 20.3 Sales per store

■ *Sales per square foot (or sales space productivity)* – this is how Mums' Stores has managed to deliver the improvement in sales per store noted above, by increasing its sales productivity by 6% compared to Dads' Stores' 4% (Figure 20.4). In terms of year-on-year improvement, this is pretty impressive, especially given its larger format.
■ *Same store sales (or comparable store sales or like-for-like sales)* – these are sales of stores that have been opened for one year or more. Because it takes time for a new store to ramp up to full productivity, analysts will often turn to this measure to filter out the effect of distortions caused by a rapid store expansion programme. Sometimes referred to as 'Comps' sales, we can see that Dads' Stores has done an extraordinary job in its established stores, which have added a whopping 17% in sales gains. Mums' Stores has also done well with an 8% gain in Comps.

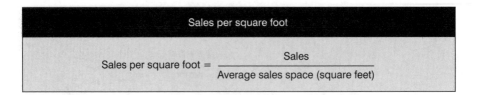

Figure 20.4 Sales per square foot

So to summarize, **Mums' Stores** has added 9 per cent to its store portfolio but, by opening smaller stores, has added only 7 per cent to its sales space. The new stores have been a slight drag on sales productivity, which has improved by only 6 per cent, whereas its established stores have improved by 8 per cent. By adopting a steady expansion plan focusing on slightly smaller stores, Mums' Stores has increased overall sales by 12 per cent

Dad's Stores has embarked on a more ambitious expansion strategy, with a 12 per cent increase in the store portfolio (with stores that are slightly larger than average, increasing sales space by 13 per cent) multiplied by a 7 per cent increase in sales per store. The new stores have clearly been a fairly high drag factor because their performance is well below same-store sales, which were 17 per cent higher. The combination of more stores and more sales per store has delivered a 20 per cent increase in sales. As these new stores come fully up to speed, they will power future sales growth.

In addition to these measures, larger retailers with a significant number of stores will track **store density**, which is expressed as stores per thousand population. For example, in a market with 55 million people a retailer with 1,050 stores would have a density of 1 store per 52,000 people (= 55m divided by 1,050). This measure, when applied to sub-markets, helps determine where there are opportunities to open more stores. For example, in some cities the density may be 1 store per 25,000 but in others the density may be 1 per 200,000, which indicates that the city with the higher number may support additional stores, unless the demographic profile is extremely unattractive. Franchise systems often use this measure to guide store development and to reassure existing franchisees that a new store will not jeopardize current business. Some quick-service restaurants have achieved densities as low as 1 store (or restaurant) per 10,000 population in mature markets. Department stores may be concerned that they are approaching saturation if density falls below 1 per 100,000. Saturation is determined by the store size and expected visit frequency. Larger stores need lower densities, and high visit frequency supports higher densities.

Almost all retailers are **seasonal** to some extent, not least because retailers use seasons to drive promotional calendars and they time refreshes of store merchandising to motivate customers to return to the store and to encourage increased expenditure. Typical retail seasons include Christmas/Holidays (December), Back to School (September), Vacations (July/August in the northern hemisphere), and the artificial seasons created around clearance sales, usually twice a year (January, August). The chart in Figure 20.5 shows the degree to which different types of retailer are seasonal, ranked in order of most sales in quarter 4 (ie most seasonal) from top in bottom.

There are probably few surprises in this table, with jewellery retailers showing 39 per cent of their sales in the quarter that contains Christmas/Holidays, and building materials and car dealers showing the least degree of seasonality with 23 per cent of their sales in this quarter. The seasonal distortion of sales across the quarters means that it is very important to compare sales to the equivalent quarter, month or week in the previous year to measure how well a retailer is performing. Some retailers will even highlight the day of the week that Christmas falls in a given year because a Saturday Christmas could mean one or two more selling days in one year compared to the prior year.

Margins

Margins are the 'earn' in the earn and turn model of the retailer and as such there are several specialist margin terms that are used in retailers as well as the concept of 'mark-up', which is sometimes used interchangeably with margin, even though these are quite different measures. Let's start with the difference between **gross margin** and **mark-up** (Figure 20.6).

For example, a garment purchased from a supplier for $80 and sold to a customer for $160 would have been marked up 100 per cent to realize a gross margin of 50 per cent, so you can see it's quite important to clarify whether the numbers you are looking at are margins or mark-ups.

Retailers in many sectors commit to buying decisions many months ahead of the products arriving in store for sale to customers. These decisions are made when suppliers show their new product ranges, negotiate volumes and prices with the retailer, and secure minimum commitments, fill rates (the rate at which the commitment will be shipped into stores) and the volume break-points at which additional discounts on prices will be given. In the course of the negotiation, both retailer and supplier consider

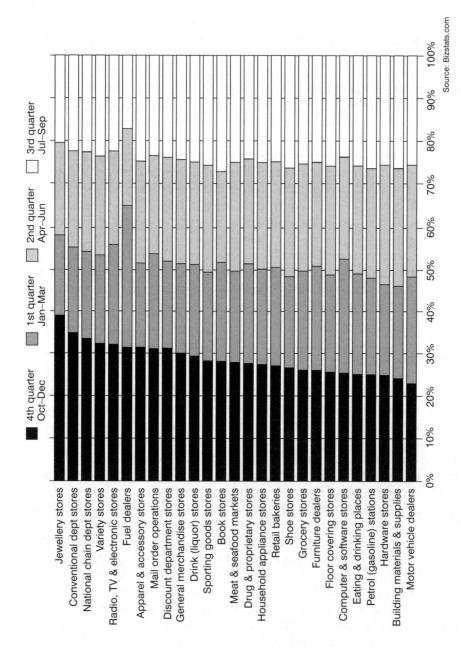

Figure 20.5 Retailer seasonality

Source: Bizstats.com

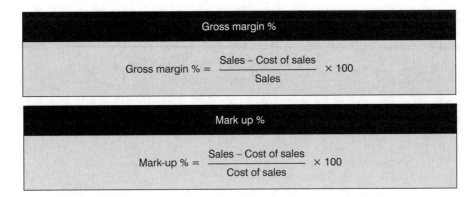

Figure 20.6 Gross margin % and mark up %

the expected street price that the consumer will pay. Ultimately the street price is the retailer's own decision, but the supplier will have worked to bring its costs into line with the expected street price and retailer gross margin. In most legal jurisdictions, suppliers can recommend a price to the retailer. In some categories (such as electricals), suppliers will have aimed at hitting particular price points with their products and engineered the specification back from the price. When the deal with the supplier is struck, the retailer has determined its **buying margin**. By the time the product arrives in store, many things may have changed:

■ Competitor retailers may be using that product as a 'loss leader' or to communicate their low prices to the market.
■ Better or more popular products may reduce the price the market is willing to pay for the product.
■ The product may not sell well, requiring the retailer to mark down its street prices to clear it off its shelves.
■ The product may have gone into short supply, enabling the retailer to mark up its prices to capitalize on its good availability.

The effect of these and many other possible factors is that the retailer is likely to achieve a gross margin different from the buying margin when it actually sells the product. The actual margin is termed the **achieved margin**. Note that both the numerator and denominator are different in these two margins (Figure 20.7).

For example, a retailer agrees to carry a new product based on an expected retail price of $99. It buys the product from the supplier at $80. Once in the

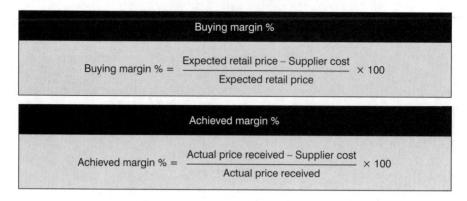

Figure 20.7 Buying margin % and achieved margin %

stores, the retailer manages to sell the product at 1 per cent below expected retail price. Look at the effect of this on the retailer's business model. First, establish the actual street price obtained, which is $98.01 (expected retail price of $99 minus 1 per cent). Thus:

■ the buying margin = 19.19% (99–80/99);
■ the achieved margin = 18.37% (98.01–80/98.01);
■ the drop in margin achieved is 4.27% (19.19–18.37/19.19).

So by reducing the street price by 1 per cent, the retailer has seen its gross margin fall by 4.27 per cent. This leveraged impact on margins is one reason why large retail chains allow their store managers only a very little discretion to mark down prices or to grant special discounts to customers. They have learnt from bitter experience that controlling prices is the key to controlling margins.

What can retailers do to manage their margins and drive them upwards? Gross margins are directly affected by both the key strategic decisions as to the retailer's core proposition and the tactical decisions taken on a daily basis to compete effectively in what is usually a highly competitive market environment. The major levers or decisions available to a retailer to manage its margins are set out in Figure 20.8.

The bigger or more powerful the retailer, the more these decisions can be driven with the collaboration and support of its suppliers. For example, major electrical retailers with large numbers of stores may command exclusive models or even entire brands to prevent customers from being able to exploit price-matching promises across retailers: Dixons Stores Group in

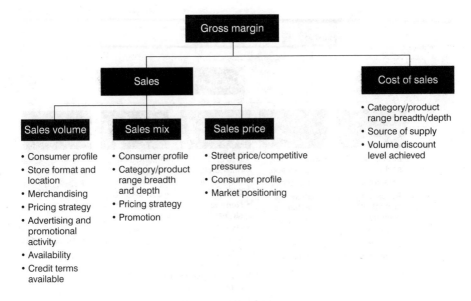

Figure 20.8 Retailer profitability levers – gross margin

the UK distributed the Compaq brand from Hewlett-Packard exclusively for a period; and Sony, Panasonic, Electrolux, etc, provide unique model numbers to each of their major retailers.

The same leverage can be applied to marketing where retailers seek promotions from suppliers that are unique to them and draw traffic to only their stores. These activities are expensive to design and implement and only make sense for the supplier for its strategic retail accounts with enough volume over which to amortize the costs.

Smaller retailers cannot look to their suppliers to customize any marketing support. The support they get from suppliers is entirely focused on promoting the suppliers' brands within any retailer's store, such as freezers to hold ice creams or fridges to hold cold drinks, both of which will be highly merchandised with the brand's messaging. (However, the cost saving to the retailer is worthwhile and will improve net margins.)

As we highlighted in Chapter 19, the retailer needs to ensure that its business volumes and margins are adequate to cover its relatively high fixed costs and earn a healthy net margin. There are other factors which it should manage to enable it to drive and improve net margins (Figure 20.9).

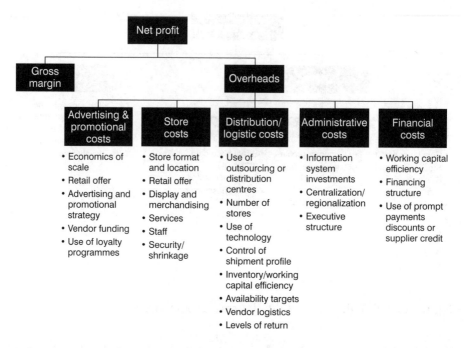

Figure 20.9 Retailer profitability levers – net margin

Many of these cost elements take time to change, as they reflect significant investment commitments and, once made, need to be leveraged over several years in order to generate the return expected. For this reason, larger retailers looking to refurbish stores and freshen up their store image will run one or more pilots in different parts of the market in order to reduce the risk of making an expensive mistake that could take a long time and/or a lot of money to correct.

Direct product cost (DPC) and direct product profitability (DPP)

Larger and more sophisticated retailers recognize that two products with the same gross margin may not deliver the same contribution to net profit, for a variety of reasons:

■ physical characteristics such as size, weight and fragility;

- rate of stock turn;
- risk of pilferage or shrinkage;
- shipping and invoicing accuracy of the products' suppliers.

These characteristics drive what are known as direct product costs (DPC). Retailers look to their suppliers to mitigate some of these costs through demanding funds to support their marketing and store costs. The net direct product costs are deducted from the gross profit (and any related other supplier rebates, etc, are added) to calculate the direct product profitability (DPP) (Figure 20.10).

An example shows how this works in practice. Shown in Figure 20.11 is part of the product portfolio of products in a computer store. You can see from this example that two products that generate a similar average gross margin can deliver a very different DPP depending on their physical characteristics. Small, high-value items such as digital cameras which the retailer can put into a vertical display containing perhaps 20 to 30 models taking up only three or four square feet of shelf space can drive very high returns on space. Similarly, they take up very little space as they go through the supply chain or in the warehouse. Perhaps their only disadvantage is the need to keep them secure against internal or external theft, as they make

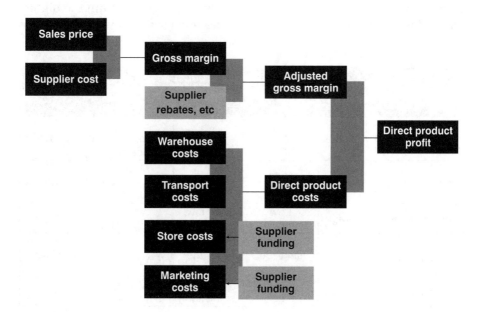

Figure 20.10 Components of direct product profit (DPP)

for attractive and easy pickings for the unscrupulous, which will add some cost. Note also how the personal computer (PC) and laptop computers trade places when you examine their DPP against their gross margins as the laptop takes up less space, weighs less and typically customers of laptops know what they want so need less attention in the store. So what? Well, which line will you find displaying more models on the retailer's shelves – the one with the better gross margin or the better DPP? Take a look next time you are in a computer store – you can guarantee that there will be almost twice as many laptops as there are PCs on display!

Within the store and within the category, retailers that use DPP measures adjust the balance of product lines and products to optimize their business model using a template along the lines shown in Figure 20.12. The retailer has to protect category integrity (eg a computer store has to have a reasonable number of PCs), so will not manage its ranging and merchandising decisions entirely based on product DPP and volume profiles. It will certainly put pressure on its suppliers to address the losers and align its marketing programmes and promotions with the actions shown in the different quadrants.

In addition to the product characteristics, some retailers will also apply a vendor-loading to the DPP to reflect the costs of doing business with that vendor. For example, a major brand that advertises heavily, driving traffic to any store that sells the product, will receive a higher loading (ie higher DPP) than a small brand that relies on the retailer for its visibility. Other

Product	Gross margin	Direct product costs			DPP
		Warehouse costs	Transport costs	Store costs	
Personal computer (PC)	Average	High (bulky)	High (heavy)	High (large footprint, advice needed)	Low
Printer	Average	High (bulky)	High (heavy)	Average (large footprint, demo attention)	Low
Consumables	Average	Low (small)	Very low (small/light)	Very low (small footprint)	High
Laptop computer	Low	Average (small but delicate)	Average	Low (small footprint)	Average
Digital camera	Average	Low (small)	Low (small/light)	Very low (small footprint)	High

Figure 20.11 Illustrative comparisons of DPC and DPP

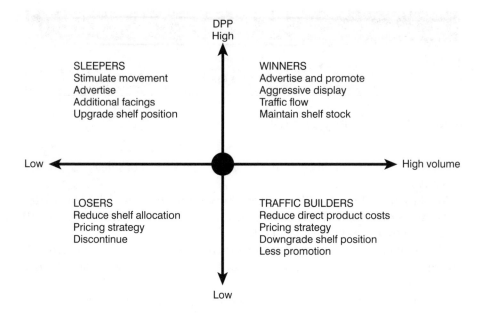

Figure 20.12 Application of DPP to segment products or categories

factors that may go into the loading include supply chain performance, credit days allowed and, of course, allowances paid by the vendor for putting the products on special display, on promotion, etc.

Turns and productivity

Inventory turns are the 'turn' in the earn and turn model of the retailer and there are several ways in which retailers look to measure the rate at which products are driving this critical part of the business model, related to their scarcest resource (after cash!) – space.

Let's start with the basic measures of how fast the retailer is turning over its inventory – inventory days and inventory turn. The time spent in inventory is known as **inventory days** or **days in inventory (DIO)** and is calculated as shown in Figure 20.13.

Note that cost of sales is used as both inventory and cost of sales are valued at cost (sales would include a margin on the product and so would distort our calculation). For our example retailer MNO from Chapter 19,

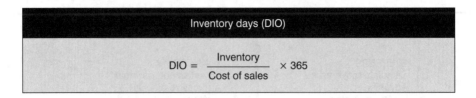

Figure 20.13 Inventory days (DIO)

inventory days are 44 days (= inventory of \$399k/Cost of sales of \$3,311k × 365 days).

Most retailers tend to talk in terms of inventory turn, which is calculated as shown in Figure 20.14. For our example retailer MNO from Chapter 19, inventory turn is 8.3 (365 days/44 days).

The retailer can measure inventory turns or days at every level from its entire inventory across all its stores and drill down by store or category, product line or vendor, right down to an individual SKU. This means that it can identify slow-moving items that are dragging down the performance of its portfolio of products in a category or store.

The disadvantage of these two measures is that they do not reflect the ticket price of the items concerned, or their profitability. So retailers use additional measures to round out their assessment of which products are earning their place on their shelves – **sales per square foot** (see also under Sales) and **profit per square foot** (Figure 20.15). These measures can also be applied at every level, from the entire sales of the retailer down to an individual SKU, provided the retailer measures its space allocation at such a low level of granularity.

Retailers accept that different categories will have different productivity profiles, with some categories delivering good sales per square foot because of their high ticket prices but perhaps average profit per square foot because of relatively low inventory turns, while other categories may deliver excel-

$$\text{Inventory turn} = \frac{365 \text{ days}}{\text{Inventory days}}$$

Inventory turn

Figure 20.14 Inventory turn

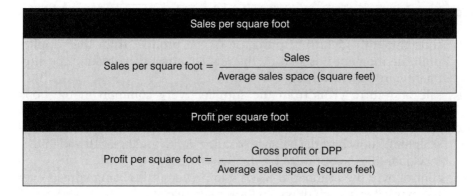

Figure 20.15 Sales and profit per square foot

lent performance across the three measures. Much of a retailer's skill lies in understanding the links and adjacencies between product lines and categories and not simply managing its product listings 'by the numbers'. For example, a photography retailer may find its leading brands of cameras turn over quite quickly, but competition on prices may mean that the profit per square foot is dismal. However, by stocking a fairly complete range of the leading brands the retailer is validating its own customer proposition and attracting a good customer footfall in the store. Every camera sale represents the opportunity to cross-sell a range of lenses, accessories and consumables that deliver an excellent profit per square foot.

What can a retailer do to improve its turn and productivity measures? There are many tactical options available, including customer-focused actions:

■ merchandising – better display and layout to simplify customer selection and purchase process; cluttered displays and muddled assortments confuse the customer... and a confused customer is not a buyer;
■ advertising – to increase demand and interest in particular items;
■ promotions – to incentivize customers to buy/buy more;
■ in-store sales assistance – to encourage trial and purchase;

and supply-chain or supplier-focused actions:

■ auto replenishment programmes – algorithm-driven systems to ensure orders for replacing line items are timed and sized for optimizing the balance between minimal inventories and suffering stock-outs;

- inventory rotation – ensuring that the oldest products are sold out first;
- consignment – deferring purchase of the product from the supplier until the moment it is sold by the retailer, effectively making the supplier finance the inventory;
- sale or return terms from the supplier (very common in the book trade);
- vendor-managed inventory – for complex categories, the leading supplier may know best the balance of range depth and breadth and inventory quantities to optimize productivity;
- control over the number of SKUs – to prevent sales being spread over too many items, each of which loses sales velocity;
- frequent shipment – reduces the level of inventory required by the retailer and minimizes the risk or period of a stock-out.

The retailer may need to combine several of these actions in order to improve performance.

In this chapter we have concentrated on the measures that are specific to retailers. However, in many ways, the mass-merchandising retailers' business model is a 'product business' and as such bears many similarities to that of the distributor. You will find that Part 2 on distributors has many relevant insights on the core business model and these will augment your understanding of the trade-offs retailers have to make to optimize their business performance. And the more specialized a retailers' business, the more its business model is similar to that of the higher-end service models covered in Part 3.

21

How to sell to retailers

What we mean by selling to retailers

It can be hard at times when dealing with retailers to remember that they are **not** the customer! They are simply a channel to reach the customer and so, when 'selling' to a retailer, you will be selling a commercial relationship that creates economic value for the business models of both supplier and retailer. Many suppliers find retailers, especially the major chains, brutal to deal with and feel that they are squeezed by the retailers' power to control access to the consumers they need to reach. In more fragmented retail channels this is less of a challenge, and as we shall show, there are some powerful ways for the supplier to work with even the largest retail chains to build economic value for both supplier and retailer by concentrating on delivering value to the consumer. Suppliers who get sucked into the 'zero-sum' game of trading blows with retailers will end up losing market access or profitability and sometimes both.

Before diving into the specifics of working with retailers, you may find it useful to revisit the key elements of a channel value proposition set out in section 17.3 (What the final tier looks for in vendor), especially the framework of growth, profit and productivity. This framework is equally valid for retailers and it will provide a useful checklist of considerations.

The sales process

As in all forms of selling, it pays to understand the party across the desk better than your competitors do and, in dealing with retailers, it is critical that you can relate to their changing world. This means understanding the major trends and forces shaping the retail sector in general as well as the consumer trends affecting the success of individual retail propositions and business models. Retailers are facing challenges as never before and, though they will rarely admit it, need their suppliers to partner with them in addressing these challenges. They can no longer win by bludgeoning their suppliers into submission. In this section we set out some of the generic forces shaping the retail landscape with their implications for retailers and thus the opportunities these open for suppliers. You will need to validate which of these forces are relevant to the retailers you want to develop as routes to market and the specific opportunities they create for you. The senior management of the top retailers recognizes the need for new levels of supplier partnership and is looking for suppliers who can raise their game above the classic 'buy–sell' relationship. We will show the various levels through which a supplier–retailer relationship can be developed, but first you need to understand the underlying challenges facing retailers.

Retailer challenges and their implications for suppliers

The picture depends who you are dealing with in the retail channel but almost every retailer is experiencing significant and pervasive shifts in consumer expectations, spending patterns, attitudes and behaviour. This is coupled with wider market trends and economic drivers:

■ globalization and the growth imperative;
■ changes in the consumer experience;
■ moving from products to services;
■ the evolving retail offer.

Globalization and the growth imperative

Until relatively recently, retailing had resisted the pressure to 'go global', on the basis that the buying habits of shoppers in different countries were too dissimilar to be able to extend proven formats from one country to another. However, successful retailers are testing this orthodoxy by looking for growth through international expansion. Examples include: Wal-Mart entering Europe, Latin America and Asia; Staples and Office Depot expanding overseas; Tesco expanding in Eastern Europe and Asia; and Carrefour consolidating its position in Latin America and the Far East. It is still early in many cases to gauge the success of these moves, but the impact on local markets has been significant. The arrival – or threatened arrival – of international players in local markets has been the catalyst for major changes, including the consolidation of local players, the formation of alliances and experiments with international operations by national retailers. These pressures have highlighted some of the limitations of the more decentralized players, who struggle to achieve consistency of brand experience.

For the most successful retailers, domestic markets are now too static to satisfy their need for sustained growth. Arguments encouraging expansion and acquisition in new territories include:

■ Shareholder pressure – for revenue growth and bottom-line improvements through economies of scale in purchasing, logistics and other cost areas.
■ Available resources – retailers are cash-rich and have traditionally enjoyed relatively favourable stock valuations.
■ Replicable formulas – leading retailers are now confident that their business models and approaches can succeed in widely differing territories.
■ Global outlook – globalization has made leading businesses look to global rather than local synergies and capabilities, including global sourcing, promotions and supplier pricing.
■ Enabling technology – global information technology management systems are now easier to set up and maintain.
■ Supplier dynamics – suppliers of consumer goods are international businesses. Regionally and globally managed retailer–supplier relationships are becoming an established feature of the retail environment.

Globalization is good news for those retailers who can carry it off. In addition to delivering much-needed growth, it offers the potential to strengthen their negotiating position with suppliers. It has also been the undoing of many famous retail brands and can take many years before success is secured. Even the mighty Wal-Mart, after over 10 years of ownership, has struggled to make its acquisitions in Germany and the UK perform in line with US benchmarks.

What do globalization and the growth imperative mean for suppliers?

Globalization makes leading retailers more powerful, and suppliers need to be proactive if they want to play an effective role. Suppliers who share their knowledge of, and expertise in, local markets are valuable allies for expanding retail businesses (to help reduce the risks of failure to adapt to local market conditions and expectations). As suppliers, you must be prepared to work with retailers on a national, regional or global basis as appropriate. Anticipating and managing potential conflicts with your own local organizations and established local retailers becomes more critical – it is pretty challenging persuading a local operation to dedicate more time and resource on what to them might be their 27th-largest account in local terms because it is the your 2nd-largest account globally, and even more challenging if the local number one account is a national player feeling threatened by the international new entrant you are perceived to be helping. Roles and responsibilities within your organization need to be reviewed to reflect new retailer relationships. Above all, retailers want to present a consistent face to the world. They look to suppliers for consistent service, quality and support. If these standards are achieved, performance by both parties will be rewarded with access to previously untapped markets.

Changes in the consumer experience

Consumers now have a greater choice of products and delivery channels than ever before. They are better equipped to make informed purchasing decisions, with easy access to high-quality information about products and services – particularly on performance and pricing – in traditional and new media formats. In addition to established industry and non-industry commentary, consumer word-of-mouth has become a key information channel in the form of published consumer reviews and referrals, particularly over the internet (just type 'I hate McDonalds' into Google and see the array of sites that appear... and how well organized some of them are). Retailers are detecting a growing preference among consumers for customized products and service offerings. Faced with a greater number and variety of complex offerings, consumers are looking for help, guidance and reassurance from brands they trust. Even for commodity items, consumers do not simply buy and respond to 'things' – they are looking for an enhanced customer experience, and shopping is only a part of it. Increasingly, consumers want to be entertained as part of the buying experience and will favour retailers who offer more than just the selection and purchase of goods. Service solutions are seen as the key to gaining a bigger share of individual customer spend. Reaching the consumer now encompasses everything from providing information, through product purchase and the provision of ancillary services, to maintenance, disposal and replacement. The brand message to the consumer is the same, but now there are many more touch points in the experience.

Using customer information

Advances in digital technologies are helping retailers to identify and target consumer needs. Both retailers and suppliers are building databases at considerable cost, but few have the resources to mine fully their data and develop extensive consumer insight. As yet, there has been limited progress in collaboration between retailers and suppliers to exploit the wealth of information being collected. Customer relationship management (CRM) technologies, when applied with intelligence and a focused strategy, can enhance the ability of retailers to track all interactions with consumers, whether in-store, online or through catalogues, and to tailor offers accordingly. The number of retailers doing this well is still small, but will start to grow.

The modal consumer

Consumers demand a variety of forms of access to products and services to suit their individual circumstances. The same consumer will behave differently depending what **mode** he or she are in – worker, family member, private individual, browser, bargain hunter, impulse shopper, convenience shopper, and so on. For proof of this, consider the different price you are prepared to pay for bottled water depending on whether you are doing the weekly grocery shop (very low), dining out in a fine restaurant (very high), stopping at a motorway service station (moderately low) or gasping of thirst at a pop concert or other big event (moderately high). Consumers now expect to be able to get what they want, when and how they want it, wherever they are.

Impact of the internet

The internet has not and will not replace traditional retailing, but it has become an important additional channel, augmenting existing store and catalogue formats. Its power will increase in line with improvements in bandwidth and usability. Consumers will continue to use established channels as well as newer ones. However, the internet is becoming an extremely powerful tool to influence product and channel choice. Trust in established brands is a key factor. Very few of the internet-only retailers have survived through to today's era of 'Web 2.0'. In markets where web-based retailing is strong, this reflects the aggressive development of the online channel by existing ('bricks-based' and catalogue-based) retail brands rather than the emergence of pure web-based retailers. The internet is well on the way to becoming a channel for the mass market and many retailers are now actively encouraging their consumers to flit seamlessly between their online and offline channels as they progress through the shopping and purchasing process.

What do these changes in the consumer experience mean for the supplier?

Retailers and their suppliers need to leverage their joint strengths and attributes in order to deliver complete product-service solutions. Neither side has a monopoly on consumer insight; nor can they go it alone. As consumer behaviour becomes increasingly modal, the opportunities to serve will be more varied, whether in-store, off-the-page or online. Retailers want to work with existing suppliers who can master multiple formats and channels, rather than look for new suppliers, but they will shift if necessary. A key focus for greater retailer–supplier collaboration is the pooling of consumer and market information in order to: target profitable segments with appropriate products and value-added services; and devise retail propositions that address the total consumer experience across channels – from information search through purchase and ownership to disposal and replacement.

Helping consumers make sense of complex new products and services – and packaging them for easy consumption – is a key success factor and a focus for retail innovation. Both suppliers and retailers must help consumers understand which offerings are relevant to them. Tesco online does this brilliantly by uploading customers' shopping lists from in-store shopping (captured through Club Card identities attached to POS data), so that they can easily find the particular loaf of bread, etc, that they usually purchase – instead of trying to spot it from the 133 types of loaf available online).

Suppliers must ensure that they measure up to the challenge of supporting and fulfilling the promise behind the extended retail offer. Suppliers do not just sell products, but also the image, culture, values and associations that support and enhance those products (otherwise why would so many of us wear clothes and shoes where the maker's brand is prominently displayed?). Competitive advantage is now determined by gaining insight into consumer lifestyle across categories, and from segmenting and targeting consumers on that basis. Suppliers need to focus on defining consumer segments based on desired experience, and on selecting the right retail partners to deliver appropriate propositions. Branding issues are becoming more complex. Consumers continue to look to trusted brands as products and channels proliferate to help them navigate through what at times is a bewildering array of choices. As a supplier, you need to determine how you can leverage your brand alongside retailer and third-party brands to ensure front-of-mind among your target segments. Brands, whether manufacturer or retailer, drive customer traffic and loyalty, and there is an increasing use of joint brand equity to enhance the consumer experience. A good example of this from the early 2000s was the joint marketing of anti-virus/parental control software by Dixons Stores (the retailer) and McAfee (the supplier). Dixon's component of the proposition was 'easy to use and install software' as its entire proposition was 'when technology stuff is sold by us, it is suitable for ordinary families'. McAfee's component of the marketing proposition was 'we know how to protect computers (and users) from nasty viruses and internet porn and worse'. It needed both components to give the proposition credibility and traction with the target market.

Moving from products to services

Product offerings themselves are evolving from pure product, through enhanced products, to related products and services and on to lifestyle solutions. As the retailers' offer moves beyond item and price, service is a potential key differentiator in the overcrowded market space. In search of new sources of growth, retailers are:

■ leveraging their existing core merchandising, customer relations, brand strength, product strength and the scale of their operations;
■ starting to offer interrelated products, services and information;

■ entering new fields where they can apply their strengths and redefine their market offerings.

Multiple channels

Successful retailers are applying their knowledge of multiple distribution channels and the strength of their partnerships and alliances to create new services and products for consumers. As a result, retailer organizations are becoming more complex, with a greater number of touch points for suppliers to manage. For example, the Dixons Store Group now has shops in a variety of formats (including Currys, Currys.*digital*, PC World, Dixons Tax Free and The Link), each of these has an online selling motion, and PC World has a business-focused, online presence as well as a corporate contracts capability and a business telecoms reseller. As a supplier you have to be very clear in which of these channels you expect your product to show up and be prepared to work to ensure that your marketing funding is aligned with your objectives, not the retailer's.

New competitors

New competitors are also offering interrelated products and services. Banks, utilities and media groups have become competitors in some contexts – and potential partners for retailers in others. Traditional retailers have inherent advantages over their new rivals, including brand loyalty, infrastructure, successful fulfilment and long-term, mutually beneficial relationships with suppliers.

What does the move from products to services mean for the supplier?

Suppliers will need to keep close to the consumer and the retailer throughout the product life cycle. Key tasks include:

■ matching and complementing new retailer skill sets;
■ ensuring consistent delivery of message, products and services;
■ setting clear objectives for serving specific segments;
■ developing a clear rationale for choosing partners;
■ building new skill sets for dealing effectively with non-traditional retailers, including e-tailers and new market entrants;
■ raising the profile of partnership management activity.

The evolving retail offer

Retailers are moving from products to offers of interrelated products and services. They are increasingly entering related fields where they can leverage their customer relations, brand power, product strength and scale. For some, these extensions are simply underpinning their traditional retailing role, for others it is a means to develop new revenue streams from new business models. There are many examples of this trend, including grocery chains offering financial services, travel services and flower delivery. DIY stores (known originally for selling wood, tools, paint, etc) now offer complete home furnishing departments, fitted kitchen services, bathroom installations and garden landscaping.

Out-of-town retail malls and shopping centres are spreading in Asia, Latin America and in southern and eastern Europe. While destination specialists are trying to enhance the total consumer shopping experience, convenience/local outlets will continue to offer the potential to satisfy the spontaneous and 'immediate' consumer demands.

Life cycle and boundary issues

Retailers are now starting to track the life cycle of technology products more closely, and are tailoring their offers to suit the level of consumer acceptance of particular technologies. As technologies move from being perceived as extraordinary to ordinary, the cost and effort involved in making the sale diminishes. Different levels of sales effort and support are required for products that have become widely accepted and moved into everyday use than is appropriate for launching new technologies onto the market. The challenge is to track this evolution carefully and adjust offers appropriately and in good time. As products commoditize over time, there is a tendency for them to move along the evolutionary chain The highly specialized product of today soon moves beyond the boutiques to the multi-specialists or mass merchandisers and is eventually sold through discounters (look at the array of 'high technology' products available in Costco, such as laptop computers, plasma-screen TVs and digital recorders). Mass merchandisers are showing a growing desire and ability to push back into the territory of the specialists who originally stole ground from the generalist retailers as 'category killers'. (Toys 'R' Us aggressive growth through breadth of range and low prices initially virtually wiped out the sale of toys from department stores, but its lack-lustre in-store merchandising and service have laid it wide open to lose the ground it claimed.)

What does the evolving retail offer mean for suppliers?

Identifying ideal business partners and conducting mutual assessments of strategic fit is a key success factor. Suppliers must be able to match the ability and desire of retailers to develop new channels – geographic as well as conceptual – with their own capability and commitment to maintain market share and competitive advantage. Your selection of priority retail accounts needs to consider how well they fit with your corporate strategy and not just focus on the potential size of business. Evolving retail formats require suppliers to showcase their products in ways that make quality, style and value immediate – especially in the virtual 'shop window' of the internet. Retailers look to their partners for experienced and expert consumer marketing and retail management advice. This is a key opportunity for suppliers to add value to their strategic relationships with retailers. Suppliers need to audit their capabilities closely and assess whether they are ready to become a strategic supplier and what obstacles might stand in the way of their selection as a strategic partner. The rewards on offer for successful strategic partnerships mean that suppliers should aspire towards this type of relationship with their retailers of choice.

Managing retail relationships at a strategic level

Given this landscape of change facing the retailers and the opportunities these create for suppliers, how should you approach the tasks of building and managing retail relationships for maximum advantage? The following framework (developed by Michael White of VIA International and Rob Abshire of Publicis) provides a powerful way of assessing the potential for relationship development and defines the approach to take with different retailers according to this potential.

The potential for developing a strategic retailer relationship depends a great deal on where a retailer sits on a spectrum which is defined at either end by two fundamentally different approaches to fulfilling consumer needs:

1. Fill demand – The challenge here is to fill a given market demand for standardized products or services. The assumption is that there is a defined market to be shared – and retailers and suppliers compete for a bigger slice of the pie. Retailers and suppliers trade with each other in order to offer items to the mass market on the most advantageous terms. Retailer–supplier relationships are transactional and focus on trading

terms, discounts, margins and supply chain issues. Consumer activity is triggered by basic considerations of price and availability.

2. Create demand – At the other end of the spectrum, the challenge is to create demand – or grow the pie – by offering highly customized packages of products and services. Based on an intimate knowledge of consumers and their needs, retailers and suppliers work closely as partners in order to offer a better shopping and ownership experience. Consumers are willing and active participants in the process of new product and service delivery and innovation.

The framework identifies four types of retail offer to the consumer, each with a corresponding retailer–supplier relationship. These relationship types are characterized as: 1 transaction-driven, 2 targeted, 3 collaborative and 4 strategic as shown mapped on the fill demand/create demand spectrum shown in Figure 21.1.

Each relationship type represents a different approach to meeting consumer needs, and no hierarchy is implied in the movement along the spectrum from one end towards the other. Retailers and suppliers will decide which type of relationship is most appropriate to their market environment and their vision for their business. For example, successful exponents of the transaction-driven model may not have an immediate need to inves-

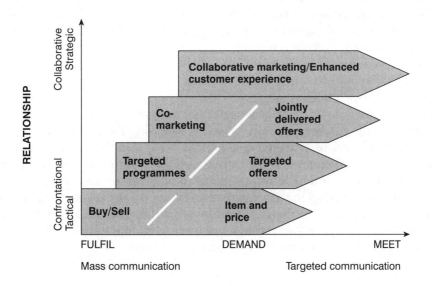

Figure 21.1 Spectrum of retailer offer and retailer–supplier relationships

tigate other options. However, the factors influencing a move into a different type of relationship and consumer offering are dictating fundamental choices about the future direction of retail. While most retailing relationships currently focus on filling demand, changes in consumer behaviour described in the previous section are prompting many retailers to investigate the business case for moving towards relationships that help create demand. The trend is clear – relationships are migrating towards the partnering end of the spectrum; however, there are still many retailers operating towards the buy/sell end.

Set out in Figures 21.2 to 21.5 are the supplier–retailer relationship management strategies suggested for each of the four retailer positions.

Clearly the opportunity to partner with major retailer accounts at the third and fourth level of this framework is going to be limited to a small number of strategic suppliers. The investment required on both sides of the relationship is significant and can only be justified when amortized across a large volume of business. Equally, a supplier that can secure this kind of relationship is going to shut the door on its nearest competitors for a significant period and, once it has won this status, it should ensure that it never loses it.

Typically, it is a stumble that undoes a strategic relationship, such as a flawed line of new products that fails to sell but which the supplier refuses to accept has missed the market, or complacency, when the supplier starts to take its status for granted. Just occasionally, it can come about with a change of personnel on either side, prompting a review of strategic relationships or simply a desire for change. If you are the competition, you need to be ready to take advantage of the openings that come and ensure that you can move swiftly to set out your strategic proposition and back it up with the investments, resources and offerings to consolidate your advance. Most retailers will review their strategic partner profile once a year and take into account how well their suppliers' competitors are performing in the market generally as well as assessing their ability to step up to a higher level of engagement. Equally, as a supplier you should be reviewing your target retailer accounts to see which ones are showing signs of movement (or intent to move) along the fill/create demand spectrum. For those target retailer accounts that show up, it may take several years, but it will pay to keep them as well informed as you can of your brand strengths, share gains and strategic partnering capabilities so that you can show a clear trend that should be ignored no longer.

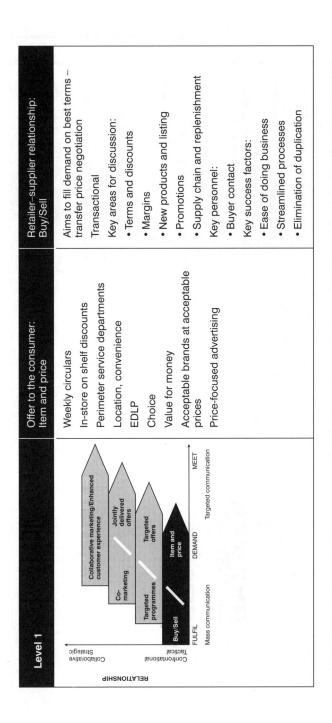

Figure 21.2 Transaction driven retailer–supplier relationship

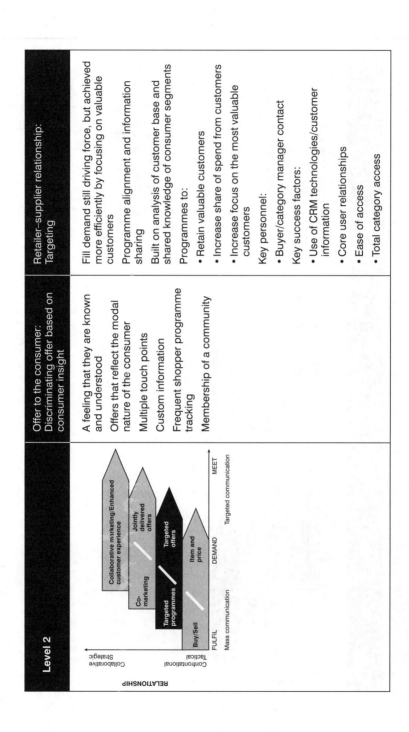

Level 2	Offer to the consumer: Discriminating offer based on consumer insight	Retailer–supplier relationship: Targeting
	A feeling that they are known and understood Offers that reflect the modal nature of the consumer Multiple touch points Custom information Frequent shopper programme tracking Membership of a community	Fill demand still driving force, but achieved more efficiently by focusing on valuable customers Programme alignment and information sharing Built on analysis of customer base and shared knowledge of consumer segments Programmes to: • Retain valuable customers • Increase share of spend from customers • Increase focus on the most valuable customers Key personnel: • Buyer/category manager contact Key success factors: • Use of CRM technologies/customer information • Core user relationships • Ease of access • Total category access

Figure 21.3 Targeted retailer–supplier relationship

Level 3	Offer to the consumer: Joint delivery of enhanced value	Retailer–supplier relationship: Co-marketing
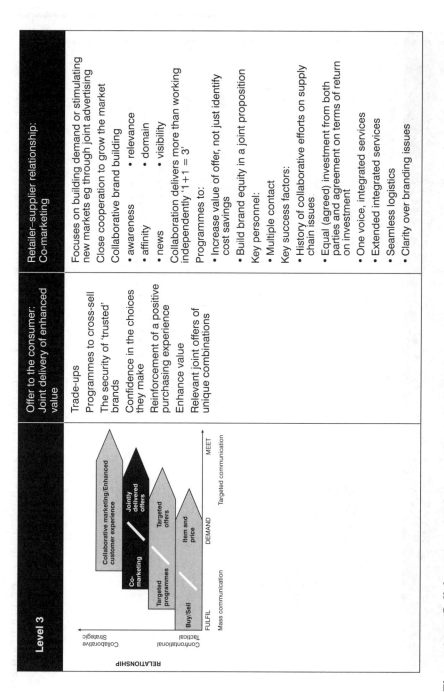	Trade-ups Programmes to cross-sell The security of 'trusted' brands Confidence in the choices they make Reinforcement of a positive purchasing experience Enhance value Relevant joint offers of unique combinations	Focuses on building demand or stimulating new markets eg through joint advertising Close cooperation to grow the market Collaborative brand building • awareness • relevance • affinity • domain • news • visibility Collaboration delivers more than working independently '1 + 1 = 3' Programmes to: • Increase value of offer, not just identify cost savings • Build brand equity in a joint proposition Key personnel: • Multiple contact Key success factors: • History of collaborative efforts on supply chain issues • Equal (agreed) investment from both parties and agreement on terms of return on investment • One voice, integrated services • Extended integrated services • Seamless logistics • Clarity over branding issues

Figure 21.4 Collaborative retailer–supplier relationship

Level 4	Offer to the consumer: Enhanced total customer experience	Retailer–supplier relationship: Customized products and services
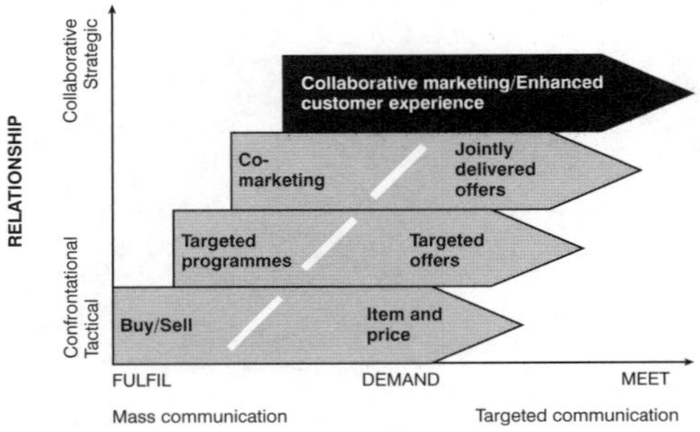RELATIONSHIP Collaborative Strategic Confrontational Tactical Collaborative marketing/Enhanced customer experience Co-marketing Jointly delivered offers Targeted programmes Targeted offers Buy/Sell Item and price FULFIL DEMAND MEET Mass communication Targeted communication	Personalized products and services accessed uniquely through specific retailers Single integrated sales and service experience Customized offers Augmented value Unique propositions A feeling that the brands involved understand their life, needs and motivation Services that incorporate product Dialogue with the supplier and retailer A relationship with the supplier/retailer that engages with and is managed through multiple touch points	Focus on creating demand with a joint venture mindset Strategic, joint-venture type partnerships with a select number of suppliers Close cooperation to grow the market Programmes to: • Develop new products and services • Use a variety of delivery channels • Minimize delays and obstacles to reaching the customer Key personnel: • Multiple contacts including board Key success factors: • Close analysis of customer base • Involve consumer in devising and developing market offerings • Proactive approach to identifying and anticipating consumer needs • Extending profit pool • Integrated e-commerce

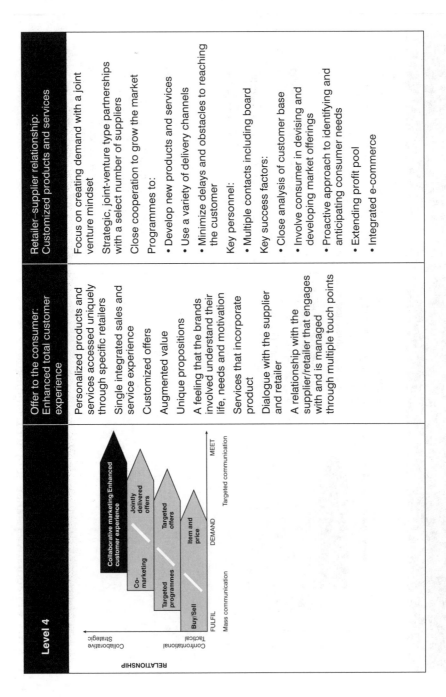

Figure 21.5 Strategic retailer–supplier relationship

Managing retail relationships at a tactical level

As we have seen, not all retailers are open to a strategic relationship and even for those that are, you will need to manage the account on a tactical level. (It's just that in some accounts you will have a strategic framework for your tactical plans and for others you will be engaged in taking any ground that you can.) Your tactical management should keep a sharp focus on the basics of supporting the retailer's core trading needs – strong brands and attractive products to be able to draw customers to its stores, a balanced mix of high-volume and high-margin lines and a steady stream of new and updated products to refresh its offering and get customers to return regularly to its stores.

When you work with retailers at a tactical level, your main points of contact will be the category buyers and merchandisers. You must be ready to engage with them because they will not give you long to make your case. First, however, you must know what **you** want and how much you are prepared to pay, so you can negotiate for it. For example, you will need to have answers ready to the following questions:

- Which product lines and SKUs do you want the retailer to list (ie to carry)?
- What level of margin are you prepared to give the retailer (by discounting from list) at what expected street price?
- Where do you want your products to be positioned in the store, in the category and on the shelf? In how many locations in the store do you want each of your products?
- For which products do you want special displays or demonstration days, etc?
- How much are you prepared to pay to be in prime locations in the stores or for mounting special displays or allowing demonstrators into the stores, etc?
- Which of your products do you want to be featured in the retailer's marketing activities, mailings, etc? What control or restrictions do you want to impose on how your products are presented (eg no competitors' products should appear on the same page as yours)?
- What proportion of your products (and which product lines) do you want to be on promotion?
- How much are you prepared to pay for appearing in the retailer's marketing and promotional activities?

- How are you physically going to get your products into the stores or the retailer's distribution centre? What level of fill rate, shipping accuracy, etc, can you commit to?
- What payment terms are you willing to accept from the retailer (could be 90 days or longer)?
- What level of returns (for reasons of product fault) do you anticipate and how much do you plan to pay the retailer for handling them?
- Are you prepared to take back unsold inventory and at what point?

Next you will need to do your homework on the buyers, to understand their objectives, the constraints under which they are operating and the targets and incentives they are striving to achieve. Most buyers will be targeted on at least the category's revenues, blended gross margin, inventory turns and the combination measure, GMROII. They may also have a sales quota! This is for the amount of marketing funds they can obtain from suppliers for the use of the retailer's special display areas (such as the 'end caps' at the end of the aisles) and its marketing activities. The framework set for buyers can vary significantly between retailers, with some having very wide latitude to negotiate with suppliers to optimize their key performance indicators and others given minimum margins and a quota for sales of the retailer's marketing platforms. Note that the more you want to move your relationship with a retailer away from 'buy–sell', the more important it is that you build relationships across the retailer's organization, beyond the buyer. An understanding of how the business model management responsibilities and metrics are allocated across the retailer's organization will enable you to align your proposition more effectively.

Buyers recognize that there are very few individual products which are going to meet all their criteria, so will adopt a portfolio approach, using some products to drive the volume through their category and others to enrich the blended gross margin and so on. You should be aware of the measures on which each of your products will perform best and sell them to the buyer on that basis, backed up by solid support. For example, highlight the size of the advertising funding you will be spending to drive the revenues of your current products, emphasizing the impact that this will have on sales volumes and stock turns. Even better if the retailer is one of a restricted number of retailers receiving the new products in time for the advertising campaign, as this will give it a differentiation (possibly make the category a destination for additional traffic to the store) and enhance its potential to earn good margins on the products. Alternatively, you may have good research which shows that customers who buy your brand of products tend to spend more in their 'average basket' than the customers of your competitors' products – ie you are helping to attract and merchandise to a higher spending and possibly more profitable segment of consumers. Buyers and merchandisers tend to know what works well in their category in their stores, so you will have to be convincing if you can claim that you can show them better ways to position, range or display your products. Your best evidence is going to come from running pilots in their stores, so negotiate to run projects that can help you and the retailer learn better how to increase sales, turns and margins.

Figure 21.6 gives a summary of the measures you should emphasize in your presentations and reviews with the retailer, depending on the retailer's business objectives and your relative strength as a brand.

It is essential you are honest with yourself as a supplier in appraising your own brand and products before engaging with the retailer. Buyers are shrewd and quick to spot if and when they are being oversold and will filter anything you may later try to sell in. It is actually even worse if you do succeed in over-selling your products as the result will be stock stuck on the shelves, earning no margin for the retailer and destroying your credibility. Even a retrospective discount to enable the retailer to clear the prod-

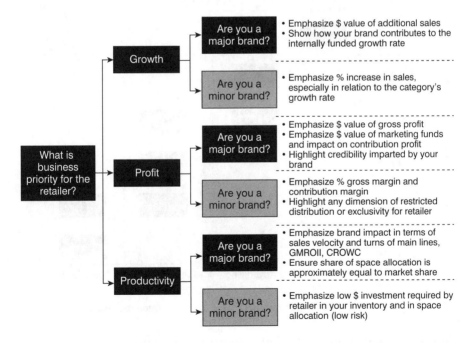

Figure 21.6 Decision tree – which measures to emphasise in different situations

ucts out (there is no such thing as a bad product, just a bad price) or an offer to take the products back will not fix the damage done. The products have not justified their place on the shelves and valuable selling days have gone when other products could have been earning and turning. It will be a long time before the retailer will entertain an approach from your brand again. To encourage you to be brutally honest, remember that the buyer is balancing a number of measures across the portfolio of products and even products that do not initially seem to justify their place in the store can be effectively positioned using this framework (courtesy of Rob Abshire of Publicis) (Figure 21.7).

To apply this framework, first locate your product on the vertical axis, which compares your product to its direct competition in terms of the consumer perception of its advantages. At the top of the axis are products that are so superior they have no discernable competition – an example might be Viagra or the Apple iPod when it was first introduced. In the middle are parity products, ie consumers cannot perceive any advantage or disadvan-

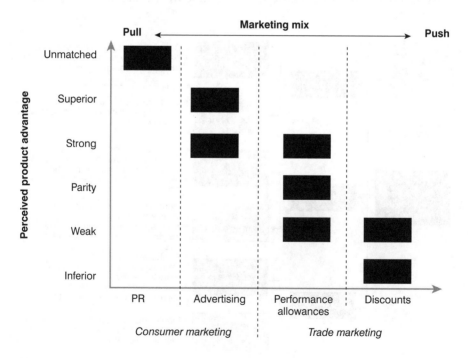

Figure 21.7 Matching the marketing mix to perceived product competitiveness

tage over other products – perhaps different brands of paper towels. And at the bottom are products that are perceived as clearly inferior to the other products in the market, perhaps a no-name brand of baked beans. Note that this axis is consumer **perception**, not reality, as it may be that the no-name is a better product, but the marketing of the competition has created this perception of inferiority.

Let's say your product is an unmatched superior one; read across and down the chart for the recommended positioning strategy with the retailer – which is to use PR only. Because of its superior perceived benefits, consumers will flock to any retailer that stocks that product, and the supplier is in the envious position of being able to virtually auction stock allocation to retailers that will give it prime positioning and the longest purchase commitments. There is no need to spend money on advertising or to pay any marketing funds to retailers. As you move down the vertical axis, you can see that the recommended approach moves from 'pull' to 'push', shifting the balance of marketing expenditure from consumer marketing activities (pull) to trade marketing activities (push). Where you have superior products the balance should be weighted to pull marketing, effectively communicating the superior benefits to the consumer, driving them into the store looking for the 'better' product.

As your products become parity products, there is no further advantage in spending significantly on advertising as the consumer is likely to perceive similar products in store and you will have paid simply to drive consumers into your competitors' arms. The best result may be to grow the category but not necessarily your own share. In fact, this is the point at which to start to pay the trade (ie the retailer) to give your product pre-eminence in the store. Thus consumers arriving in store will tend to perceive an 'acceptable set' of products, but will be influenced to select your product through its in-store merchandising and placement. Some consumer marketing will still be needed to ensure that consumers are aware of the brand and place your products into the acceptable set, not least because competitor brands will be attempting something similar. Occasionally continued consumer marketing can create a perception of product superiority, even when none exists, or evoke such strong imagery that brand affinity becomes a desirable attribute – cigarette advertising used to do this very effectively before it was banned. Note how Apple has introduced advertising for its iPod for the first time, some three years after its initial introduction, as it feels the pressure to refresh the brand affinity of the whole iPod brand evoked by the classic white cables from the earphones. At launch, nothing more than good PR was needed to promote the superior user interface, but now many MP3 players can offer similarly good user interfaces.

As your products move into the inferior part of the spectrum, the framework suggests focusing almost entirely on trade marketing, moving initially into 'performance allowances', which are payments made to retailers for 'performing' certain functions, such as premium shelf positioning or putting the products on promotion. As your products continue to descend further, the remaining approach is to pay the trade to sell them by enriching their margin. You can go further by offering one of your major retail accounts an 'end-of-line' exclusive and selling it the entire final run of the product's production. This enables the retailer to offer an exclusive product and set the street price it wants without fear of price comparison by consumers. This can be an effective way of flushing obsolete products out of the channel without causing channel conflict, assuming you use other retailers or retailer types to launch your new ranges. Suppliers that introduce a new range each season will typically have launch accounts, often more specialist, that will give the new range prominent positioning and will not discount the products, then following launch, the suppliers will widen distribution into more generalist retailers and finally, just prior to the next launch, channel the old range into discounters or offer it as an exclusive to one of the generalist retailers.

Selling in to the retailer's buying cycle and open-to-buy

Retailers plan ahead between 6 and 12 months by season. If you want your products in the next Christmas/Holiday season, you will need to be sharing your proposals for the new products and seasonal promotions sometime between March and June that year. Many retailers' annual performance is critically dependent upon the success of the six- to eight-week Christmas/Holiday season and they need to ensure that they select the right suppliers and products to deliver success. This is the time when the consumer proposition is key and will dominate the negotiations. What are you going to be able to offer that will bring the customers in and encourage them to shop? How will you help the retailer to break out of the clutter and command attention? You will need to demonstrate that your products will deliver top margins and volumes to secure the best sites in the stores as these will be at an absolute premium. Equally, this is the time of year when every brand will be fighting for attention and the price you will need to pay to even match your usual 'share of voice' (share of the advertising spend) will be between two and four times higher than average. If you are a major brand with substantial budgets this period will tend to play to your advantage as you can afford the kind of consumer marketing that will show up in shaping awareness and preference. However, if you are a smaller brand, this may not be the time to compete. You may be better off allocating your more limited budgets to periods where there is less intensity and your communications will show up.

One concept that is critical to understand when dealing with buyers is that of 'open to buy' funds. Open-to-buy is the difference between planned purchases and inventory already ordered (this includes inventory on hand, in transit and any outstanding orders), ie the dollar amount of merchandise that a buyer can order for a particular period. Open-to-buy can be calculated in either units or money. In order to take advantage of special buys or to add new products, some of the open-to-buy dollars are held back. This also allows the retailer to react to fast-selling items and quickly restock shelves. Retailers maintain an open-to-buy plan for their business as a whole, but also plan for each category of merchandise they stock.

Open-to-buy usually refers to the amount of cash any particular buyer has available for the next key trading period (could be monthly, but typically relates to a season). Faster-turning categories will return cash to the retailer more quickly and generate a bigger open-to-buy fund. Buyers will be charged with earning a return on their open-to-buy funds and the better the return, the greater the amount of open-to-buy funds allocated. Equally, the bigger the open-to-buy funds allocated, the more senior the buyer.

Managing open-to-buy is vital in controlling inventory levels and retailers need to make sure that they control product supply to avoid both stockouts and excess inventories building up. To do this they have to forecast sales and decide what level of forward cover they need. Open-to-buy systems normally operate using a flow calculation. This is shown in the following simple example where the closing stock for the first period is a result of adding the opening stock, on order and open to receive, and then subtracting the forecast sales. This closing stock then becomes the opening stock for period 2 and so on. Figure 21.8 gives an example of how the control works (with thanks to John Hobson of The Planning Factory Limited).

Each period is therefore dependent on the previous periods' stock levels in the determination of its own open-to-buy. Here's how the table works:

■ *Forecast sales* – in order to prime the system retailers need to make an estimate of the sales that will occur by period. Usually this is achieved

	Period 1	Period 2	Period 3	Period 4	Period 5	Period 6
Forecast sales	100	150	200	150	100	100
Periods' forward cover	3	3	3	3	3	3
Stock required	500	450	350	300	300	300
Opening stock	200	500	450	350	300	300
Intake requirement	400	100	100	100	100	100
On order	200	100				
Open to receive	200	0	100	100	100	100
Closing stock	500	450	350	300	300	300

© John Hobson, The Planning Factory

Figure 21.8 Worked example of open-to-buy controls

by creating a financial budget for the entire season and then breaking it down (or 'phasing' it) by period or season.

■ *Periods' cover and stock requirement* – the entry in 'periods' cover' is critical to the operation of the system. 'Cover' means the amount of stock that a retailer will hold, and it is normally related to forecast sales for a given number of periods, hence the term 'periods' cover'. In very simple open-to-buy systems the calculations are performed using 'flat cover'. Thus if 3 periods' cover is required and the forecast for the current month is 100 then the stock requirement will be 3 × 100 or 300. In more sophisticated systems 'forward cover' is used. This means that rather than multiplying the current period by 3, the system would add up the next 3 periods' forecast sales. With seasonal merchandise this can make a large difference. Consider the effect of the two different methods where the sales forecast is 100, 200 and 300 for the next 3 periods. Flat cover in the first period would produce a stock requirement of 300, while forward cover would produce a requirement of 600.

■ *Opening stock* – the value of opening stock is a flow calculation. In open-to-buy planning the first entry will be an estimate, probably based on the last season. From the second period onwards, the figure is the closing stock from the previous period.

■ *Intake requirement* – the intake requirement is calculated by subtracting the opening stock from the stock requirement.

■ *On order* – the on-order quantity shows the items due for delivery in the relevant period.

- *Open to receive* – the open to receive is calculated by subtracting the on-order quantity from the intake requirement. It is important to realize that we are looking at the intake of goods here and not the placing of an order. The goods in any given open to receive may be ordered in any number of preceding periods, depending on lead-times.
- *Closing stock* – this is normally calculated by taking the opening stock, subtracting sales, and adding the on-order and open-to-receive quantities. Although some systems omit the open to receive and thus generate a cumulative open to buy.

No retailer will share these calculations with you (unless you are the category captain) but by understanding the concept and asking intelligent questions about the open-to-buy situation, you can time and target your conversations with buyers much more effectively.

Should you deal with retailers direct or through a wholesaler?

Retailers are final-tier resellers and thus represent one of possibly a number of feasible routes to market. However, their dominance of the consumer sector has made them a powerful and demanding channel to sell through, requiring dedicated and professional resources. Many smaller suppliers simply do not have the scale to support this level of investment and hand this role off to wholesalers, or partner with a service provider, accepting the dilution of their ability to influence how retailers position their product. Figure 21.1 gives a comparison of three possible alternatives available.

Each model has its advantages and disadvantages, which are unique to the resources and scale of the individual supplier and its products. There is no substitute for a detailed analysis of the full costs of selling through and servicing retailers under each option, with a projection of how the business will grow over the next two to three years. This period is the minimum time that it will take to establish and operate a distribution model before considering migrating to a different one.

Summary

Retailers have a tough business model to operate. They have to work with suppliers to succeed but aim to make their suppliers work as hard as

WHOLESALER	PURE DIRECT	SERVICE PROVIDER
Supplier delivers to wholesaler in bulk	Supplier delivers to retailer in bulk to one central point	Supplier delivers to service provider in bulk (under agency model)
	Retailer has responsibility to break bulk, finish products and deliver to store level	Service provider breaks bulk, finishes product and delivers to store level
		Supplier pays fee to service provider
Wholesaler owns buy/sell relationship with retailer	Supplier owns buy/sell relationship with retailer at classic wholesalers' T&Cs and prices	Supplier owns buy/sell relationship with retailer at wholesalers' T&Cs and prices
		Supplier retains fee from retailer for services provided by SP (see above)
Wholesaler recommends the assortment and street pricing	Supplier recommends the assortment and street pricing	Supplier recommends the assortment and street pricing
Wholesaler performs in-store merchandising of total category	Third party performs in-store merchandising of total category	Third party performs in-store merchandising of total category
	Supplier carries out full-blown category management	Supplier carries out full-blown category management
Wholesaler has key relationship with retailer	Supplier engages in strategic account management with retailer	Supplier engages in strategic account management with retailer
Wholesaler has financial exposure to retailer	Supplier has financial and administration exposure to retailer	Supplier has financial and administration exposure to retailer

Figure 21.9 Alternative models for managing retailers

possible in bringing customers into the store, earning good margins from fast-turning products and bringing customers back again. The current pressures on retailers are creating opportunities for suppliers to build strategic partnerships that create a competitive advantage for both parties by focusing on creating value for consumers. Only a few suppliers can hope to achieve this top-level status, but by making a strong commercial proposition to buyers, most suppliers can secure many of their objectives for effective market access through the retail channel. With or without a strategic partnership, suppliers need to make a realistic assessment of the role their products can play in a category buyer's portfolio and sell in their economic strengths, backed by a willingness to pay for the consumer or trade marketing that is appropriate. Retail is an expensive channel to go to market, but its scale and reach deliver sales volumes and growth acceleration that can transform a brand's position in the market. It pays to research the channel well, identify the opportunities of best fit with the retail accounts that address the target consumer for your products and deliver a well-timed proposition that hits the buyer's objectives. And above all, focus on the retailer's key challenges, getting customers to the store, getting them to shop the store and buy the most profitable products and getting customers to return.

Key Ratios

Ratio	Calculation	Interpretation	Ratio increase means...
Achieved margin %	$\dfrac{\text{Actual price received} - \text{Supplier cost}}{\text{Actual price received}} \times 100$	Used to compare to buying margin % by retailers	Good performance
Average project size	$\dfrac{\text{Total (project) sales}}{\text{Number of projects}}$	Effectiveness measure – as size drives utilization	Good performance
Average store size	$\dfrac{\text{Actual sales space}}{\text{Average number of stores}}$	Indicator of a retailer's core proposition	Large changes mean shift in core proposition
Buying margin %	$\dfrac{\text{Expected retail price} - \text{Supplier cost}}{\text{Expected retail price}} \times 100$	Used as benchmark for achieved margin %	Good performance
Contribution margin %	$\dfrac{\text{Sales} - \text{Cost of sales} - \text{Variable costs}}{\text{Sales}} \times 100$	Profitability measure – shows true return on sales	Good performance
Contribution margin return on inventory investment (CMROII)	$\dfrac{\text{Contribution profit}}{\text{Inventory}} = \underbrace{\dfrac{\text{Contribution profit}}{\text{Sales}}}_{\text{'Earn'}} \times \underbrace{\dfrac{\text{Sales}}{\text{Inventory}}}_{\text{'Turn'}}$	Productivity measure – shows true return on capital tied up in inventory	Good performance
Contribution margin return on working capital (CMROWC)	$\dfrac{\text{Contribution profit}}{\text{Working capital}} = \dfrac{\text{Contribution profit}}{\text{Sales}} \times \dfrac{\text{Sales}}{\text{Working capital}}$	Productivity measure – shows true return on working capital	Good performance
Days payable outstanding (DPO)	$\dfrac{\text{Accounts payable}}{\text{Cost of sales}} \times 365 \text{ days}$	Shows time taken to pay suppliers	Good performance (up to a limit, beyond that can be bad)

Ratio	Calculation	Interpretation	Ratio increase means...
Days sales outstanding (DSO)	$\dfrac{\text{Accounts receivable}}{\text{Sales}} \times 365 \text{ days}$	Shows time taken to collect payment from customers	Bad performance
Gross margin %	$\dfrac{\text{Sales} - \text{Cost of sales}}{\text{Sales}} \times 100$	Basic profitability measure – indicates value added	Good performance
Gross margin return on inventory investment (GMROII)	$\dfrac{\text{Gross profit}}{\text{Inventory}} = \dfrac{\text{Gross profit}}{\text{Sales}} \times \dfrac{\text{Sales}}{\text{Inventory}}$ 'Earn' $\times$ 'Turn'	Productivity measure – shows basic return on capital tied up in inventory	Good performance
Gross Margin Return on Working Capital (GMROWC)	$\dfrac{\text{Gross profit}}{\text{Working capital}} = \dfrac{\text{Gross profit}}{\text{Sales}} \times \dfrac{\text{Sales}}{\text{Working capital}}$ Working capital = Inventory + Accounts receivable – Accounts payable	Productivity measure – shows basic return on working capital	Good performance
Inventory days (DIO)	$\dfrac{\text{Inventory}}{\text{Cost of sales}} \times 365$	Shows time taken to sell inventory	Bad performance
Inventory turn	$\dfrac{365 \text{ days}}{\text{Inventory days}}$	Shows speed at which inventory is turning over	Good performance
Mark-up %	$\dfrac{\text{Sales} - \text{Cost of sales}}{\text{Cost of sales}} \times 100$	Shows amount of profit added to cost of product	Good performance
Net margin %	$\dfrac{\text{Sales} - \text{Cost of sales} - \text{Overhead costs} - \text{Interest}}{\text{Sales}} \times 100$	Profitability of business activity for a period	Good performance

Ratio	Calculation	Interpretation	Ratio increase means...
Operating margin %	$\dfrac{\text{Sales} - \text{Cost of sales} - \text{Overhead costs}}{\text{Sales}} \times 100$	Profitability of trading operations for a period	Good performance
Potential growth capacity %	Net margin after tax % × Working capital turn	Rate of sales growth that can be financed internally	Good performance
Profit per square foot	$\dfrac{\text{Gross profit or DPP}}{\text{Average sales space (square feet)}}$	Profitability of sales space in a retailer	Good performance
Recoverability	$\dfrac{\text{Final contract price paid by customer}}{\text{Total resources used} \times \text{Standard prices}}$	Proportion of billable work that customers will pay for	Good performance
Return on capital employed (ROCE)	$\dfrac{\text{Net profit before tax}}{\text{Total assets} - \text{Non-interest-bearing liabilities}}$	Productivity of capital employed in the business	Good performance
Return on invested capital (ROIC)	$\dfrac{\text{Operating profit after tax}}{\text{Invested capital}}$ $= \dfrac{\text{Net profit after tax} + \text{Interest}}{\text{Total assets} - \text{Excess cash} - \text{Non-interest-bearing current liabilities}}$	Productivity of capital employed in the trading operations of the business (or allocated to the relevant part of the business)	Good performance
Return on net assets (RONA)	$\dfrac{\text{Operating profit}}{\text{Cash} + \text{Working capital} + \text{Fixed assets}}$	Productivity of assets employed in the business	Good performance
Sales per square foot	$\dfrac{\text{Sales}}{\text{Average sales space (square feet)}}$	Productivity of sales space in a retailer	Good performance

Ratio	Calculation	Interpretation	Ratio increase means...
Sales per store	$$\dfrac{\text{Sales}}{\text{Average number of stores}}$$	Productivity of stores in a retailer	Good performance
Sales pipeline	$$\dfrac{\text{Booked sales plus probability of expected sales}}{\text{Average monthly targeted sales}}$$	Size of order book and expected sales	Good performance
Utilization	$$\dfrac{\text{Billable time}}{\text{Standard time}} \times 100$$	Productivity of people in a service business	Good performance (up to a limit, beyond that can be bad)
Value creation (VC)	Operating profit after tax − (Invested capital × WACC)	Profits generated in excess of cost of capital employed	Good performance
Working capital turn	$$\dfrac{365 \text{ days}}{\text{Working capital days}}$$	Shows speed at which working capital is turning over	Good performance

Glossary of technical terms

accounting principles   The principles governing the preparation of financial statements.

accounts payable (US term)   Persons or business to whom amounts are due for goods or services purchased on credit (also known as 'trade payables'). Also includes other amounts payable within 12 months from the date of the balance sheet. (UK term is creditors.)

accounts receivable (US term)   Amounts owing to the company. Accounts receivable are amounts owed from customers. (UK term is debtors.)

accumulated depreciation   The cumulative amount of depreciation written off a fixed asset at a balance sheet date.

achieved margin   The actual gross margin achieved on selling products. It is then compared to the buying margin.

acid test – quick ratio   Liquid assets divided by current liabilities. 'Liquid assets' are normally represented by cash plus debtors; but long-term debtors (if any) would be excluded. If inventories were reckoned to be 'liquid' (for example, in a retailing chain with a very rapid rate of stock turnover) then they too might, exceptionally, be included.

advocate channel   A channel that influences the awareness and preferences of the end-customer, by acting as a specifier (such as an architect) or as a paid adviser (such as a technical consultant or independent financial adviser). Although this is not a channel that a supplier can sell its products through, it is a critical channel to include in a channel strategy as a 'sell-with' channel.

amortization   The reduction in value of a liability over a period due to regular repayments.

asset turnover   Measure of the utilization of the assets of the business, ie how many dollars of sales each dollar invested in assets produces.

balance sheet   Statement of the assets, liabilities and shareholders funds of a company at particular date. International accounting standards require that share capital, reserves, provisions, liabilities, fixed assets, current assets and other assets must be separately identified.

basis point   A basis point is 1 hundredth of 1 per cent or 0.01 per cent.

book value   The monetary amount of an asset as stated in its balance sheet. It usually represents acquisition cost less accumulated depreciation. In the case of land (or land with buildings on it), marketable securities or foreign currencies book value can be market value.

borrowing ratio (gearing ratio)   Ratio of debt to equity. Normally expressed as percentage. 100 per cent and over is high. Most public companies aim for 50 per cent or less.

break-even   The volume of activity or sales in units at which the contribution profit earned on those sales is exactly equal to the fixed costs in the business. At this volume the business makes neither a profit nor a loss.

buying margin   The gross margin expected when making a purchasing commitment. In some sectors, such as clothes retailing, this can be many months before the products arrive in the stores ready to be sold.

capacity utilization   The proportion of a service provider's billable capacity (measured in time terms such as hours or days) that is absorbed by billable activity on customer projects. High capacity utilization means that the service provider is very busy and is good for the business.

capital commitments   The amount of contracts for capital expenditure not provided for and the expenditure authorized by the directors but not contracted for that must be disclosed in the accounts.

capital employed   Capital employed is long-term capital. It consists of equity capital (ordinary share capital and reserves) plus long-term liabilities. Looked at from the asset side, capital employed equals net assets (= fixed assets plus working capital = total assets less current liabilities).

cash budget/cash flow   A plan of future cash receipts and payments based on specified assumptions concerning sales growth, credit terms, etc.

cash-to-cash cycle   The time taken for the cash paid out to suppliers for products to be returned to the business having been invested in inventory and receivables from credit customers, measured in days.

channel   A route to market for a supplier. Sometimes used loosely ('the channel') to describe only the indirect channel or trade channel, but when applied correctly refers to any specific route to market, which can include the direct channels such as sales force, catalogue, direct mail and the web.

channel value proposition   The relationship offering of a supplier to its trade channel partners. Perceived by the channel as the strategic and commercial value of a relationship with a particular supplier. It is built up from the comprehensive array of terms and conditions in the contract supported by the sales and marketing programmes, inter-business process investments, relationship support, strategic alignment and many other aspects of the relationship.

contribution   Contribution profit (or margin) is the gross profit less other variable costs incurred.

co-op funds   Marketing funds allocated as a fixed percentage of sales by a supplier to be spent by a channel player on driving increased sales through that player.

comps sales   *see* **same store sales**

corporate reseller   A final-tier player that specializes in selling into corporate customers, usually in the realm of information technology, business equipment, etc.

cost of goods sold or cost of sales   The price paid for getting goods and services to the point and condition where they are ready for sale.

cost structure   The profile of the overhead costs incurred by a business. Can also be used in reference to the balance between fixed and variable costs.

cost to sell   The costs incurred in *generating* a sale through a channel. Typically these costs are buried in traditional management accounting analyses and need to be extracted or estimated using an activity-based costing approach.

cost to serve   The costs incurred in *fulfilling* a sale through a channel, and can include all the costs over the life cycle of the product, including warranty, service and support as well as the relationship management costs. Typically these costs are buried in traditional management accounting analyses and need to be extracted or estimated using an activity-based-costing approach.

creditors (UK term) Persons or business to whom amounts are due for goods or services purchased on credit (= 'trade' creditors). Also includes other amounts owing within 12 months from the date of the balance sheet. (US term is accounts payable.)

credit period The amount of time that it takes a person who has made a purchase on credit to pay.

cross-sell The sales technique of adding sales of other product lines to the core product when engaged with a customer. An example is the adding of accessories and consumables to the core purchase.

current assets Those assets which are either already cash or can reasonably be expected to become cash within one year from the date of the balance sheet. Examples: accounts receivable, inventories.

current liabilities Liabilities which are expected to be paid within one year from the date of the balance sheet (eg trade creditors, proposed dividend, current taxation).

current ratio Ratio of current assets to current liabilities.

current taxation Tax payable within one year from the date of the balance sheet.

days inventory outstanding (DIO) A measure of how long the business holds its inventory between purchase and sale, expressed in days. Used to show how quickly the inventory is turning.

days payable outstanding (DPO) A measure of how long the business is taking to pay its suppliers' credit invoices, expressed in days.

days sales outstanding (DSO) A measure of how long customers are taking to pay their credit invoices, expressed in days.

debtors (UK term) Amounts owing to the company. Trade debtors are amounts owed from customers. (US term is accounts receivable.)

depreciation Expense recording the using up of fixed assets through operations. Accountants usually measure it by allocating the historical (acquisition) cost less scrap value of the asset on a straight-line or reducing-balance basis. Amount of depreciation must be disclosed in the profit and loss account. The accumulated (provision for) depreciation is deducted from the cost in the balance sheet to give the net book value.

Depreciation (of fixed assets) is the process of allocating part of the cost of fixed assets as expense to a particular accounting period. Accumulated depreciation is the total amount so provided to date for assets still held by the company; it must be shown separately in the balance sheet or in the notes to the accounts.

Net book value (NBV) is the difference between the cost of a fixed asset (or, in some cases the amount of its valuation) and the accumulated depreciation in respect of that asset. It does not represent market value.

Residual value is the amount for which a fixed asset can be sold at the end of its useful life. The expected residual value is taken into account in calculating depreciation during the asset's life by writing off a constant percentage of the asset's original cost.

The reducing-balance method writes off a constant percentage of the declining net book value of a fixed asset shown at the start of each accounting period. The percentage rate used is higher than for the straight-line method.

Accelerated depreciation is any depreciation method which charges higher amounts in the early years of an asset's life than in the later years. Reducing balance is one such method.

DIO   *see* **days inventory outstanding**

direct channel   A route to market that involves the supplier in dealing directly with its customers and not going to market through intermediaries. Examples of direct channels are any type of sales force which calls on customers, catalogues, direct mail and the web.

distributor   A business that buys from suppliers and sells to other types of channel player (usually in the final tier) who in turn sell on to end customers. It does not sell directly to end customers.

DPO   *see* **days payable outstanding**

DSO   *see* **days sales outstanding**

earnings per share (EPS)   Net profits after tax divided by the number of ordinary shares. This measure is often used to compare the overall performance of a business to the previous year.

end cap   The display located at the end of an aisle in a retail store. Typically these locations attract an above-average level of passing customer traffic or footfall and stand out from the normal shelves, so are regarded as a premium location.

equity share capital   Any issued share capital which has unlimited rights to participate in either the distribution of dividends or capital.

final tier   The generic name given to channel players that sell to end customers. Refers to their location in a channel or distribution model as the final tier before reaching the customer.

financial statements   Statements showing the financial position (balance sheet), profit for a period (income statement) and the sources and uses of funds for a period (funds flow statement).

fixed assets   Assets held for use in the business rather than for re-sale. In general the movement for the year should be shown in the accounts.

footfall   The number of customers entering a store or passing through a particular section of the store.

gearing   The ratio of net borrowings to capital employed. A measure of how much of the money in the business is owed; also known as leverage.

GMROII   Gross margin return on inventory investment (GMROII) can be calculated by multiplying gross margin (earn) by the sales to inventory ratio (turn). A measure of the productivity of different products in inventory.

GMROWC   Gross margin return on working capital (GMROWC) is calculated by dividing gross profit by working capital. A measure of how efficiently working capital is being used.

Gold-tier dealer or partner   A dealer or partner that is in the top tier of a Gold/Silver/Bronze three-tier partnership model. A Gold-tier dealer or partner may be in the top tier through the volume of sales it makes or through meeting the top accreditation requirements.

goodwill   The excess of the price paid for a business acquired over the fair value of its identifiable assets acquired less liabilities assumed.

gross margin   Gross profit divided by sales expressed as a percentage.

gross profit   The difference between sales and cost of sales or cost of goods sold. Also known as the trading margin.

historical cost   The usual basis of valuation in published financial statements. Favoured because it is more objective and more easily verifiable by an auditor. Its use can be attacked on conceptual grounds, especially in times of inflation. In practice historical cost is usually replaced by market valuations for land, marketable securities and financial assets denoted in foreign currencies.

holding company   Company which controls another company, called its subsidiary. The balance sheet of holding company must show separately its investment in subsidiaries (including basis of valuation) and amounts owing to and owed by subsidiaries. Holding companies are required to publish consolidated accounts which combine the financial statements of all the companies in the group.

income statement (US term)   A financial statement summarizing the results of a business's trading activities for a period. (UK term is profit and loss account.)

indirect channel   Any route to market that involves a supplier selling through intermediaries such as distributors or final-tier trade players.

intangible assets   Goodwill, patents and trademarks, intellectual property of any sort, brands, etc. There are strict rules governing how intangible assets should be valued.

inventory (US term)   Raw materials, work-in-progress and finished goods, usually valued at the lower of cost or market value. (UK term is stock.)

inventory days   Measures the average number of days inventory is held before it is sold.

inventory turn   Measure of working capital management, which represents how many times the inventory has been sold and replaced in a given period.

liabilities   Amounts owing by a company.

liquidity   The ease with which current assets and current liabilities can be transformed into cash.

listing fees   Fees demanded by retailers from suppliers for including the suppliers' products in their stores, ie to include them in their list of products.

marketing funds   The money allocated by a supplier to be spent by a channel player according to rules defined by the supplier to ensure the marketing drives sales for the supplier through the channel player. Can be allocated on a discretionary basis or in direct proportion to sales, in which case they are often termed co-op marketing funds.

mass merchant   A type of retailer that offers a very broad array of categories in its stores, catalogues or online. Leading retail mass merchants include discount store and department store operators, and some of the larger grocery chains have some stores that include such large non-food sections that they could also be considered to be mass merchants.

minority interest   That part of a subsidiary company's shareholders' funds that is not held by the holding company. Usually shown as a separate item on the liabilities side of a consolidated balance sheet.

net current assets   Current assets less current liabilities.

net margin (before or after tax)   Net profit divided by sales expressed as a percentage. Can be applied to net profit before tax or after tax.

net profit (before or after tax)   Net profit is the operating profit less interest. Can be expressed as before tax or after tax.

net present value   Net present value is the present value of future cash flows discounted back using an interest rate which is normally the company's cost of capital.

net assets   Total assets less total liabilities.

net worth   Assets less liabilities in the proprietorship section of a balance sheet, usually referred to as shareholders' funds or share capital and reserves.

operating profit   The profit made after deducting overheads from the gross profit, but before deducting interest.

overheads   The selling, general and administrative costs incurred by a business that are not included in cost of sales (or cost of goods sold).

overtrading   Running the business at a level of sales above that which can be supported by the capital available within the business.

parent company   *see* **holding company**

payable days   Measures the average number of days it takes to pay for purchases on credit.

planograming/ planogram   Planograming is the process of working out the layout and display of product categories, product lines and individual SKUs in a retail store to maximize sales or profitability. The result is a planogram, which is a map of where categories are sited in the store and where each product sits on the shelf.

potential growth capacity   Measures the amount by which the company can grow using its existing financial resources.

professional services firm   Any type of business selling professional services such as lawyers, accountants, consultants, etc, either to private individuals or to companies,

provision   An estimate of the loss in the value of an asset which is charged against the profits. Examples include provisions for future warranty costs, bad debts and inventory obsolescence. Can also refer to providing for a known liability of which the amount cannot be determined with accuracy such as the outcome of outstanding litigation or claims against the business.

ranging   Deciding on the range of products to offer in a retail store, including the assortment of how many models and sizes to offer in each category and in what depth.

retained profits   Profits which are retained and not paid out as dividends. Also called accumulated profits when shown in the balance sheet and represents the retained profits since the business was started.

receivables   *see* **accounts receivable**

receivable days   *see* **days sales outstanding**

recoverability   The proportion of billable activity (valued at sales prices) that can be billed to a customer by a service provider.

reseller   A trade channel player that buys and resells products to end customers. A term used mainly by suppliers as it describes the role the player fulfils for them.

reserve   A specific application of retained earnings which prevents them from being available for distribution to shareholders. An example is capital redemption reserve, which is created when retained earnings have been used to buy back shares, and is needed to prevent the capital of the business being reduced. The term reserve is often used inappropriately as a vague term or even a substitute for the meaning applied to provision or even surpluses of cash.

return on capital employed (ROCE)   Net profit before tax (EBIT) divided by shareholders funds expressed as a percentage.

return on invested capital (ROIC)   Operating earnings after tax divided by invested capital (total assets less excess cash minus non-interest-bearing liabilities). This is often used to assess the value creation capabilities of a firm in an intuitive way. It is a measure of the operating business performance, with the treasury aspects (ie excess cash) stripped out.

return on net assets (RONA) (before or after tax)   Net profit (before or after tax) divided by net assets employed expressed as a percentage. A measure of how well the company is utilizing its assets to produce a return on shareholder investment.

return on shareholders' funds (ROSF)   Profit after tax divided by equity shareholders' funds expressed as a percentage.

revenues (US term)   The value of all goods and services sold in a period. (UK term is sales.)

sales (UK term)   The value of all goods and services sold in a period. (US term is revenues.)

sales pipeline   The measure of revenue visibility equal to the average number of months sales booked as orders (or orders plus expected value of outstanding bids). Can also be used in a more generic way to refer to a business's view of the number of enquiries or leads, prospects, bids or proposals and unfulfilled orders outstanding that gives it some ability to predict its future levels of sales or revenues.

sales cycle   The time it takes on average for a lead to be converted into a confirmed order.

same store sales   These are sales of stores that have been opened for one year or more. Because it takes time for a new store to ramp up to full productivity, analysts will often turn to this measure to filter out the effect of distortions caused by a rapid store expansion programme. Sometimes referred to as 'comps' sales.

sell-with channel   *see* **advocate channel**

seasonality   The sensitivity of a business to uneven sales over the year. A seasonal business is one that is highly uneven such as one selling suntan lotions in the UK. Seasons can be artificial, not just related to nature's seasons, for example Back to School and the end of the public sector financial year, which often involves a rush to spend unused budgets to ensure they are not cut in future years.

share capital   The ownership of a share gives the shareholder a proportionate ownership of the company. The share capital is stated in the balance sheet at its par (nominal) value.

shareholder   Member of a company through ownership of shares in the company. Shareholders are the capital backers of a business, either by investing directly or by buying the shares second-hand. Private companies' shares are usually traded directly between individuals; public companies' shares can be traded through the stock markets.

shareholders' funds   The proprietorship section of a company balance sheet. Includes the share capital, any share premium and the retained earnings.

short-term loan   A loan with an original maturity of less than 12 months.

SKU   An acronym for stock-keeping unit. Each different size and weight and packaging of a product is a unique SKU, so the 250 g box, the 450 g box and the 450 g box with a special promotion are each individual SKUs.

SPIFF   A special reward given by manufacturers or service sources to a dealers' sales team for encouraging the sale of their own products, usually run as a very short-term programme, such as a 'SPIFF day'. (SPIFF is possibly an acronym for sales promotion incentive for funds.)

stock (UK term)   Raw materials, work-in-progress and finished goods, usually valued at the lower of cost or market value. (US term is inventory.)

store density   A measure of the size of a store chain, which is the number of stores per thousand population. For example, in a market with 55 million people a retailer with 1,050 stores would have a density of 1 store per 52,000 people (= 55m divided by 1,050).

straight-line depreciation   Cost less estimated scrap value of an asset divided by its estimated economic life.

subsidiary   Company that is owned by another company (either entirely or substantially, defined by technical rules).

trade channel   A route to market that comprises intermediaries that sell to the end customer (*see also* indirect channel). Sometimes loosely called 'the trade'.

trading margin   *see* **gross margin**

unsecured loan or borrowings   Money borrowed by a company without the giving of security.

up-sell   The sales and marketing technique of encouraging a customer to buy a better, more expensive or higher-margin product when considering a purchase. Many suppliers offer a range comprising of 'good, better, best' products to encourage the customer to trade up. Some also offer a basic model that is so stripped down that its only real feature is a low price to generate customer interest on which up-selling techniques can be engaged.

utilization   The key measure of productivity used in service providers. It can be applied to the entire service part of the business, individual divisions or teams and even each individual billable member of staff. High utilization means that a high proportion of the time of billable staff is going into productive, revenue-generating work. Excessively high utilization over time will lead to burnout and quality issues.

value creation (destruction)   Operating profits generated in excess of the cost of capital. If profits exceed cost of capital, management has created value and if the reverse is true, management has destroyed value.

vendor   Term for supplier often used by distributors and channel players.

weighted average cost of capital (WACC) The average cost of capital, representing the expected cost of all of a company's sources of capital. Each source of capital, such as equities, bonds and other debt, is weighted in the calculation according to its prominence in the company's capital structure.

wholesaler *see* **distributor**

working capital Inventory plus accounts receivable less accounts payable. This represents the capital required by a business to fund its trading cycle. As the business grows it will need more working capital, unless it can improve the working capital cycle.

working capital cycle Measures the average number of days working capital is tied up in the business. The lower the figure, the more efficiently working capital is being recycled.

working capital requirement Measures the amount of working capital required in a company given its level of sales and how quickly its working capital is recycled.

working capital turn Measures how many times the company generates its working capital during a period. The higher the turn, the better the generation capacity.

work-in-progress Partly completed manufactured goods.

yield Another term for return. Usually means to the annual return generated by an asset or investment.

Index

NB: page numbers in *italic* indicate figures

With over 42 years of publishing, more than 80 million people have succeeded in business with thanks to **Kogan Page**

www.koganpage.com

KoganPage